Comparative Law Yearbook of International Business

Comparative Law Yearbook of International Business

Volume 43

Christian Campbell

The Center for International Legal Studies

The Center for International Legal Studies is a nonprofit research and publications institute established and operating under Austrian law, with its international headquarters in Salzburg, Austria.

The Center has operated since 1976 in Salzburg, and it has close cooperation with the faculties of law of the University of Salzburg, Boston University and Suffolk University in the United States, Lazarski University in Poland, Eötvös Loránd University in Hungary, and numerous other universities and educational institutions in Europe.

The *Comparative Law Yearbook of International Business* prints matter it deems worthy of publication. Views expressed in material appearing herein are those of the authors and do not necessarily reflect the policies or opinions of the *Comparative Law Yearbook of International Business*, its editors, or the Center for International Legal Studies.

Manuscripts proposed for publication may be sent by email to:

The Editor

Comparative Law Yearbook of International Business
christian.campbell@cils.org

Summary of Contents

Table of Contents

Editor's Note

The *Comparative Law Yearbook of International Business*, published under the auspices of the Center for International Legal Studies, in this 43rd volume spans an arc of timely and challenging concerns for business law practitioner and academics alike. It discusses:

- how arbitrability of intellectual property rights (IPRs) disputes might improve worldwide IPR enforcement;
- how the "disregard of legal entity" may be used to establish implied consent by a person or entity that is not a signatory to an arbitration agreement;
- how an effective cross-border insolvency framework under the Indian insolvency and bankruptcy code can borrow from the UNCITRAL Model Law's and other jurisdictions' approaches to the tension between "universality" and "territoriality";
- how a promising new mediation act for Pakistan may help resolve a backlog of millions of cases in a jurisdiction with a patchwork of traditional and modern ADR mechanisms;
- how the EU seeks to balance the taxation of digital services;
- how Brazil is addressing the taxation of offshore indirect transfers;
- how private equity capital structures in the unique market of professional sports create opportunities as well as risks;
- how Securities Market Regulation theory plays a role in the organization and development of active securities markets, particularly in emerging markets; and
- how non-signatories can be bound by arbitration agreements in Brazil through "disregard of legal entity" to ascertain implied consent.

The authors are practitioners and academics from Brazil, England, France, India, Pakistan, Singapore, the United States and Uzbekistan. They offer a broad and diverse perspective on some of today's pressing business law issues in a shrinking world.

Editor: Christian Campbell

Assistant Editors: Ellie Persellin (J.D. cand. Georgetown) and Choy Chen (L.L.B. cand. Anhui University)

Acknowledgments

The Editor would like to acknowledge the assistance of Ms. Ellie Persellin and Ms. Choy Chen in organizing and editing the 43rd volume of the Yearbook.

Formulating an Effective Cross-Border Insolvency Framework under the Indian Insolvency and Bankruptcy Code

Meenakshi R. Kurpad

230, First Floor, 39th ‘c’ Cross, 9th Main, 5th Block, Jayanagar
560041 Bangalore
India
Phone number: (+91) 967 4917033
Email address: mrk2193@colombia.edu

Piercing the Corporate Veil to Ascertain Implied Consent to Arbitrate: A Comparative Perspective from Brazil

Caetano Berenguer

Sergio Bermudes Advogados
Praça XV de Novembro, 20 – 7º e 8º
andar – Centro – CEP
20010-010 Rio de Janeiro
Brazil
Phone number: +55 (21) 3221 9000
Email address: caetanoberenguer@sbadv.com.br

Gustavo Favero Vaughn

Cesar Asfor Rocha Advogados
Rua Iguatemi n. 151, 29th Floor Itaim Bibi
01451-011 São Paulo
Brazil
Phone number: +1 (718) 724-4310
Email address: gustavovaughn@car.adv.br

Arbitrability of Intellectual Property Rights Validity Disputes

Jayems Dhingra

Tiberias Management Consultants Pte. Ltd.
20, Ayer Rajah Crescent, #09-17
Singapore 139964

Singapore
Phone number: +65 9785 9896
Email address: jayems@tiberiasmc.com

A New Mediation Act? The Way Forward for Pakistan

Mian Sheraz Javaid

MK Consultus
72-y Street 19 Phase III, DHA, Lahore,
54792
Pakistan
Phone number: +92 (0) 300 400 9000
Email address: mian.javaid@mkconsultus.com

Tariq Mahmood

Glendene,
Woodstock Close
Newcastle-under-Lyme
ST5 0RP
United Kingdom
Phone number: 0044-7896953303
Email address: t.mahmood@33bedfordrow.co.uk
chtariq1uk@yahoo.co.uk

Taxing Offshore Indirect Transfers in Brazil: Discussions on International Tax Policies and Recommendations for Reform

Juliana Midori Kuteken

Rua Mateus Grou, 398, apt. 11, district of Pinheiros
05415-040. São Paulo – SP
Brazil
Phone number: +55 (11) 99960-4476
E-mail address: juliana.kuteken@gmail.com

Back to the Future: Looking for a European Tax System

Olivier Péjout

21 Avenue de la Canéda
Sarlat-la-Canéda
24200
France
Phone number: 0033684132417

Email address: olivierpejout@gmail.com

Private Equity's Arrival in American Sports Leagues

Tanner Schenewark

182 Columbus Avenue, Apt 2FN
10023 New York, NY
USA
Phone number: (385) 424-2638
Email address: tanner.schenewark@gmail.com

Securities Market Regulation Theories and Perspectives on Their Improvement

Otabek Narziev

Tashkent State University of Law, TSUL
Sayilgokh str. 35
100047 Tashkent, Uzbekistan
Phone number: +998978300737
Email address: otabeknarziev@yahoo.com

Formulating an Effective Cross-Border Insolvency Framework under the Indian Insolvency and Bankruptcy Code

Meenakshi R. Kurpad*
L.L.M., Class of 2020, Columbia Law School

Introduction

In 2016, India introduced the Insolvency and Bankruptcy Code (Code) largely in response to the nonperforming crisis that plagued the domestic banking and financial sector for nearly two decades. However, given the large and growing presence of Indian businesses abroad, as well as multinational corporations in India, a bankruptcy code without a cross-border insolvency framework was a task half done. This chapter analyzes the nascent cross-border insolvency legal regime in India and makes recommendations for establishing an effective cross-border insolvency regime. In particular, it argues for the adoption of the UNCITRAL Model Law on Cross-Border Insolvency with certain modifications. Further, it also argues for the adoption of alternatives in the form of bilateral treaties and cross-border protocols in addition to the Model Law.

This chapter is divided into five sections. Section I provides a brief overview of the theories of cross-border insolvency and the UNCITRAL Model Law on cross-border insolvency. Section II seeks to acquaint the reader with the economic events leading up to the introduction of the Code. It outlines India's economic and political background, the nonperforming assets (NPAs) crisis, and the introduction of the Code. Section III examines the cross-border insolvency legal framework in India. It begins by highlighting the importance of having an effective cross-border insolvency

* I would like to thank Prof. Edward Morrison for his guidance and supervision of this chapter in addition to detailed discussions and comments. I would also like to thank Hon. Martin Glenn at the Southern District of New York Bankruptcy Court for his inputs on cross-border insolvency protocols. I am grateful to Jane Manners, Vasujith Ram, Shouvik Kumar Guha, and Krishnendu Sen for their detailed comments and inputs. All errors remain mine.

framework from an Indian legal perspective. It then analyzes the laws preceding the Code as well as provisions under the Code that govern cross-border insolvencies. By examining cases of cross-border insolvencies involving multinational Indian corporations, this chapter highlights the deficiencies in the current regime addressing cross-border insolvencies. Section IV makes recommendations to establish an effective cross-border insolvency regime in India. First, it highlights the benefits of adopting the Model Law. Second, it highlights the usefulness of bilateral treaties in enhancing cooperation and coordination between nations regarding cross-border insolvency. Third, using the *Jet Airways* case as an example, it illustrates the effectiveness of cross-border insolvency protocols as a viable alternative. It recommends that the Insolvency and Bankruptcy Board of India (IBBI) adopts a practice guide on cross-border insolvency protocols based on the UNCITRAL Practice Guide. Fourth, it recommends that the specialized commercial law courts in India adopt the Judicial Insolvency Network (JIN) Guidelines, thereby enhancing cooperation and communication with other courts while dealing with cross-border insolvency cases in each other's jurisdictions. Section V concludes.

What Is Cross-Border Insolvency?

Theories of Cross-Border Insolvency

The theoretical approaches to cross-border insolvencies represent a spectrum with pure universalism[1] at one end and pure territorialism[2] at the other.[3] On one end of the spectrum lies pure universalism, which advocates that the insolvency law of the debtor shall apply to all assets of such debtor, regardless of where they are located.[4] Territoriality is based on the premise that a country applies its own cross-border insolvency law to all assets

1 Nigel John Howcroft, *Universal v. Territorial Models for Cross-Border Insolvency: The Theory, the Practice, and the Reality That Universalism Prevails*, 8 U.C. DAVIS BUS L. J. 366, 370 (2008).

2 Ryan Halimi, *An Analysis of the Three Major Cross-Border Insolvency Regimes*, INTERNATIONAL IMMERSION PROGRAM PAPERS 47, 47 (2017), available at http://chicagounbound.uchicago.edu/international_immersion_program_papers/47.

3 Nigel John Howcroft, *Universal v. Territorial Models for Cross-Border Insolvency: The Theory, the Practice, and the Reality That Universalism Prevails*, 8 U.C. DAVIS BUS L. J. 366, 370 (2008).

4 Nigel John Howcroft, *Universal v. Territorial Models for Cross-Border Insolvency: The Theory, the Practice, and the Reality That Universalism Prevails*, 8 U.C. DAVIS BUS L. J. 366, 370 (2008).

located within its jurisdiction without deferring to any other country's laws.[5]

The two traditional approaches to cross-border insolvency have been heavily criticized, primarily for their inability to accommodate real-life situations. This criticism invariably leads to the adoption of "middle of the road" models, such as modified universalism and cooperative territorialism, that seek to address the shortcomings of the traditional models.[6] Modified universalism generally operates on the principles of access and recognition of proceedings, provision of timely relief, and cooperation and coordination among jurisdictions.[7]

Territorialism

The territorialist theory of cross-border insolvency applies domestic insolvency law to cross-border cases without deferring to laws of other nations or international law.[8] Under the territorialist approach, creditors claim priority over assets of the insolvent corporation, including assets in a foreign jurisdiction.[9] Proponents of the territorialist approach argue that claims are disposed of faster (since there is no need to worry about foreign proceedings) and that by giving domestic creditors greater preference, more domestic capital will flow to local businesses.[10] Territorialism also emphasizes national sovereignty, whereby courts in a certain country must have the sole authority to control all assets within its physical boundaries.[11] Jurisdictions that have adopted a territoriality model of cross-border insolvency include Brazil, Russia, and China.

---

5 Ryan Halimi, *An Analysis of the Three Major Cross-Border Insolvency Regimes*, INTERNATIONAL IMMERSION PROGRAM PAPERS 47, 47 (2017), available at http://chicagounbound.uchicago.edu/international_immersion_program_papers/47.

6 Paulo Fernando & Campana Filho, *The Legal Framework for Cross-Border Insolvency in Brazil*, 32 HOUS. J. INT'L L. 97, 106-107 (2009).

7 The Model Law envisages these principles. *See* UNCITRAL Model Law on Cross Border Insolvency, 1997, available at http://www.uncitral.org/uncitral/en/uncitral_texts/insolvency/1997Model.html.

8 Sean E. Story, *Cross-Border Insolvency: A Comparative Analysis*, 32 ARIZ. J. INT'L & COMP. L. 431, 433 (2015).

9 Sean E. Story, *Cross-Border Insolvency: A Comparative Analysis*, 32 ARIZ. J. INT'L & COMP. L. 431, 433 (2015).

10 Ryan Halimi, *An Analysis of the Three Major Cross-Border Insolvency Regimes*, INTERNATIONAL IMMERSION PROGRAM PAPERS 47, 47 (2017), available at http://chicagounbound.uchicago.edu/international_immersion_program_papers/47.

11 Phoebe Hathorn, *Cross-Border Insolvency in the Maritime Context: The United States' Universalism vs. Singapore's Territorialism,* 38 TUL. MAR. L.J. 239, 241 (2013).

Universalism

A "pure" universalist model is one that treats all insolvency proceedings across jurisdictions as a single proceeding.[12] Courts who would otherwise have jurisdiction transfer or "give up" their jurisdiction over those assets to the centralized court overseeing the entire bankruptcy. Proponents of universalism argue that it is a more efficient method, as it substantially reduces the transaction costs involved in multiple insolvency proceedings.[13]

Modified Universalism

The modified universality approach was proposed shortly before the introduction of the Model Law in 1997.[14] Modified universalism evolved as a hybrid between the extremes of pure territorialism and pure universalism and seeks to combine the advantages of both.[15] This approach to cross-border insolvency is premised on voluntary cooperation, where courts are encouraged to cooperate with courts of other jurisdictions but are not obliged to cooperate. The premise of modified universalism is the recognition of a foreign "main" proceeding—the central proceeding in a cross-border insolvency matter—while allowing for ancillary or "non-main" proceedings.[16] Advocates of the modified universalist model argue that it is rooted in efficiency as it emphasizes the reduction of transaction costs to the greatest extent possible.

The UNCITRAL Model Law

The United Nations Commission on International Trade Law (UNCITRAL) formulated the Model Law on Cross-Border Insolvency (Model Law) in 1997. Prior to the adoption of the Model Law, recognition of

---

12 Sean E. Story, *Cross-Border Insolvency: A Comparative Analysis*, 32 ARIZ. J. INT'L & COMP. L. 431, 432 (2015).

13 Phoebe Hathorn, *Cross-Border Insolvency in the Maritime Context: The United States' Universalism vs. Singapore's Territorialism,* 38 TUL. MAR. L.J. 239, 242 (2013).

14 In their article titled '*The Cross-Border Insolvency Concordat: Principles to Facilitate the Resolution of International Insolvencies*,' Anne Nielsen, Mike Sigal, and Karen Wagner examined a hybrid approach to cross-border insolvencies.

15 Anne Nielsen, Mike Sigal & Karen Wagner, *The Cross-Border Insolvency Concordat: Principles to Facilitate the Resolution of International Insolvencies*, 70 AM. BANKR. L.J. 533, 534 (1996).

16 Sean E. Story, *Cross-Border Insolvency: A Comparative Analysis*, 32 ARIZ. J. INT'L & COMP. L. 431, 434 (2015).

foreign insolvency proceedings was difficult in many countries.[17] With the growth of conglomerates aided by globalization and expansion of trade and investment, national insolvency laws were not equipped to deal with insolvencies cutting across borders.[18] Multiple domestic insolvency proceedings led to inexplicable delay, inconsistency among legal regimes, higher costs, and inefficiencies.[19]

The modified universalist approach adopted in the Model Law sought to address the inconsistencies in recognition of foreign proceedings, as enforcement and recognition of judgments were particularly complicated and tedious in certain jurisdictions. The Model Law was adopted by the UNCITRAL on May 30, 1997. A core principle of the Model Law is rooted in the modified universalist approach to recognition of foreign proceedings; the law groups these proceedings into foreign "main" proceedings and foreign "non-main" proceedings.[20] The foreign main proceeding is determined by the center of main interests (or COMI) of the corporate debtor.[21] While COMI has not been defined under the Model Law, case law illustrates that examining the significant places of business and operations[22] of a corporate debtor helps to determine COMI. The Model Law is particularly aimed at making recognition of foreign proceedings as expeditious as possible, so as to secure a debtor's assets across jurisdictions.[23]

---

17 Jay Lawrence Westbrook, *An Empirical Study of the Implementation in the United States of the Model Law on Cross Border Insolvency,* 87 AM. BANKR. L.J. 247, 250 (2013).

18 United Nations Commission on International Trade Law, *Model Law on Cross-Border Insolvency with Guide to Enactment and Interpretation*, U.N. COMM'N ON INT'L TRADE LAW, 1, 20 U.N. SALES NO.:E.14.V.2 (July 2014), available at https://www.uncitral.org/pdf/english/texts/insolven/1997-Model-Law-Insol-2013-Guide-Enactment-e.pdf.

19 United Nations Commission on International Trade Law, *Model Law on Cross-Border Insolvency with Guide to Enactment and Interpretation*, U.N. COMM'N ON INT'L TRADE LAW, 1, 20 U.N. SALES NO.:E.14.V.2 (July 2014), available at https://www.uncitral.org/pdf/english/texts/insolven/1997-Model-Law-Insol-2013-Guide-Enactment-e.pdf.

20 United Nations Commission on International Trade Law, *Model Law on Cross-Border Insolvency with Guide to Enactment and Interpretation*, U.N. COMM'N ON INT'L TRADE LAW, 1, 20 U.N. SALES NO.:E.14.V.2 (July 2014), available at https://www.uncitral.org/pdf/english/texts/insolven/1997-Model-Law-Insol-2013-Guide-Enactment-e.pdf.

21 United Nations Commission on International Trade Law, *Model Law on Cross-Border Insolvency with Guide to Enactment and Interpretation*, U.N. COMM'N ON INT'L TRADE LAW, 1, 20 U.N. SALES NO.:E.14.V.2 (July 2014), available at https://www.uncitral.org/pdf/english/texts/insolven/1997-Model-Law-Insol-2013-Guide-Enactment-e.pdf.

22 *In re Stanford International Bank Limited & Others* [2009] EWHC 1441 (Ch).

23 Jay Lawrence Westbrook, *An Empirical Study of the Implementation in the United States of the Model Law on Cross Border Insolvency,* 87 AM. BANKR. L.J. 247, 251 (2013).

Recognition and Enforcement of Insolvency Judgments

In 2018, UNCITRAL adopted a new model law that would govern the recognition and enforcement of insolvency judgments, with a focus on cross-border insolvencies.[24] The primary aim of the Model Law is to give effect to interim judgments in insolvency proceedings covering multiple jurisdictions. However, the Model Law is yet to be adopted by a UN Member State.

Background

Economic and Political Background

India gained independence after over two hundred years of British colonialism in 1947. In the four decades that followed, India adopted a protectionist economic system, hoping to enhance domestic production and create self-sufficiency. British colonial rule left India with few resources and a large population in poverty. Historians pegged India's share of world income at 22.6 percent in 1700; by 1952, it had decreased to a mere 3.8 percent.[25] In its nearly seventy-three years of independence, Indian economic policy has moved from socialism and state primacy to liberalization.[26]

In the early stages as a newly independent nation, India adopted a mixed economic model that was part-state and part-market, hoping to draw a middle ground between capitalism and communism.[27] India's first Prime Minister, Jawaharlal Nehru, formulated a development model that emphasized the primacy of the state over the individual enterprise and established a substantial public sector.[28] The 1950s and 1960s focused on making India

---

24 *Model Law on Recognition and Enforcement of Insolvency-Related Judgments (2018)*, United Nations Commission on International Trade Law, available at https://uncitral.un.org/en/texts/insolvency/modellaw/mlij.

25 Angus Maddison Development Centre Studies the World Economy: Historical Statistics 261 (2003).

26 *A Short History of Indian Economy 1947-2019: Tryst with Destiny & Other Stories* Livemint (August 14, 2019, 11:43 PM IST), https://www.livemint.com/news/india/a-short-history-of-indian-economy-1947-2019-tryst-with-destiny-other-stories-1565801528109.html.

27 Lydia Powell, *India's Modern Economic History: A Brief Review*, The Globalist, https://www.theglobalist.com/indias-modern-economic-history-a-brief-review/.

28 *A Short History of Indian Economy 1947-2019: Tryst with Destiny & Other Stories* Livemint (August 14, 2019, 11:43 PM IST), https://www.livemint.com/news/india/a-short-history-of-indian-economy-1947-2019-tryst-with-destiny-other-stories-1565801528109.html.

self-sufficient in agricultural production to feed its population, culminating in the Green Revolution (developing high-yield varieties of wheat and rice) and the White Revolution (increasing milk production).[29] The wars with China and Pakistan during the 1960s, as well as the Bangladesh Liberation War in 1971, slowed economic progress once again. Further, the nationalization of banks in 1969 laid the foundation for politically influenced lending, particularly to the agricultural sector, as farmers comprised an important vote bank for the then Indian government.[30]

However, by the late 1970s, this "mixed model" proved to be a disaster, and coupled with the Indian Emergency between 1975 and 1977, paved the way for the decade with the slowest growth for Independent India. In the 1980s, India's economy grew at a slow pace of 1.7 percent, termed as the infamous "Hindu Growth."[31] Further, there was growing dissatisfaction among Indians on the country's reliance on foreign aid and loans.

India's planned socialist economy went through a major breakdown when in 1991, India underwent a severe balance of payments crisis. As the value of the Indian Rupee was adjusted, the country's central bank, the Reserve Bank of India (RBI), ran out of foreign reserves to deflect the decline in value.[32] In the late 1980s, India's current account deficit had widened as India shifted from import substitution to export-led growth, introducing measures to liberalize and encourage exporters such as easing licensing requirements and tariffs.[33] However, the value of imports increased at a faster pace, leading to a deterioration of the fiscal situation due to greater expenses from a wider current account deficit.[34] Yet, India

---

29 *A Short History of Indian Economy 1947-2019: Tryst with Destiny & Other Stories* LIVEMINT August 14, 2019, 11:43 PM IST), https://www.livemint.com/news/india/a-short-history-of-indian-economy-1947-2019-tryst-with-destiny-other-stories-1565801528109.html.

30 *A Short History of Indian Economy 1947-2019: Tryst with Destiny & Other Stories* LIVEMINT (August 14, 2019, 11:43 PM IST), https://www.livemint.com/news/india/a-short-history-of-indian-economy-1947-2019-tryst-with-destiny-other-stories-1565801528109.html.

31 Davis Rodrik & Arvind Subramanian, *From "Hindu Growth" to Productivity Surge: The Mystery of the Indian Growth Transition*, 52(2) INTERNATIONAL MONETARY FUND STAFF PAPERS 193, 194 (2005).

32 Valerie Cerra & Sweta Chaman Saxena, *"What Caused the 1991 Currency Crisis in India?"* IMF WORKING PAPER WP/00/157 3 (2000), https://www.imf.org/external/pubs/ft/wp/2000/wp00157.pdf.

33 Valerie Cerra & Sweta Chaman Saxena, *"What Caused the 1991 Currency Crisis in India?"* IMF WORKING PAPER WP/00/157 3, 4 (2000), https://www.imf.org/external/pubs/ft/wp/2000/wp00157.pdf.

34 Valerie Cerra & Sweta Chaman Saxena, *"What Caused the 1991 Currency Crisis in India?"* IMF WORKING PAPER WP/00/157 3, 4 (2000), https://www.imf.org/external/pubs/ft/wp/2000/wp00157.pdf.

continued to borrow to finance the current account deficit. The Middle East Gulf crisis of 1990 was the last straw and precipitated the crisis in India as the value of petroleum imports spiked and the current account further deteriorated.[35] Considered to be the watershed moment for the Indian economy since independence, the Indian government sold 20 tonnes of gold to UBS Investment Bank (part of UBS Group AG) so that a USD 240 million loan could be secured from the Bank of England and the Bank of Japan.[36]

The balance of payments crisis was turned into an opportunity by the then Indian government to introduce long-needed economic reforms. Former RBI governor (and later Prime Minister) Dr. Manmohan Singh had warned the government of its fiscal delinquency as early as 1982.[37] Upon his appointment as Finance Minister, Dr. Singh represented the 1991 budget that would launch the Indian economy into two decades of unprecedented growth, placing India as one of the fastest-growing economies.

India's economic growth in the next twenty years was remarkable. Foreign direct investment poured in, facilitating growth and development across various industrial sectors. The services industry, particularly information technology, boomed, thus creating millions of jobs for Indians.

Prior to the introduction of economic reforms in 1991, the growth of Indian corporations was largely left to the control of the government. The decades preceding liberalization, termed as the license-quota era, determined which entities would be allowed to engage in manufacturing and services. This invariably led to a situation where primarily those with considerable political and administrative connections could engage in business.[38]

The rise of the Indian conglomerate has been synonymous with economic liberalization beginning in 1991 and the development of India's and Asia's financial markets since then. This economic liberalization, coupled

---

35 Valerie Cerra & Sweta Chaman Saxena, *"What Caused the 1991 Currency Crisis in India?"* IMF WORKING PAPER WP/00/157 3, 5 (2000), https://www.imf.org/external/pubs/ft/wp/2000/wp00157.pdf.

36 *A Short History of Indian Economy 1947-2019: Tryst with Destiny & Other Stories* LIVEMINT (August 14, 2019, 11:43 PM IST), https://www.livemint.com/news/india/a-short-history-of-indian-economy-1947-2019-tryst-with-destiny-other-stories-1565801528109.html.

37 Ankit Mital, *The Long Road to the 1991 Economic Crisis*, LIVEMINT (July 8, 2016, 5:05 AM IST), https://www.livemint.com/Sundayapp/E0rCYXfJyjWd2qsENV3KOO/The-long-road-to-the-1991-economic-crisis.html.

38 Shyam Sunder, *A Roadmap for Indian Conglomerates*, FORTUNE INDIA (November 7, 2018), https://www.fortuneindia.com/opinion/road-map-for-indian-conglomerates/102660.

with the steady inflow of foreign direct investment, has enabled the rapid internationalization of Indian companies.[39] In the first quarter of 2019, India received foreign direct investment totaling USD 16.33 billion, in comparison to USD 12.75 billion in the first quarter of 2018.[40] Indian conglomerates such as Reliance Industries Limited operate on a global scale in a myriad of sectors, including energy, oil and gas, minerals, manufacturing, agriculture, and financial services.[41] Given the growing importance of India's place in the global economy and the Indian conglomerate, having a well-defined cross-border insolvency regime becomes critical.

Political Considerations

In 2004, the United Progressive Alliance with Dr. Manmohan Singh as its Prime Minister was elected to power, and following a slew of successful economic measures, was reelected in 2009. However, the second tenure was marred with high-profile and significant economic scandals, such as the coal allocation scam, spectrum scam, and the mismanagement of funds for the 2010 Commonwealth Games.

The right-leaning Bhartiya Janata Party (BJP) won a huge majority in 2014 and elected Narendra Modi to be the new Prime Minister. A known nationalist, he was elected based on his economic promises to revitalize India's growth. The new government sought to focus on the promotion of industrial development within India through a new economic campaign called "Make in India." The current Indian government is keen on improving the ease of doing business in India and has liberalized licensing and regulatory requirements to an extent.

Restricted Entry: Open, but Not too Open

India continues to be a highly regulated exchange-controlled jurisdiction even today. Foreign investment is regulated under the Foreign Exchange Management Act, 1999 (FEMA) and by the Department for the Promotion

---

39 Jaya Prakash Pradhan & Karl Sauvant, *Introduction: The Rise of Indian Multinational Enterprises: Revisiting Key Issues Sauvant K.P, in* THE RISE OF INDIAN MULTINATIONALS 1, 1 (Jaya Prakash Pradhan, Ayesha Chatterjee & Brian Harley eds., 2010).

40 *FDI up 28 Per cent in April-June 2019*, HINDU BUSINESS LINE (September 26, 2019), https://www.thehindubusinessline.com/economy/foreign-direct-investment-up-28-in-april-june-2019/article29340468.ece.

41 Reliance Steel & Aluminium was ranked 275 in the Fortune 500 list for 2019. *See* Fortune, "Global 500" (Fortune, March 31, 2018), https://fortune.com/fortune500/2019/search/?name=Reliance.

of Industry and Internal Trade (DIPP), which regulates how much foreign investment may be made in each of the specified sectors.[42] The RBI also regulates foreign investment through both debt and equity.[43] This legacy most probably comes from the lessons of British colonial rule, as many historians argue that large parts of the erstwhile Mughal Empire's wealth were used by the British East India Company and, later, the British Empire.[44] Although foreign creditors are not treated distinctly from domestic creditors, the law and the regulators want to limit the outflow of revenue from Indian territory.

The current government's nationalist drive coupled with a focus on domestic creditor recovery also illustrates why the adoption of the Model Law has not gone forward. The Code's primary focus still remains maximization of local creditor recovery and cleaning up the mess created by the NPAs crisis.

The Nonperforming Assets Crisis

NPAs are assets that do not generate income for the lender.[45] They are, in essence, a deadweight loss to banks as they divert resources from deposits and hinder the bank's capacity to lend.[46] While NPAs have always been a concern for the Indian banking and financial sector, the problem has become acute in the recent past. Bad debts have risen from INR 150 billion in March 2012 to over INR 8.4 trillion in December 2017[47] and subsequently to INR 7.27 trillion in September 2019.[48]

---

42 The DIPP formulates the Foreign Direct Investment Policy on an annual basis. Industries are classified as "sectors" and are subject to a specified investment cap. *See Foreign Direct Investment*, DEPARTMENT FOR PROMOTION OF INDUSTRY AND INTERNAL TRADE, GOVERNMENT OF INDIA, available at https://dipp.gov.in/foreign-direct-investment/foreign-direct-investment-policy.

43 The RBI issues a multitude of regulations that govern any form of cross-border transactions, including external commercial borrowings and trade credits.

44 William Dalrymple, *The East India Company: The Original Corporate Raiders*, THE GUARDIAN (March 4, 2015, 00:59 EST), https://www.theguardian.com/world/2015/mar/04/east-india-company-original-corporate-raiders.

45 Neeraj Tiwari, *Resolution of NPA in India: The Role of Asset Reconstruction Companies*, 7 PRATT'S J. BANKR. L. 552, 553 (2011).

46 Neeraj Tiwari, *Resolution of NPA in India: The Role of Asset Reconstruction Companies*, 7 PRATT'S J. BANKR. L. 552, 553 (2011).

47 Press Trust of India, *Banks' gross NPAs at Rs. 8.41 lakh crore*, THE ECONOMIC TIMES (March 9, 2018 05:56 PM IST), https://economictimes.indiatimes.com/industry/banking/finance/banking/banks-gross-npas-at-rs-8-41-lakh-crore-in-dec/articleshow/63234553.cms.

48 Press Trust of India, *NPAs of Public Sector Banks Stand at Rs. 7.27 Lakh Crore as on H1FY20: Govt*, LIVEMINT (February 3, 2020 06:46 PM IST), https://

NPAs in India began to first develop in the aftermath of the Asian crisis of 1997. This was coupled with the fact that the Indian banking sector had focused on lending based on governmental policies[49] and was made even more acute by the bank nationalization of 1969. Decades of inefficient lending practices, lack of supervision and monitoring, and corruption have riddled the Indian banking system with huge NPAs, especially affecting public sector banks.[50]

In the last decade, there have been various approaches toward resolving the issue of NPAs that plague the Indian banking system. These include the setting up of asset reconstruction companies, taking active measures to develop the corporate bond market, and strengthening creditor rights by enacting and implementing a specialized insolvency law.

A Much-Awaited Bankruptcy Code

The introduction of the Indian Insolvency and Bankruptcy Code, 2016 (the Code) has heralded significant reform and has sought to resolve the bad loans crisis plaguing the Indian banking sector. The Code was enacted in May 2016 after decades of ineffective debt collection laws and regulation, and its significance is highlighted by the shift from a debtor-in-possession model to a creditor-in-possession model.[51] However, the Code lags behind in formulating a framework for cross-border insolvency, considering that many Indian companies have multinational operations, own assets abroad, and are constantly making acquisitions overseas. A strong case was made by the Insolvency Law Committee for the ratification of the Model Law.[52] Accordingly, in June 2018, the Indian Ministry of Corporate Affairs issued

---

www.livemint.com/industry/banking/npas-of-public-sector-banks-stand-at-rs-7-27-lakh-crore-as-on-h1fy20-govt-11580733371206.html.

49 Anshu SK Pasricha, *On Financial Sector Reform in Emerging Markets: Enhancing Creditors' Rights and Securitizing Non-performing Loans in the Indian Banking Sector—An Elephant's Tale*, 55 BUFF L.REV 325, 329 (2007-2008).

50 Anshu SK Pasricha, *On Financial Sector Reform in Emerging Markets: Enhancing Creditors' Rights and Securitizing Non-performing Loans in the Indian Banking Sector-An Elephant's Tale*, 55 BUFF L.REV 325, 330 (2007-2008).

51 A debtor-in-possession model allows the debtor filing for bankruptcy to continue to be in charge of the business of the insolvent corporation. On the other hand, a creditor-in-possession model empowers the creditors to take over the insolvent corporation and manage its business affairs.

52 Report of the Insolvency Law Committee on Cross-Border Insolvency, MINISTRY OF CORPORATE AFFAIRS, GOVERNMENT OF INDIA, October 16, 2018, available at https://www.mca.gov.in/Ministry/pdf/CrossBorderInsolvencyReport_22102018.pdf.

a notification inviting public comments on the draft chapter on cross-border insolvency (Draft).[53] As of the writing of this chapter, the Draft (or Part Z, if and when incorporated into the Code) has not yet been ratified into law by the Indian Ministry. The Draft was introduced as a bill in mid-2018, and yet there seems to have been no movement in incorporating it into the Code nearly a year and a half later.

Cross-Border Insolvency in India

In the Indian context, cross-border insolvency may be triggered in three situations: one, where creditors seek to enforce their security interests over the foreign assets of an Indian debtor; two, when creditors seek to enforce rights over Indian assets of a foreign debtor; and three, when Indian creditors wish to enforce their rights over foreign assets of a foreign debtor.[54] While the second scenario seems straightforward and is likely to proceed under the Code, cross-border insolvency becomes complex in cases of assets situated abroad. In such situations, creditors would want to prevent the sale of such foreign assets, preserve the bankruptcy estate and ensure that their legal remedies are not subordinated to the rights of other creditors.[55]

The Importance of a Cross-Border Insolvency Framework

The current Indian government was elected to power largely due to electoral promises to enhance economic development, including the promise to improve the ease of doing business in India and strengthen the creditor rights framework in light of the growing NPAs crisis in India (which continues to be ongoing).[56] The absence of legal certainty in creditor

---

53 Public Notice, *Suggestions Invited on Draft on Cross-Border Insolvency*, MINISTRY OF CORPORATE AFFAIRS, GOVERNMENT OF INDIA, June 20, 2018, available at http://www.mca.gov.in/Ministry/pdf/PublicNoiceCrossBorder_20062018.pdf.

54 Ran Chakrabarti, *India's Proposed Cross Border Insolvency Regime: Will It Trump the Gibbs Rule?*, MONDAQ (July 24, 2018), http://www.mondaq.com/india/x/721994/Insolvency+Bankruptcy/Indias+Proposed+Cross+Border+Insolvency+Regime+Will+It+Trump+The+Gibbs+Rule.

55 Ran Chakrabarti, *India's Proposed Cross Border Insolvency Regime: Will It Trump the Gibbs Rule?*, MONDAQ (July 24, 2018), http://www.mondaq.com/india/x/721994/Insolvency+Bankruptcy/Indias+Proposed+Cross+Border+Insolvency+Regime+Will+It+Trump+The+Gibbs+Rule.

56 Beginning in the mid-2000s, Indian banks granted loans to corporations based on expected growth and returns, particularly in the infrastructure sector. In the aftermath of the global financial crisis, the Reserve Bank of India sought to revert a liquidity crisis

rights, particularly in cases of cross-border corporate debt investments, hinders this policy goal.

Another untested but pertinent issue with respect to cross-border insolvency involves subsidiaries and affiliates of global conglomerates incorporated in India. Although some conglomerates do operate on a franchise in India, there are many multinational corporations with Indian subsidiaries that may become subject to insolvency. For instance, when Forever 21 filed for bankruptcy protection under Chapter 11 of the U.S. Bankruptcy Code, its Indian operations were largely unimpacted because it operated through a franchise agreement with Aditya Birla Fashion and Retail Limited.[57] However, in the event that a foreign or an Indian multinational corporation with subsidiaries in India or abroad files for bankruptcy, the lack of an effective cross-border framework may create legal uncertainty.

Laws Governing Cross-Border Insolvency Outside the Code

For nearly a century, insolvency and bankruptcy laws in India were highly underdeveloped. Despite its tremendous growth post-independence in 1947 and emergence as one of the world's fastest-growing economies, outdated colonial-era laws were in existence until recently. Yet, cases of cross-border insolvency are not new to India, and the Indian legal system has struggled to arrive at comprehensive resolutions in the absence of a cross-border framework.

British Colonial Rule (British Raj)

The biggest remnant of India's history as a former British colony is seen in the country's legal system, which largely functions on British antecedents even today. A major chunk of India's laws, including the penal code, the contract law statute, and real property laws, are colonial-era legislation.[58]

---

by encouraging banks to lend. However, this led to a steep rise in defaults and the emergence of India's twin balance sheet problem—where both banks and Indian companies came under financial stress. *See* Ahita Paul, *Examining the Rise of Non-performing Assets in India*, PRS LEGISLATIVE RESEARCH, September 13, 2018, available at https://www.prsindia.org/content/examining-rise-non-performing-assets-india.

57 Suneera Tandon, *Forever 21 India Business Will Not Be Impacted by Bankruptcy Filing in US*, LIVEMINT (September 30, 2019, 6:46 PM IST), https://www.livemint.com/companies/news/forever-21-india-business-will-not-be-impacted-by-bankruptcy-filing-11569849131133.html.

58 The Indian Penal Code, 1860, the Indian Contract Act, 1872, and the Transfer of Property Act, 1882 were all enacted during British colonial rule and remain in force (with minimal amendments) even today.

Until 2016, two colonial-era laws governed insolvency—the Provincial Insolvency Act, 1920 and the Presidency Towns Insolvency Act, 1909.[59] However, these laws continue to apply only in cases of individual insolvencies and do not address insolvencies involving any corporate form.[60]

Foreign Judgments under the Civil Procedure Code, 1908

The law governing civil procedure in India, the Code of Civil Procedure, 1908 (CPC), is another piece of colonial-era legislation. Foreign judgments and decrees are recognized and may be enforced under §44A of the CPC, which recognizes the principle of comity.[61] However, the recognition of a foreign judgment under the CPC is limited, and a foreign decree may be enforced under §44A only if it fulfills the requirements of §13 of the CPC. For instance, a foreign decree cannot be enforced if it was not passed on the merits, was founded on an incorrect view of international law or a refusal to recognize Indian law, is opposed to public order, or was obtained by fraud.[62] While these grounds for enforcing a foreign decree are legitimate, courts have been reluctant to allow for the enforcement of foreign decrees, except in limited circumstances.

The (Old) Companies Act, 1956 and the (New) Companies Act, 2013

The Companies Act, 1956 (Old Companies Act) and the revamped Companies Act, 2013 (Companies Act) provide for the winding-up of companies in the event of failure to repay debt.[63] The Old Companies Act did not have express provisions for foreign creditors to enforce their claims in India, although foreign companies incorporated outside India but doing business in India could be wound up as an unregistered company.[64] The Companies Act incorporates the same provision.[65]

59 S. Gupta & M.A. Batki, *India*, *in* INTERNATIONAL BANK INSOLVENCIES: A CENTRAL BANK PERSPECTIVE 95, 95 (Mario Giovanoli & Gregor Heirich eds., 1999).
60 Adam Feibelman, *Consumer Finance & Insolvency Law in India: A Case Study*, 36 BROOK INT. L.J. 75, 107 (2010).
61 Nidhi Shetye, *International Insolvency: An Indian Perspective on Cross-Border Treatment of Cases,* 39 FORDHAM INT'L L.J. 1045, 1054 (2016).
62 CODE CIV. PROC. (1908) § 13.
63 Companies Act, No. 1 of 1956, INDIA CODE (1956) §§ 484-520. *See also* Companies Act, No. 18 of 2013, INDIA CODE (2013) §§ 270-365.
64 Companies Act, No. 1 of 1956, INDIA CODE (1956) § 584.
65 Companies Act, No. 18 of 2013, INDIA CODE (2013) § 376.

Sick Industrial Companies Act and the Board for Financial Reconstruction

During the 1980s, shortly before India's balance of payments crisis, industries in India were plagued with growing "sickness" or financial distress. Based on the recommendations of the T. Tiwari Committee, the Indian Parliament enacted the Sick Industries Companies (Special Provisions) Act, 1985 (SICA) which established the Board of Industrial and Financial Reconstruction.[66] However, the process of reorganization or liquidation of financially distressed companies under the SICA was often used by corporate debtors to obtain a stay on security enforcement by creditors, and the process was long and cumbersome.[67]

Cases of Cross-Border Insolvency

Cross-border insolvencies are not new to India. During the British Raj, the Madras High Court witnessed what was the first cross-border insolvency protocol as early as 1908.[68] In this particular case, an Anglo-Indian merchant sought to liquidate a bank partnership after the death of one of its partners.[69] The deceased partner held assets in both India and England, and trustees were appointed in London and Madras to distribute the assets of the erstwhile partnership, ultimately entering into an agreement to allow distribution across borders.[70] This case illustrates how cross-border aspects are critical to any insolvency or liquidation process, demonstrating the need to highlight these aspects in Indian bankruptcy law.

Long before the Code was enacted, the Supreme Court of India recognized the right of foreign creditors to enforce their claims under the Old Companies Act. In *Rajah of Vizianagaram v. Official Receiver*,[71] the corporate debtor was a company incorporated in England during the

---

66 The Sick Industries Companies (Special Provisions) Act, No. 1 of 1986, INDIA Code (1985) § 4.

67 Lalit Kumar, *Our Bankruptcy Laws Are a Mess*, THE HINDU BUSINESS LINE (March 10, 2015), https://www.thehindubusinessline.com/opinion/our-bankruptcy-laws-are-a-mess/article22512647.ece.

68 *In re P. Macfayden & Co. Ex parte Vizinagaram Co.Ltd* [1908] 2 K.B. 817, 817. This case went on appeal from the Madras High Court to an English court, which was a common practice during British colonial rule.

69 *In re P. Macfayden & Co. Ex parte Vizinagaram Co.Ltd* [1908] 2 K.B. 817, 818, 819. This case went on appeal from the Madras High Court to an English court, which was a common practice during British colonial rule.

70 *In re P. Macfayden & Co. Ex parte Vizinagaram Co.Ltd* [1908] 2 K.B. 817, 819. This case went on appeal from the Madras High Court to an English court, which was a common practice during British colonial rule.

71 AIR 1962 SC 500.

British Raj under the English Companies Act and was engaged in mining in Kodur in India.[72] The company was unable to pay its debts, resulting in the appointment of a liquidator and claims filed by foreign creditors, which were rejected by the company on the basis that the liquidation proceedings were exclusive to Indian creditors.[73] The Supreme Court rejected the company's argument and held that foreign creditors could validly enforce their claims in the event of the winding-up of unregistered foreign companies in India.[74]

Another interesting case that arose prior to the enactment of the Code was the case of *Intesa Sanpaulo S.P.A v. Videocon Industries*[75] before the High Court of Bombay. Intesa Sanpaulo S.P.A., an Italian bank incorporated under the laws of Italy, had formed a consortium with Intesa Mediocredito S.P.A (Italian Banks) to extend a facility amounting to EUR 35 million to VDC Technologies S.P.A (VDC), a wholly owned subsidiary of Eagle Corporation Limited, a company incorporated in the Cayman Islands, which was itself a wholly owned subsidiary of Videocon.[76] Videocon was a corporate guarantor for this facility and was liable not only for default of the loan but also for the debt in case of change in the share capital of either Eagle or VDC.[77] VDC defaulted on the loan, resulting in dilution of shares in Eagle and VDC,[78] and filed a petition for winding-up as a statutory creditor against Videocon. In a first ruling of its kind, the Bombay High Court allowed the Italian Banks to file such a claim, ruling that any statutory creditor (Indian or foreign) may bring an action for winding-up.[79]

While Indian courts have been proactive in addressing cross-border issues in the absence of a formal law, there remains a lot of legal uncertainty that can only be resolved by a comprehensive cross-border insolvency law.

---

72 AIR 1962 SC 500.
73 AIR 1962 SC 500.
74 AIR 1962 SC 500.
75 Intesa Sanpaulo S.P.A. v. Videocon Industries Limited [2014] 183 Comp Cas 395 (Bom).
76 Intesa Sanpaulo S.P.A. v. Videocon Industries Limited [2014] 183, paragraph 5 Comp Cas 395 (Bom). The appellants (Videocon) appealed the commercial division bench order, but the division bench dismissed the appeal. *See* Videocon Industries Limited v. Intesa Sanpaulo S.P.A. MANU/MH/2686/2014.
77 Intesa Sanpaulo S.P.A. v. Videocon Industries Limited [2014] 183, paragraphs 6, 7 Comp Cas 395 (Bom).
78 Intesa Sanpaulo S.P.A. v. Videocon Industries Limited [2014] 183, paragraph 13 Comp Cas 395 (Bom).
79 Intesa Sanpaulo S.P.A. v. Videocon Industries Limited [2014] 183, paragraph 47 Comp Cas 395 (Bom).

Cross-Border Insolvency under the Code and the Proposed Framework

The Code has not been completely silent on the issue of cross-border insolvency. It recognizes foreign creditors as "financial creditors" who may enforce their rights under the Code either by filing a petition before the National Companies Law Tribunal (NCLT)[80] or by filing claims as a financial creditor once a resolution professional has been appointed for the corporate debtor. Sections 234 and 235 of the Code are the primary provisions under the Code that deal with cross-border insolvency. Section 234 empowers the IBBI to issue letters of request to a court in a particular jurisdiction to allow them to access and deal with assets.[81] Section 235 makes provisions for entering into bilateral treaties for reciprocal treatment of insolvency proceedings. However, these provisions have not yet been ratified into law. The Draft, which seeks to incorporate a cross-border insolvency regime based on the Model Law, has not yet been implemented, despite having been released as a bill over a year ago.

This chapter examines two cases that illustrate the issues that arise in the absence of an effective cross-border framework.

Essar Group

In the early 1950s, Nand Kishore Ruia left the North Indian state of Rajasthan to establish an export business called the Essar Group for iron ore mining in Madras (now Chennai).[82] Upon his death in 1969, control of the family business shifted to Shashi and Ravi Ruia, who set out to expand the business to include shipping, construction projects, oil and gas, mining

---

80 The National Companies Law Tribunals were established across states in India with the introduction of the (New) Companies Act, 2013. The benches of the NCLT sit at New Delhi, Allahabad, Ahmedabad, Hyderabad, Bangalore, Chandigarh, Chennai, Cuttack, Guwahati, Jaipur, Kochi, Kolkata and Mumbai. The appellate court, the National Companies Law Appellate Tribunal (NCLAT), is at New Delhi.

81 India Insolvency and Bankruptcy Code, 2016 § 234.

82 BW Online Bureau, *The Return of the Ruias*, Business World (November 8, 2014), http://www.businessworld.in/article/The-Return-Of-The-Ruias/08-11-2014-62369/; *see also* Suveen Sinha, *$13 Billion Deal for the Ruias of Essar: Lucky or Unlucky?*, The Hindustan Times (October 15, 2016, 16:58 IST), https://www.hindustantimes.com/business-news/13billion-deal-for-the-ruias-of-essar-lucky-or-unlucky/story-FiY3psKABjNw1ikgEQYJkL.html.

and steel.[83] Post-liberalization, Essar also ventured into telecommunications with Hutchison Essar in the early 2000s.[84] From a small town export business, Essar grew to become one of India's biggest conglomerates in the manufacturing, steel, and natural resources industries, with operations all across the world, including the United Arab Emirates, Africa, United Kingdom (U.K.), and the United States (U.S.).

The development of the Code is synonymous with the Essar Steel insolvency. In June 2017, India's largest bank, State Bank of India (SBI), along with Standard Chartered Bank, filed insolvency petitions before the NCLT at Ahmedabad.[85] Essar Group's troubles began with a global downturn in the steel industry, and Essar Steel accumulated over INR 69.19 billion of debt as of July 2019.[86] Further, Essar Steel featured among the "Dirty Dozen" list of corporate defaulters (prepared by India's central bank, the RBI) that were referred to be resolved under the Code.[87] While the Essar case has largely been domestic, creditors to its subsidiaries and affiliates in the UAE and Cyprus have filed claims as foreign creditors before the NCLT.[88] In the absence of any formal cross-border regime, bilateral treaties between India and the implicated countries, or a cross-border protocol, claims against assets owned by Essar's subsidiaries abroad are yet to be addressed.

Videocon Industries

Videocon Industries Limited ("Videocon") is an Indian multinational conglomerate that manufactures consumer electronics and home

---

83 BW Online Bureau, *The Return of the Ruias*, BUSINESS WORLD (November 8, 2014), http://www.businessworld.in/article/The-Return-Of-The-Ruias/08-11-2014-62369/.

84 Hutchison Essar was later acquired by Vodafone in 2007. *See* Andrew Parker, *Vodafone Acquires Hutchison Essar Stake*, THE FINANCIAL TIMES (May 8, 2007), https://www.ft.com/content/0c6cb68a-fdb1-11db-8d62-000b5df10621.

85 C.P. (I.B.) No. 40/7/NCLT/AHM/2017 and C.P. No. (I.B.) No. 39/7/NCLT/AHM/2017, https://ibbi.gov.in/2ndAugust17inthematterofEssarSteelsLtdCPIBNo407NCLTAhm2017.pdf.

86 Ishita Guha, *SC on Essar Steel: CoC Decision Final; Ruling Clears Way for Arcelor-Mittal*, LIVEMINT (November 15, 2019, 10:57 AM IST), https://www.livemint.com/companies/news/sc-on-essar-steel-coc-decision-final-ruling-clears-way-for-arcelormittal-11573795214708.html.

87 Gopika Gopakumar, Alekh Archana & Sahib Sharma, *RBI Tells Banks to File Cases Against 12 Big Loan Defaulters in a Month*, LIVEMINT (June 17, 2017, 12:49 AM IST), https://www.livemint.com/Politics/bTsvgLK63zmErEicmIbf3I/Bhushan-Essar-Steel-among-12-firms-being-moved-to-insolvenc.html.

88 *List of Creditors of Essar Steel India Limited (Summary of Status of Claims from Creditors as of 19 January 2018)*, available at http://www.essarsteel.com/upload/pdf/list_of_creditors5.pdf.

appliances and is regarded as India's first homegrown consumer durables company.[89] However, stiff competition from its Asian and European counterparts, particularly the entry of Korean family-run businesses or Korean Chaebols in the Indian market, impacted Videocon's growth in the late 2010s.[90] As an Indian multinational conglomerate, Videocon owns assets and operates in Brazil, Oman, Australia, Cayman Islands, the Netherlands, People's Republic of China and Indonesia.[91]

On 1 January 2018, NCLT admitted the insolvency petition[92] filed by SBI, to which Videocon owes around INR 11,175.25 crores.[93] The petition did not originally include overseas subsidiaries of Videocon that hold substantial oil assets.[94] However, after the committee of creditors began to invite bids for the overseas oil and gas assets, Videocon asked the NCLT to include assets owned by its Brazilian and Indonesian subsidiaries within the corporate insolvency resolution process.[95] Banks such as SBI have argued that bringing overseas assets into the realm of domestic insolvency proceedings does bring up cross-border insolvency issues that have not yet been addressed in the Code, and the NCLT is yet to rule on this aspect.[96]

---

89 *How Videocon Turned from Making Rs. 800 Crore Profit to a Debt-Ridden Firm*, BUSINESS TODAY (January 24, 2019 11:26 AM IST), https://www.businesstoday.in/sectors/banks/videocon-industries-insolvency-sbi-venugopal-dhoot/story/278647.html.

90 Sayantani Kar, *Match on for Videocon*, BUSINESS STANDARD (January 21, 2013, 02:54 IST), https://www.business-standard.com/article/management/match-on-for-videocon-110051700043_1.html.

91 Videocon Annual Report 2017-2018, http://www.videoconindustriesltd.com/Documents/Videocon per cent20Industries per cent20Ltd_2018.pdf.

92 Under the Code, upon a default (of a minimum of INR 100,000) by the corporate debtor, a creditor may file an application before the commercial courts (the NCLT or the NCLAT) to initiate corporate insolvency resolution proceedings against the corporate debtor. Since the Code was adopted, most insolvency proceedings have been made by creditors by way of involuntary petitions against the corporate debtor.

93 Financial Claim Summary as of November 12, 2018, Videocon Industries, http://www.videoconindustriesltd.com/document/33.pdf.

94 Bhavya Dilipkumar, *Videocon Requests NCLT to Include Overseas Oil Assets in Insolvency Process*, THE ECONOMIC TIMES (August 22, 2019, 7:46 AM IST), https://economictimes.indiatimes.com/industry/banking/finance/videocon-requests-nclt-to-include-overseas-oil-assets-in-insolvency-process/articleshow/70779728.cms.

95 Bhavya Dilipkumar, *Videocon Requests NCLT to Include Overseas Oil Assets in Insolvency Process*, THE ECONOMIC TIMES (August 22, 2019, 7:46 AM IST), https://economictimes.indiatimes.com/industry/banking/finance/videocon-requests-nclt-to-include-overseas-oil-assets-in-insolvency-process/articleshow/70779728.cms.

96 Bhavya Dilipkumar, *Videocon Requests NCLT to Include Overseas Oil Assets in Insolvency Process*, THE ECONOMIC TIMES (August 22, 2019, 7:46 AM IST), https://economictimes.indiatimes.com/industry/banking/finance/videocon-requests-nclt-to-include-overseas-oil-assets-in-insolvency-process/articleshow/70779728.cms.

Recommendations for Establishing an Effective Cross-Border Insolvency Regime

Adopting the Model Law

None of the BRIC (Brazil, Russia, India and China) nations have adopted the Model Law, and Brazil, Russia, and China have explicitly adopted a territorialist approach to cross-border insolvency proceedings. While an analysis of the factors that contribute to a territorial framework's success or failure is beyond the scope of this chapter, it is safe to conclude that at a minimum, such a framework has not proven as effective in countries such as Brazil where it has been tried.[97]

Is the Indian cross-border insolvency framework synonymous with adopting the Model Law? The Model Law does not require reciprocity.[98] Therefore, as long as proceedings under the Code are recognized by a Model Law jurisdiction (that does not adhere to the reciprocity requirement), there is no hurry for India to adopt the Model Law.

However, adopting the Model Law has many advantages. It has been adopted by as many as 46 jurisdictions,[99] including major economies such as the U.S., which embodies the Model Law in Chapter 15 of the U.S. Code (Chapter 15), and the U.K. Being a common law jurisdiction, Indian courts often rely on U.S. and English case law in the absence of precedent under Indian law. By adopting the Model Law, Indian courts would have ample precedent and guidance in deciding cross-border insolvencies. The Model Law embraces modified universalism at its best; it is a straightforward regime that seeks to enhance cooperation and recognition by allowing for ancillary proceedings in support of the "main" proceeding.[100] Further, the adoption of the Model Law will enable emerging common law jurisdictions such as India to handle complex cross-border insolvencies. The

---

97 Foreign creditors of Brazilian conglomerates often file for reorganization in the United States to facilitate faster restructuring. *See In re Rede Energia SA* 515 B.R. 69 (Bkrtcy. S.D.N.Y. 2014).

98 United Nations Commission on International Trade Law, *Model Law on Cross-Border Insolvency with Guide to Enactment and Interpretation*, U.N. COMM'N ON INT'L TRADE LAW, 1, 20 U.N. SALES NO.:E.14.V.2 (July 2014), available at https://www.uncitral.org/pdf/english/texts/insolven/1997-Model-Law-Insol-2013-Guide-Enactment-e.pdf.

99 *Status UNCITRAL Model Law on Cross-Border Insolvency (1997)*, UNITED NATIONS COMMISSION ON INTERNATIONAL TRADE LAW, available at http://www.uncitral.org/uncitral/en/uncitral_texts/insolvency/1997Model_status.html.

100 Morshed Mannan, *Are Bangladesh, India and Pakistan Ready to Adopt the UNCITRAL Model Law on Cross-Border Insolvency,* 25 INT'L INSOLVENCY REV. 195, 214 (2016).

adoption of the Model Law would provide a strong impetus to the growth of legal infrastructure dealing with cross-border insolvency and other sophisticated commercial matters.

Further, Indian courts seem to have already embraced a form of the modified universalism even before the enactment of the Code. As a common law jurisdiction, Indian courts give emphasis to the principle of comity and have been facilitative of a cooperative approach, as illustrated in the recent judgment in *State Bank of India v. Jet Airways (India) Limited*,[101] where the National Companies Law Appellate Tribunal (NCLAT) recognized and allowed for parallel insolvency proceedings in the Netherlands.[102]

The Code must embody the principles in the Model Law and specifically provide for interim relief in the case of cross-border insolvencies. U.S. courts make provisions for interim relief in the event that recognition is pending.[103] This ensures that the debtor's assets are not disposed of and creditor interests are protected.[104] The Draft in its current form provides for relief only after recognition of a foreign proceeding has been made[105] and therefore must accommodate interim relief while recognition is pending. This ensures timely relief by Indian courts.

The introduction of a fully formalized cross-border insolvency regime largely depends on the availability of supporting infrastructure to implement such a regime.[106] The establishment of the NCLT and the NCLAT has helped to create a specialized corporate law court system, enabling quicker and more effective resolution of complex corporate transactions. However, the NCLT and NCLAT are still grappling with the nuances of the Code and mounting domestic insolvency matters, which gives them little room to take on more complex matters, including cross-border insolvency matters,

---

101 Jet Airways (India) Ltd. (Offshore Regional Hub/Offices through its administrator Mr. Rocco Mulder) v. State Bank of India Company Appeal (AT) (Insolvency) No. 707 of 2019.

102 Jet Airways (India) Ltd. (Offshore Regional Hub/Offices through its administrator Mr. Rocco Mulder) v. State Bank of India Company Appeal (AT) (Insolvency) No. 707 of 2019.

103 11 U.S.C. § 1519 (a).

104 Phoebe Hathorn, *Cross-Border Insolvency in the Maritime Context: The United States' Universalism vs. Singapore's Territorialism,* 38 TUL. MAR. L.J. 239, 253 (2013).

105 § 18, *Draft Part on Cross-Border Insolvency for suggestions*, MINISTRY OF CORPORATE AFFAIRS, GOVERNMENT OF INDIA, June 20, 2018, available at http://www.mca.gov.in/Ministry/pdf/PublicNoiceCrossBorder_20062018.pdf.

106 Steven T. Kargman, *Emerging Economies and Cross-Border Insolvency Regimes: Missing BRICs in the International Insolvency Architecture (Part II)*, 7 INSOLVENCY & RESTRUCTURING INT'L 6, 8 (2013).

which may also be time-sensitive. Therefore, in addition to the adoption of the Model Law, entering into bilateral and regional agreements as well as the use of formal cross-border insolvency protocols are viable alternatives.

Bilateral Treaties

While the Model Law has proven to be beneficial in the jurisdictions that have adopted it, it is not without limitations. The jurisdictions that have adopted the Model Law have uncovered ambiguities and inconsistencies in the text and difficulties in attaining harmonization. For instance, different foreign courts have determined COMI on a varying set of factors. While courts in the U.S. have determined COMI on the basis of the registered office of a corporate debtor,[107] the European Union seeks to determine COMI based on the place where the debtor conducts administration and operations on a regular basis.[108] Another ambiguity lies in the public policy exception, which has proven to be extremely difficult to harmonize; what is "manifestly contrary to the public policy" is largely determined by domestic legal policy.[109] Lastly, the Model Law functions heavily on the common law principles of comity, which civil law jurisdictions are reluctant to rely on.

In such situations, bilateral insolvency agreements play an important and crucial role in facilitating cooperation and recognition of foreign proceedings in cross-border insolvencies.[110] This chapter argues that, by entering into broader bilateral insolvency agreements, particularly between a common law jurisdiction and a civil law jurisdiction, the gap between the legal approaches toward cross-border insolvencies may be bridged.

While useful, negotiating and entering into bilateral insolvency agreements involve huge costs and considerable time. When time is of the

---

107 Ethan Meredith, *Bilateral Insolvency Agreements: A Two-Sided Solution for Reciprocity in Cross-Border Insolvency,* 8 GEO. MASON J. INT'L COM. L. 379, 392 (2017) (citing *In re SPhinX Ltd* 371 B.R. 10 (S.D.N.Y 2007)).

108 Council Regulation 2015/848 of the European Parliament and of the Council of May 20, 2015 on insolvency proceedings, 2015/848, 2015 O.J. (L141).

109 Steven T. Kargman, *Emerging Economies and Cross-Border Insolvency Regimes: Missing BRICs in the International Insolvency Architecture (Part II)*, 7 INSOLVENCY & RESTRUCTURING INT'L 6, 393 (2013).

110 *See generally* Ethan Meredith, *Bilateral Insolvency Agreements: A Two-Sided Solution for Reciprocity in Cross-Border Insolvency,* 8 GEO. MASON J. INT'L COM. L. 379 (2017). The author highlights the benefits of entering into a bilateral insolvency agreement between the United States and France.

essence in cross-border insolvencies that span multiple jurisdictions, bilateral insolvency agreements may not be the most favorable approach outside the Model Law framework.

Cross-Border Insolvency Protocols

The financial crisis illustrated the full extent of the complexity involved in cross-border insolvencies. For instance, eighty foreign affiliates of the *Lehman Brothers* group commenced insolvency proceedings across sixteen jurisdictions.[111] While the Model Law facilitated some ease in parallel proceedings, it could not match the extent of the complications that arose out of *Lehman*. This is where a cross-border insolvency protocol came to the rescue.[112] Since then, cross-border protocols have gained traction in plugging the gaps that the Model Law could not address.

Cross-border protocols are instrumental in getting parties to agree on a framework for the resolution of cross-border disputes that arise out of insolvency, with the backing of judicial recognition. Protocols are drafted outlining how proceedings would be recognized and how parties may exercise their right to appear and be heard before courts.[113] Once the protocols are drafted, they are presented before the bankruptcy courts for approval and enforcement.[114]

Cross-border insolvency protocols play a crucial role in helping judicial systems of emerging economies acclimatize themselves to cross-border insolvency issues as bankruptcy and insolvency laws develop.[115] Cross-border insolvency protocols provide ample precedent for courts to develop expertise and understanding of intricate cross-border issues and

---

111 *Debtors' Disclosure Statement* by Lehman Brothers Holdings Inc. filed before the United States Bankruptcy Court, Southern District of New York, at p. 28, available at https://www.sec.gov/Archives/edgar/data/806085/000119312511239866/dex991.htm #rom224677_21.

112 *Debtors' Disclosure Statement* by Lehman Brothers Holdings Inc. filed before the United States Bankruptcy Court, Southern District of New York, at p. 28, available at https://www.sec.gov/Archives/edgar/data/806085/000119312511239866/dex991.htm #rom224677_21.

113 Kevyn D. Orr, Dan T. Moss & Anna M. Wetzel, *Courts, Cooperation, and More: A review of U.S. Cross-Border Insolvency Protocols-Part I,* Jones Day, July 2017, available at https://www.jonesday.com/en/insights/2017/07/courts-cooperation-and-more-a-review-of-us-crossborder-insolvency-protocols--part-1.

114 Chapter 15 of the U.S. Bankruptcy Code allows for recognition and enforcement of such cross-border protocols.

115 § 18, *Draft Part on Cross-Border Insolvency for suggestions*, Ministry of Corporate Affairs, Government of India, 20 June 2018, available at http://www.mca.gov.in/Ministry/pdf/PublicNoiceCrossBorder_20062018.pdf.

act as a guide in cooperation and coordination among proceedings in multiple venues.[116]

The doctrine of comity has played a crucial role among common law jurisdictions in the recognition of proceedings even before the Model Law.[117] In the decades preceding the adoption of the Model Law, the doctrine of comity enhanced judicial cooperation, although it does not offer the same degree of predictability and reliability as full-fledged cross-border insolvency law.[118] Yet, its importance should not be understated: the doctrine of comity continues to be encompassed within the Model Law and is the basis for the principles of recognition and reciprocity. I argue that, from an Indian perspective, the adoption of cross-border insolvency protocol guidelines that can be used in restructuring documentation proves to be the best step forward. Further, as seen in the *Jet Airways* case, Indian courts seem to be warming up to the idea of formal protocols as a sort of interim step, as incorporating a cross-border insolvency framework into the Code takes time.

Jet Airways: Paving the Way for Cross-Border Insolvency Protocols

Economic reforms of the early 1990s spearheaded the growth of the domestic aviation industry. A forerunner in this growth was Jet Airways (India) Limited (Jet Airways). Incorporated in 1992, Jet Airways grew exponentially to become India's first private multinational airline company, second only to India's national airline, Air India. As of the first quarter of 2019, Jet Airways still possessed a market share of 11.9 percent according to India's aviation regulator, the Directorate General of Civil Aviation (DGCA).[119]

---

116 Paul H. Zumbro, *Cross-Border Insolvencies and International Protocols—An Imperfect but Effective Tool*, BUSINESS LAW INTERNATIONAL 157, 158 (2010).

117 United Nations Commission on International Trade Law, *Model Law on Cross-Border Insolvency with Guide to Enactment and Interpretation*, U.N. COMM'N ON INT'L TRADE LAW, 1, 20 U.N. SALES NO.:E.14.V.2 (July 2014), available at https://www.uncitral.org/pdf/english/texts/insolven/1997-Model-Law-Insol-2013-Guide-Enactment-e.pdf.

118 United Nations Commission on International Trade Law, *Model Law on Cross-Border Insolvency with Guide to Enactment and Interpretation*, U.N. COMM'N ON INT'L TRADE LAW, 1, 20 U.N. SALES NO.:E.14.V.2 (July 2014), available at https://www.uncitral.org/pdf/english/texts/insolven/1997-Model-Law-Insol-2013-Guide-Enactment-e.pdf.

119 April 2019 Traffic Report, DIRECTORATE GENERAL OF CIVIL AVIATION, http://dgca.nic.in/reports/Traffic_reports/Traffic_Rep0119.pdf.

On April 17, 2019, Jet Airways suspended all flights after months of negotiations over restructuring efforts with banks and operational creditors. On June 20, 2019, official insolvency proceedings were commenced before the NCLT in Mumbai.[120] However, Jet Airways' woes were not limited to India alone. It was declared bankrupt in the Netherlands when it failed to pay its European creditors.[121] The NCLT rejected the Dutch administrator's plea to legally recognize the proceedings (for enforcement of security and restructuring of Jet Airways' subsidiary in the Netherlands).[122] The NCLAT, in an attempt to develop the nascent cross-border insolvency framework in India, allowed the Dutch administrator to participate in meetings of the committee of creditors (without a vote), and more importantly, upheld the enforcement of the cross-border insolvency protocol clause in the restructuring documentation.[123] The protocol was an agreement entered into between the resolution professional of the corporate debtor[124] and the administrator for the subsidiary under Dutch law.[125] The protocol distinguished between the insolvency proceedings in India and the proceedings in the Netherlands and stated that Jet Airways would be subject to both proceedings.[126] Clause 3 of the Protocol states that the parties to the agreement recognize that the Indian proceedings would be the "main" insolvency proceedings and the Dutch proceedings would be the "non-main" insolvency proceedings:

> The Parties recognize that the Company being an Indian company with its centre of main interest in India, the Indian Proceedings are the main insolvency proceedings and the Dutch Proceedings are the non-main insolvency proceedings:

---

120 State Bank of India v. Jet Airways (India) Limited CP 2205 (IB)/MB/2019.

121 State Bank of India v. Jet Airways (India) Limited CP 2205 (IB)/MB/2019, paragraphs 12, 13.

122 State Bank of India v. Jet Airways (India) Limited CP 2205 (IB)/MB/2019, paragraphs 12, 13.

123 *Jet* Airways (India) Ltd. (Offshore Regional Hub/Offices through its administrator Mr. Rocco Mulder) v. State Bank of India Company Appeal (AT) (Insolvency) No. 707 of 2019.

124 The Code envisages a creditor-in-possession model. Under the Code, the resolution professional is appointed by the committee of creditors to undertake and supervise the management of the corporate debtor.

125 Jet Airways (India) Ltd. (Offshore Regional Hub/Offices through its administrator Mr. Rocco Mulder) v. State Bank of India Company Appeal (AT) (Insolvency) No. 707 of 2019.

126 Jet Airways (India) Ltd. (Offshore Regional Hub/Offices through its administrator Mr. Rocco Mulder) v. State Bank of India Company Appeal (AT) (Insolvency) No. 707 of 2019.

(a) Coordination—To promote international cooperation and the coordination of activities in the Proceedings; and to provide for the orderly, effective, efficient, and timely administration of the Proceedings in order to reduce their cost and maximize recovery for creditors.
(b) …
(c) …
(d) …
(e) Communication—To promote communication among the Parties and the CoC; and to provide, wherever possible, for direct communication among NCLT, NCLAT and Dutch Bankruptcy Court.
(f) Information and Data Sharing—To provide for the sharing of relevant information and data among the Parties in order to promote effective, efficient, and fair Proceedings, and to avoid duplication of effort and activities by the parties.
(g) Preservation—To identify, preserve, and maximize the value of the Company's worldwide assets for the collective benefit of all creditors and other interested parties.
(h) Claims Reconciliation—To coordinate an efficient and transparent claims process.
(i) Maximize value of assets/recoveries—To cooperate in marshalling the assets of the Company in order to maximize value of assets/recovery for all of the Company's creditors.
(j) Comity—To maintain the independent jurisdiction, sovereignty, and authority of NCLT, NCLAT, and Dutch Bankruptcy Court.[127]

This judgment illustrates the potential and effective use of contractual protocols in cross-border insolvency matters. Although the ruling of the NCLAT has given precedence to domestic insolvency proceedings under the Code, the recognition of cross-border insolvency protocol allows room for cooperation between the Dutch and Indian administrators in the resolution process.

However, this case also illustrates the struggle between the approaches to cross-border insolvency from an Indian perspective. While creditors

127 Jet Airways (India) Ltd. (Offshore Regional Hub/Offices through its administrator Mr. Rocco Mulder) v. State Bank of India Company Appeal (AT) (Insolvency) No. 707 of 2019.

may make applications to the NCLT or the NCLAT to recognize a particular proceeding as a "main" proceeding, it largely rests on the discretion of the courts, leaving room for uncertainties.

The cross-border insolvency protocol adopted in the *Jet Airways* case is the first of its kind and has paved the way for the use of such protocols in future cross-border insolvencies involving India as a jurisdiction. So that cross-border insolvency protocols are more effective as an alternative to the Model Law, this chapter argues that the IBBI should adopt a practice guide on formulating cross-border insolvency protocols based on the UNCITRAL Practice Guide.[128] Like the UNCITRAL Practice Guide, the practice guide may seek to provide sample clauses, which serve as useful guidance to ensure uniformity and establish a market precedent while also ensuring fairness to the parties. Having standardized and uniform protocols that are fair to parties in a cross-border insolvency dispute are also likely to be recognized and enforced by courts.

Adoption of the JIN Guidelines

The JIN, an institutionalized network of judges and lawyers who practice insolvency and bankruptcy law, formulated the Guidelines for Communication and Cooperation between Courts in Cross-Border Insolvency Matters (JIN Guidelines), which has garnered wide recognition and adoption since its inception in Singapore in October 2016.[129] The key objective of the JIN Guidelines is to enhance efficiency in cross-border proceedings by reducing transaction costs associated with information asymmetry. The JIN Guidelines stipulate that all courts where insolvency proceedings have been commenced notify each other of present and potential issues[130] and adopt time-saving procedures to prevent delay in the coordination of

128 In 2009, the UNCITRAL formulated the Practice Guide on Cross-Border Insolvency Cooperation that provides guidelines for formulating Cross-Border Insolvency Agreements, including protocols. *See* UNCITRAL Practice Guide on Cross-Border Insolvency Cooperation, U.N. COMM'N ON INT'L TRADE LAW, 1, 1 (July 2009), available at https://www.uncitral.org/pdf/english/texts/insolven/Practice_Guide_english.pdf.

129 Judicial Insolvency Network, "*Guidelines for Communication and Cooperation between Courts in Cross-Border Insolvency Matters,*" (2016), available at http://www.jin-global.org/jin-guidelines.html.

130 Judicial Insolvency Network, "*Guidelines for Communication and Cooperation between Courts in Cross-Border Insolvency Matters,*" Guideline 1 (2016), available at http://www.jin-global.org/jin-guidelines.html.

requests.[131] The JIN Guidelines encourage direct communications between courts through videoconference or telephone conference, which may or may not allow for parties to be present.[132] Further, the JIN Guidelines allow courts to appear before a foreign court, subject to approval by that foreign court.[133] Since its formulation, the JIN Guidelines have been adopted by the Southern District of New York (SDNY), the U.S. Bankruptcy Court for the District of Delaware, Singapore, the U.K., and Hong Kong.[134]

The *Jet Airways* case is the first of many cross-border insolvencies to come before Indian courts, and the development of a workable and certain framework on cooperation and communication with other courts is crucial. Therefore, this chapter argues that Indian courts (particularly the NCLT and the NCLAT, which are the adjudicating bodies that deal with insolvencies in India) must adopt the JIN Guidelines to foster more efficient communication in cross-border insolvencies with courts in other jurisdictions.

Conclusion

Although businesses are increasingly global, financial distress is confined by jurisdictional boundaries. This has been the bane of the territorialist approach to cross-border insolvencies. While the Code has been central to the much-needed overhaul of bankruptcy laws and strengthening of creditor rights in India, it has been blind to the global nature of Indian conglomerates and multinational corporations. In that sense, the Code is incomplete without a cross-border insolvency framework. It is important to recognize that a cross-border insolvency framework cannot be complete by adopting the Model Law alone; indeed, it is only one of the tools of an effective

131 Judicial Insolvency Network, "*Guidelines for Communication and Cooperation between Courts in Cross-Border Insolvency Matters,*" Guideline 3 (2016), available at http://www.jin-global.org/jin-guidelines.html.

132 Judicial Insolvency Network, "*Guidelines for Communication and Cooperation between Courts in Cross-Border Insolvency Matters,*" Guidelines 7 & 8 (2016), available at http://www.jin-global.org/jin-guidelines.html.

133 Judicial Insolvency Network, "*Guidelines for Communication and Cooperation between Courts in Cross-Border Insolvency Matters,*" Guideline 10 (2016), available at http://www.jin-global.org/jin-guidelines.html.

134 Paul H Zumbro & Omid H Nasab, *Two Is Company but Three Is a (Better) Crowd: The Southern District of New York Joins Delaware and Singapore in Adopting Cross-Border Insolvency Guidelines*, 11 INSOLVENCY AND RESTRUCTURING INT'L 21 (2017).

regime. Cross-border insolvency protocols are critical due to their role in fostering quicker resolution and reduction of the large transaction costs that are associated with cross-border litigation. The *Jet Airways* case has highlighted the imperative role of cross-border protocols; it is vital for the Code to embrace the legal infrastructure that fosters this role.

Piercing the Corporate Veil to Ascertain Implied Consent to Arbitrate: A Comparative Perspective from Brazil

Caetano Berenguer

Litigation and Arbitration Partner at Sergio Bermudes Advogados, Rio de Janeiro and Sao Paulo, Brazil

Gustavo Favero Vaughn

L.L.M. Candidate at Columbia Law School, Litigation and Arbitration Associate at Cesar Asfor Rocha Advogados, Sao Paulo, Brazil

Introduction

This chapter considers the following question: under Brazilian Law, can the theory of disregard of legal entity be used as a means of ascertaining implied consent to arbitrate by a person or entity that is not a signatory to an arbitration agreement?

Arbitration is essentially based on the autonomy (free exercise of volition) of the parties. That usually means that only parties who have expressly consented to the arbitration agreement are bound by the obligation to refer their dispute to arbitration. In relatively straightforward cases, in which, for example, there are only two parties to a contract containing an arbitration clause, issues as to the subjective limits of the agreement to arbitrate are unlikely to arise. However, as the recent practice of arbitration in Brazil has revealed, the use of arbitration to resolve disputes in complex transactions (e.g., multiparty or multi-contract situations) may raise fundamental questions as to whether (and to what extent) a non-signatory to a contract may be considered to have effectively consented to arbitration proceedings.

One specific question that arises in such cases is whether (and, again, to what extent) arbitrators should look for implicit consent in disputes involving multiple persons, not all of whom have expressly manifested their agreement to arbitrate a dispute. A particularly thorny issue is whether an arbitral tribunal has powers to disregard legal personality (pierce the corporate veil) in order to join or maintain a non-signatory as a party to an arbitration. This is the issue we examine in this chapter, in the light of subjective and objective arbitrability.

Under Brazilian Law, material (substantive) aspects of the disregard doctrine, such as the scope of its application, are regulated principally by Article 50 of the Civil Code, whereas procedural matters are governed by Articles 133 through 137 of the Civil Procedure Code. Although the disregard doctrine has been the subject of frequent analysis by Brazilian legal scholars, practitioners and judges, the debate surrounding its applicability to arbitration is relatively recent and has not been as thoroughly explored as other aspects. The issue recently came to the fore following a split ruling by the Brazilian Superior Court of Justice holding that an arbitration agreement could be deemed binding on non-signatories following the disregard of the corporate veil.[1]

The aim of this chapter is to present an overview of the possible use of the disregard doctrine under Brazilian Law as a means of ascertaining a non-signatory's implied consent to arbitration. To that end, we set out a brief analysis of the current legislation, legal theory and relevant case law.

Consent as the Basis of Arbitral Jurisdiction

The use of arbitration as a means of resolving disputes is only possible with the consent of the parties. This consent is, in the words of Sergio Bermudes, the "bedrock of the 'flourishing institute' of arbitration."[2] Consequently, lack of consent or an invalid expression of consent renders arbitration impossible.[3] Arbitration is therefore a "creature of the contract."[4] The parties, in the exercise of their volition, agree to resolve a dispute by

1 Brazilian Superior Court of Justice, Case Number 1.698.730-SP, reporting Justice Bellizze (2018).

2 Sergio Bermudes, Arbitragem: um instituto florescente, *Revista de Arbitragem e Mediação*, v. 50, pp. 387-389 (2016).

3 Julian Lew and Loukas Mistelis, et al., *Comparative international commercial arbitration*, Kluwer Law International, p. 99 (2003).

4 *United Steelworkers of America v. American Manufacturing Co.*, 80 S.Ct. 1363, 1364 (1960); George A. Bermann, The self-styled "autonomy" of international arbitration, in William W. Park (ed.), *Arbitration international*, Oxford University Press, v. 36, p. 223 (2020).

arbitration and this agreement is recorded in a procedural convention (the arbitration agreement).[5]

Under Brazilian Law, the arbitration agreement may take the form of an arbitration clause in a contract or in a separate agreement to arbitrate (a submission agreement). As per Articles 4 and 9 of the Brazilian Arbitration Act (Law 9307/1996), the main difference between the arbitration clause and submission agreement is the timing: arbitration clauses precede the dispute, whereas the submission agreements are entered into after a specific dispute has arisen. The scope of the agreement to arbitrate is therefore limited.[6]

Party autonomy is material in arbitration in that parties have a very considerable degree of freedom to decide on the structure and organization of the proceedings. That includes choosing the seat of arbitration; the size and composition of the arbitral tribunal; the applicable law to the merits and to the procedure.

In essence, the parties may, by agreement, shape the arbitration proceedings according to their agreed will.[7] That is one of the many advantages of arbitration, enabling optimization of the jurisdictional provision in the light of the parties' specific needs. For instance, given the procedural flexibility of arbitration, it is possible for parties from Civil Law jurisdictions to structure proceedings that follow a Common Law model and vice versa, or even adopt a hybrid model. The main restriction on this freedom of choice under Brazilian Law is that the agreement between the parties must not breach public policy and good custom (Article 2, paragraph 2, of the Brazilian Arbitration Act).

The contractual nature of arbitration in no way diminishes its "jurisdictional essence." Arbitrators are impartial and independent judges of fact and law under the Brazilian legal system and their rulings are fully binding on the parties. An arbitral award, like a court order, can form res judicata and is enforceable under Article 515 of the Brazilian Civil Procedure Code. As Dolores Bentolila correctly states: "to claim that an arbitrator lacks

---

5 Carlos A. Carmona, Flexibilização do procedimento arbitral, *Revista Brasileira de Arbitragem*, n. 24, p. 11 (2009).

6 Blackaby Nigel and Constantine Partasides, et. al., *Redfern and Hunter on international arbitration*, 6. ed., Oxford University Press, p. 72 (2015).

7 Franco Ferrari and Friedrich J. Rosenfeld, Límites a la autonomía de las partes en arbitraje internacional, *Revista de Arbitraje Comercial y de Inversiones*, v. 10, p. 337 (2010).

jurisdictional power is tantamount to saying he or she is not an arbitrator at all."[8]

There are therefore very solid reasons for parties to opt for arbitral resolution of their disputes. The issue that then arises is how to deal with individuals and entities that did not expressly agree to referral of disputes to arbitration.

The Brazilian Arbitration Act (Article 4, paragraph 1) requires that the agreement to arbitrate must be in writing, but does not specify the type or form of document to be used.[9] This statutory provision is consistent with Article II of the New York Convention on the Recognition and Enforcement of Foreign Arbitral Awards and other pro-arbitration conventions.[10]

The Brazilian Arbitration Act contains additional provisions regarding consent to arbitration in certain specific circumstances. In standard form (adhesion) contracts, for example, the arbitration clause will be effective only if it is the adhering party (considered to be the more "vulnerable" in the contractual relationship) that takes the initiative to commence the arbitration or if said party expressly agrees in writing to arbitration, in a separate document in which the arbitration provision is highlighted and specifically signed by said adhering party.

Furthermore, in disputes involving consumer rights, Article 51, Item VII, of the Brazilian Consumer Protection Code prohibits the "compulsory" use of arbitration. Consequently, arbitration clauses in consumer contracts bind the supplier but not the consumer.[11] Arbitration will be feasible in such circumstances only if the consumer files the proceedings or does not object to commencement by the supplier/manufacturer.

The question that arises is how arbitrators and judges may ascertain the existence of consent to arbitrate in the absence of a specific arbitration clause or agreement to arbitration, assuming that they are allowed to do so at all. Express consent may be construed from signed documents or correspondence exchanged between the parties and that clearly demonstrate their intention to be bound by an arbitration agreement, even if the

---

8 Dolores Bentolila, Arbitrators as lawmakers, *International Arbitration Law Library*, v. 43, p. 17 (2017).

9 *See* Brazilian Superior Court of Justice, Case Number 1.569.422-RJ, reporting Justice Bellizze (2016).

10 Gary B. Born, *International commercial arbitration*, 2. ed., The Hague: Kluwer Law International, p. 659 (2014).

11 Felipe V. Sperandio, Convenção de arbitragem, in Daniel Levy and Guilherme Setoguti (org), *Curso de arbitragem*, São Paulo: Thomson Reuters Brasil, p. 113 (2018).

arbitration clause was not then properly executed.[12] Implied consent may be deduced from the non-signatory party's conduct, such as participation in the performance of the main contract or active participation in the performance of the contractual obligations by a group of companies of which said party is a member.[13] In both cases, the consent must be unambiguous.

Ascertaining Consent to Arbitration in Brazil: General Overview and Case Law

Given its contractual origin, arbitral jurisdiction cannot extend beyond the scope of the originating arbitration agreement, nor can it be extended to persons who did not consent to it.[14] As such, the general rule is that arbitrators lack jurisdiction over non-signatories to an arbitration agreement.

However, in Brazil, certain legal doctrines have been applied for the purpose of authorizing the joinder/participation of parties that are apparently not privy to the arbitration agreement. The "group of companies doctrine" and the doctrine of "related contracts" are two prominent examples. These doctrines often enable a court or tribunal to ascertain implicit consent by a party that, for whatever reason, is reluctant to participate in the arbitration despite having previously agreed (albeit indirectly) to be bound by the duty to arbitrate.[15]

One common misapprehension is that construing the consent of a non-signatory to the arbitration clause is tantamount to the extension of the clause to a third party. That is not accurate. It is not a question of extending—in the sense of expanding, broadening—the scope of the arbitration clause. It is rather a matter of identifying the real parties to the

12 Bernard Hanotiau, Non-signatories, groups of companies and groups of contracts in selected Asian countries: a case law analysis, *Journal of International Arbitration*, v. 32, p. 594 (2015).

13 Stavros Brekoulakis, Parties in international arbitration: consent v. commercial reality, in Stavros Brekoulakis, Julian Lew, et. al. (eds), *The evolution and future of international arbitration*, International Arbitration Law Library, v. 37, p. 121 (2016).

14 Humberto Theodoro Jr., Arbitragem e terceiros—litisconsórcio fora do pacto arbitral—outras intervenções de terceiros, *Revista de Direito Bancário e do Mercado de Capitais*, v. 14, pp. 357-386 (2001).

15 *See* Arnoldo Wald, A arbitragem, os grupos societários e os conjuntos de contratos conexos, *Revista de Arbitragem e Mediação*, v. 2, p. 31 (2004).

dispute.[16] The aim is to determine which parties have effectively agreed to resolve disputes before an arbitral tribunal. It does not, strictly speaking, involve a "third party" that is unrelated to the dispute.

This was an issue that arose in litigation between the U.S. investment fund MatlinPatterson and Gol, a Brazilian airline company. The dispute in that case resulted from the sale of Varig Airlines to Gol by the fund, in 2007. A few months after the acquisition, Gol uncovered information that led it to believe that the sellers, including MatlinPatterson, had manipulated information from Varig's balance sheet and omitted liabilities, thereby causing Gol to pay more for the company than it was actually worth.

As the Varig sale agreement included an ICC arbitration clause, the dispute was referred to an arbitral tribunal. MatlinPatterson argued that it was not bound by the arbitration clause in the sale agreement as it was not a signatory to said contract. The fund was only a signatory to the fifth amendment of the sale agreement, and the fifth amendment did not contain an arbitration clause.

The arbitral tribunal issued a partial award holding that MatlinPatterson had vicariously consented to the arbitration agreement via signature of the fifth amendment to the sales agreement.[17] MatlinPatterson then filed a lawsuit before the Brazilian Judiciary seeking to set aside the arbitration award, restating its objection to the arbitral tribunal's jurisdiction and arguing that the fifth amendment to the main contract did not contain an arbitration clause in relation to the sale of Varig.[18]

The fund's argument was rejected by the State Court of São Paulo. Referring to the arbitral award, the court concluded that there was an evident corporate bond between the fund and the seller company. Furthermore, it stated that the fund had signed an instrument (the fifth addendum to the contract) that was clearly connected to the sale agreement. On that basis, drawing on both the group of companies doctrine and the related contracts doctrine, the court ruled that the fund was not entitled to argue that it was not bound by the arbitration provision. Such conduct would constitute *venire contra factum proprium* which is prohibited under Brazilian Law.

In different circumstances, the Brazilian Superior Court of Justice drew on the related contracts doctrine in ruling that the parties to swap contracts

---

16 Eduardo Lamy et. al., A "extensão" da cláusula compromissória arbitral pela teoria dos contratos coligados, in Olavo Ferreira and Paulo Lucon (org), *Arbitragem*: atualidades e tendências, Ribeirão Preto: Migalhas, p. 257 (2019).

17 Case Number 15.372-JRF.

18 Case Number 0214068-16.2010.8.26.0100.

were bound by an arbitration clause in the underlying main contract, as the agreements were related contracts in a single transaction. The court held that when there are related contracts, the contractual rules established in the main contract must be followed in the accessory agreements.[19]

Two other precedents from the São Paulo State Court of Appeal are worthy of note. In both, the court applied the group of companies doctrine in order to construe consent to arbitration by non-signatory parties.

In *Anel v. Trelleborg*, the São Paulo State Court of Appeal dismissed the appeal of Trelleborg Industri against an order of the first instance court which had applied the effects of an arbitration agreement against Trelleborg Sweden, a non-signatory. The Appeal Court ordered Trelleborg Industri to list its Brazilian affiliate, Trelleborg Brazil, as a respondent to arbitration proceedings commenced by Anel.

The arbitration dispute arose out of two agreements by means of which Trelleborg Brazil had acquired a 60 percent stake in a Brazilian company, *Trelleborg Pav. Anel* also had a holding in Trelleborg Pav and was also a signatory to the agreements. Following the acquisition, Anel discovered that another company from the Trelleborg group of companies had acquired a Brazilian company, Avs Brazil Getoflex, which was one of Trelleborg Pav's main competitors in Brazil. Anel argued that the acquisition of Avs Brazil Getoflex by members of the Trelleborg group of companies constituted unfair competition and violated Trelleborg Pav's *affectio societatis*. On that basis, Anel sought to commence arbitration proceedings.

However, Trelleborg Brazil and its parent company, Trelleborg Industri, refused to participate in the arbitration and Anel referred the matter to court. Trelleborg Industri contested the proceedings on the grounds that as it was a non-signatory to the agreements, it could not be compelled to refer the matter to arbitration. The first instance court granted the order requested by Anel and Trelleborg Industri appealed.

The São Paulo State Court denied the appeal, finding that Trelleborg Industri, as the parent company, had played an active role in the transaction, and that correspondence and the terms of the negotiation had been set out both in Portuguese and in English, in order to enable input from the Swedish company. The court held that it was clear that Trelleborg Industri

19 Brazilian Superior Court of Justice, Case Number 1.639.035-SP, reporting Justice Sanseverino (2018).

was aware of the negotiations and of the terms of the agreements entered into, including the arbitration clause.[20]

In the second precedent, the State Court of Appeal of São Paulo rejected an appeal in which Gp Capital Partners and Smiles sought to set aside an arbitration award that had been issued against them. The grounds for the appeal were that the plaintiff companies were not signatories to the contract that had given rise to the arbitration. The court held that it was clear on the facts of the case that the plaintiffs had led the respective negotiations and had furnished a guarantee for the transaction.

The background to the dispute was as follows: the controlling shareholders of a company named Imbra assigned the controlling shares to Almeria, by means of a contract that included an arbitration clause. Almeria was controlled by Baladare, which acted as an intervening party in the agreement. Baladare was controlled by Smiles, which was in turn controlled by Gp Capital Partners.

The court found that the executives of Gp Capital Partners had negotiated the terms of the contract, and had directed the commercial operation, taking control of the process, before eventually negotiating the transfer of the shareholding to another company, named Arbeit.

The São Paulo Court of Justice rejected Gp Capital Partners and Smiles' appeal.[21] The court, in this instance, found that it was not necessary to disregard corporate entity, or to broaden the scope of the arbitration agreement. Moreover, the court stated that the existence of a group of companies did not in itself lead to a presumption *jure et de jure* of the consent to the arbitration agreement by non-signatory members of the group.[22] Rather, the court held that it was clear that Gp Capital Partners had agreed to the arbitration clause contained in the contract for the sale of Imbra shares, even though it had not actually signed it.

It is clear from these rulings that Brazilian case law accepts that a party may be deemed to have agreed to arbitration even in the absence of express consent. However, it is also clear that the courts will not readily make such a finding. The doctrine of affiliated (related) contracts or the group of companies doctrine will not in themselves be sufficient, in the absence of further concrete elements demonstrating consent. It is incumbent on the

---

20 São Paulo State Court of Justice, Appeal Number 267.450.4/6-00, reporting Appellate Judge Constança Gonzaga (2006).

21 São Paulo State Court of Justice, Appeal Number 0035404-55.2013.8.26.0100, reporting Appellate Judge Pereira Calças (2015).

22 *See* Olivier Caprasse, A arbitragem e os grupos de sociedades, *Revista de Direito Bancário e do Mercado de Capitais*, v. 21, pp. 339-386 (2003).

court or tribunal to establish the true intent of the parties involved in a commercial operation, with regard to the resolution of disputes by arbitration.[23]

The Disregard Doctrine and the Pursuit of Consent in Brazil

We now turn specifically to the application of the disregard of legal entity doctrine in arbitration.

The Legal Discipline of the Disregard Doctrine

Under Article 50 of the Brazilian Civil Code, the disregard doctrine may be applied to prevent or remedy misuse of a legal entity and to enable enforcement against individual members of the business entity of losses caused by misuse of purpose.[24] In civil procedure, a party may apply for an order for disregard at any stage of the proceedings (Article 134 of the Brazilian Civil Procedure Code), in order to assure the enforceability of a potential or existing court decision.

The circumstances that authorize piercing the corporate veil to enable enforcement of the individual assets of a company's members/shareholders are set out in various statutory provisions.[25] For the purposes of this chapter, we consider three main statutes: the Civil Code, the Consumer Protection Code and the Civil Procedure Code.

Turning first to the Civil Code, Article 50 provides that the judge, in the event of misuse of the legal entity, may order the piercing of the corporate veil so that the effects of certain obligations are extended to the private assets of directors, officers or partners of the legal entity who directly or indirectly benefited from the abusive conduct.

Article 50 refers to two possible grounds for a finding of abuse of legal entity: ultra vires misuse of the company's object or the existence of

---

23 Gustavo Tepedino, Consensualismo na arbitragem e teoria do grupo de sociedades, *Revista dos Tribunais*, v. 903, pp. 9-25 (2011).

24 Brazilian Superior Court of Justice, Case Number 1.721.239-SP, reporting Justice Sanseverino (2018).

25 Brazilian Law provides for several instances in which a corporation may have its corporate veil lifted, as a means, for example, to ensure reparation for damages caused to the environment. However, a detailed analysis of these specific fields of application of the disregard doctrine remains outside the scope of this chapter.

unwarranted commingling. The first of these grounds set out in paragraph 1 is characterized by acts that are intentionally performed for an unlawful purpose, as to undermine the rights of creditors. Commingling means the absence of de facto separation between the assets of the company and the personal property of its members/partners. This may arise in the three hypotheses set out in Article 50, paragraph 2: (i) repeated use of company assets to fulfill private obligations of a partner, member or officer, or vice versa; (ii) the transfer of company assets or liabilities without effective consideration (counter performance), except for assets of relatively insignificant value; and (iii) other acts that are inconsistent with the autonomy of company assets. Article 49-A Sole Paragraph of the Brazilian Civil Code explains that the separation of assets owned by legal entities serves as an instrument for risk allocation, so as to stimulate business ventures, generate jobs, increase taxation and income as well as fostering innovation for the benefit of all.

Article 50 embraces the so-called Major Theory of the disregard doctrine. That means that piercing the corporate veil requires effective proof of abuse of the legal entity.[26] A mere shortfall of assets or the occurrence of irregular (unlawful) cessation of a company's activities is in itself not deemed sufficient for piercing the veil, in accordance with the "Major Theory."[27]

Brazilian Law also admits the inverse disregard of legal entity. In such circumstances, the legal entity (company) may be held liable for the debts of its individual members, partners or officers, when the requirements of Article 50 of the Civil Code are met.[28] This would apply, for example, in the event of a director or partner placing their assets with the company in order to hide them from creditors.[29]

There is also a provision for disregarding corporate personality under the Brazilian Consumer Protection Code. Article 28 of the Code authorizes the judge to lift the corporate veil in the event of, *inter alia*: abuse of right; excessive use of market power; or illegal activity to the detriment of consumers. Furthermore, the disregard doctrine may be applied under the

---

26 Brazilian Superior Court of Justice, Case Number 1.672.689-SP, reporting Justice Bellizze (2020).

27 Brazilian Superior Court of Justice, Case Number 1.812.292-RO, reporting Justice Salomão (2020).

28 Brazilian Superior Court of Justice, Case Number 1.180.956-SP, reporting Justice Ferreira (2020).

29 Brazilian Superior Court of Justice, Case Number 1.810.414-RO, reporting Justice Falcão (2019).

Consumer Protection Code when a corporation files for bankruptcy, insolvency, dissolution, or cessation of the business as a result of mismanagement, and when the legal personality in some way presents an obstacle to the redress for losses caused to consumers.

Brazilian Consumer Law, unlike the Civil Code, adopts the so-called Minor Theory of the disregard of the legal entity, which enables lifting of the corporate veil even in the absence of proof of misuse of purpose or unwarranted commingling.[30]

Up until 2015, the Brazilian Civil Procedure Law did not set out a specific regime for the disregard doctrine, so that it was governed primarily by case law, and legal theory. The scenario changed with the introduction of the current Civil Procedure Code, which dedicates an entire chapter to procedural aspects of the disregard doctrine (Articles 133-137).

The new Brazilian Civil Procedure Code treats the disregard of legal entity, both direct and inverse, as an "incidental" procedural matter, meaning that an order piercing the corporate veil may be issued within the substantive proceedings, provided that the legal requisites are satisfied. There is no need to commence separate proceedings.

The parties or the Prosecutor's Office may request the lifting of the corporate veil. The filing of the application may lead to a stay of the substantive proceedings, unless the request is made prior to or at the outset of the lawsuit. Following the request, notice will be served requiring the affected shareholders or officers to present their defense and state the evidence they wish to produce in order to defend themselves.

The application for an order to pierce the corporate veil will be issued by means of an interlocutory ruling. The order may be appealed pursuant to Article 1.015, Item IV, of the Civil Procedure Code or under Article 137 if the order is made at second instance.

Legal Theory as to the Application of the Disregard Doctrine in Arbitration

So far as arbitration is concerned, one important question that arises is whether an arbitral tribunal, if it finds that a company is being misused or that there has been unwarranted commingling of assets among shareholders or between members of an economic group, may direct disregard of the corporate personality and require the shareholders or individual group

30 Brazilian Superior Court of Justice, Case Number 1.766.093-SP, reporting Justice Cueva (2019).

members to submit to arbitration even when these individuals are non-signatories to the arbitration agreement.

There is considerable disagreement between Brazilian legal scholars on this issue. The authoritative commentator Carlos Alberto Carmona categorically states that the decision to exclude state jurisdiction and opt to resolve a legal dispute by arbitration cannot be deduced, imagined, construed or extended.[31] Even in circumstances in which the arbitrators perceive an unwarranted commingling between corporations of the same economic group, or between companies and their shareholders and/or officers, it would not be possible to join in the arbitration those who have not consented to the arbitration agreement.

This author states that disregard of the legal entity under Article 50 of the Brazilian Civil Code cannot be invoked by arbitrators to oblige non-signatories to submit to the arbitration agreement.[32] The principle that parties to arbitration agreements must be exercising their free volition is paramount and acts as a limitation on arbitral jurisdiction, which in turn excludes the possibility of forcing into arbitration a person or entity that did not voluntarily consent to it.

Professor Carmona concludes that in the event of the unwarranted commingling, it will be the remit of a state judge (and not an arbitrator) to issue any measures designed to broaden the effects of the arbitral award.[33]

Professor Renato Beneduzi takes a similar view, asserting that there is no room, in Brazilian Law, for use of the disregard doctrine to force a non-signatory to submit to the jurisdiction of an arbitral tribunal.[34] The issue, according to Beneduzi, is one that lies beyond the limits of the arbitration agreement, and therefore outside the jurisdiction of the arbitral tribunal.

The author suggests two possible solutions. The first would be for the interested party to file a lawsuit against the non-signatory, based on the alleged ultra vires act or commingling of assets, and seeking a court order for disregard of corporate personality. Any subsequent award made in the arbitration proceedings against the company could then be enforced against the assets of individual members in line with the provisions of the court order for disregard. A second alternative would be to apply for disregard of the legal entity within proceedings for the enforcement of the

31 Carlos A. Carmona, *Arbitragem e processo*, 3. ed., São Paulo: Atlas, p. 83 (2009).
32 Carlos A. Carmona, *Arbitragem e processo*, 3. ed., São Paulo: Atlas, p. 83 (2009).
33 Carlos A. Carmona, *Arbitragem e processo*, 3. ed., São Paulo: Atlas, p. 83 (2009).
34 Renato R. Beneduzi, Desconsideração da personalidade jurídica e arbitragem, *Revista de Processo*, v. 290, pp. 473-492 (2019).

arbitral award, which is possible under the terms of Article 515, Item VII, of the Brazilian Civil Procedure Code.[35] No separate lawsuit would be necessary. As Professor Beneduzi correctly points out, this solution is likely to be advantageous to the party seeking to enforce the arbitration award, by increasing the number of parties from whom the required redress can be obtained.

Professors Fredie Didier Jr. and Leandro Aragão also take the view that the disregard doctrine, which they consider to be a civil sanction, may only be ordered in judicial proceedings, and not in arbitration. They agree that an award by an arbitral tribunal on a request for disregard would extend beyond the boundaries of the arbitration agreement.[36]

These authors conclude that the disregard doctrine is not applicable in determining the parties to arbitration, for two reasons: (i) the events that might be relied on as justification for an order to pierce the corporate veil would inevitably be non-arbitrable matters and (ii) piercing the corporate veil as a means to force non-signatories to arbitrate would be a violation of the principle of party autonomy, therefore incompatible with the contractual nature of arbitration.[37]

In his Doctorate thesis, Professor Guilherme Recena Costa analyzes the use of the disregard doctrine from two perspectives: as a means of enabling enforcement against the assets of a non-signatory and for the purpose of obliging non-signatories to participate in arbitration proceedings.

For this latter purpose, the author refers to "attributive" disregard of corporate entity for the purposes of "identification" of parties.[38] As a general example of this "attributive" use, he cites the example of a shareholder that incorporates a legal entity in an attempt to avoid the personal effects of a non-compete clause; by means of attributive disregard (identification), both the shareholder and the legal entity may be made subject to the non-compete provision, thus rendering the evasive maneuver ineffective.

---

35 Renato R. Beneduzi, Desconsideração da personalidade jurídica e arbitragem, *Revista de Processo*, v. 290, pp. 473-492 (2019).

36 Fredie Didier Jr. and Leandro Aragão, A desconsideração da personalidade jurídica no processo arbitral, in Francisco Cahali et. al. (org), *Arbitragem*, São Paulo: Saraiva, p. 271 (2016).

37 Fredie Didier Jr. and Leandro Aragão, A desconsideração da personalidade jurídica no processo arbitral, in Francisco Cahali et. al. (org), *Arbitragem*, São Paulo: Saraiva, p. 272 (2016).

38 Guilherme R. Costa, *Partes e terceiros na arbitragem*, Doctorate thesis, University of São Paulo, p. 146 (2015).

In relation to consent to arbitrate, Guilherme Recena Costa states that only this attributive use of the disregard doctrine is relevant. In other words, if the corporate veil is pierced, it may enable identification of additional individual members of a group of companies or individual shareholders that can be deemed to have consented to an arbitration agreement to which they are not signatories.[39] However, Recena Costa questions the value of application of disregard in these circumstances, given that the same result (identifying consent to arbitrate by non-signatories to the arbitration agreement) could be obtained by the application of the good faith principle and equitable estoppel.[40]

He is even more cautious with regard to use of the disregard doctrine as a means of moving against the assets of a non-signatory to the arbitration agreement. Piercing the corporate veil in this manner would require examination of facts (e.g., ultra vires abuse of the company by a shareholder) that are beyond the scope of the arbitration agreement. It would require the arbitrators to examine the conduct of non-signatories and define consequences for it. Such use of the disregard doctrine, according to the author, is for the state court, rather than an arbitration panel, to decide. Recena Costa echoes the view of other scholars to the effect that, once the arbitration award has been issued, the interested party can apply to court, if necessary, for an order lifting the corporate veil, so as to enable enforcement against a non-signatory to the arbitration agreement.

Paula Butti Cardoso states that there is no legal justification for disregarding the legal personality of a signatory to an arbitration agreement as a means of compelling a non-signatory to participate in arbitral proceedings.[41] The purpose of veil piercing is to guarantee the enforceability of a jurisdictional award, and any application for disregard for this purpose should be made to a state court.

She argues that compelling a non-signatory party to engage in arbitration should not be used as a sanction for dysfunctional use of a legal entity. To hold otherwise would be to undermine the consensual nature of arbitration, which would be unacceptable. In her view, the corporate personality of a legal entity should be respected even in circumstances in which it is

---

39 Guilherme R. Costa, *Partes e terceiros na arbitragem*, Doctorate thesis, University of São Paulo, p. 146 (2015).

40 Guilherme R. Costa, *Partes e terceiros na arbitragem*, Doctorate thesis, University of São Paulo, p. 147 (2015).

41 Paula B. Cardoso, *Limites subjetivos da convenção de arbitragem*, Master thesis, University of São Paulo, p. 154 (2013).

established that the company that signed the arbitration agreement acted merely as the instrument of a non-signatory controller.[42]

More recently, Rafael Xavier wrote that construing tacit adherence to the arbitration agreement should be clearly distinguished from disregarding the legal entity. In his view, a finding of tacit adherence requires a finding of actual consent, whereas applying the disregard doctrine is merely a means of establishing liability for ultra vires acts;[43] hence, Article 50 of the Civil Code would not be an appropriate means of binding a non-signatory to arbitration.[44] Xavier considers that the objective limits of arbitration are in no way a bar to an arbitral tribunal piercing the corporate veil, once proceedings are underway, in order to establish the liability of an existing party.[45] His argument is that it cannot be used in order to compel a non-signatory to participate in the proceedings.

In other words, arbitrators would first have to establish grounds for joining the non-signatory to the proceedings through a theory based on consent (e.g., the doctrine of related contracts, or estoppel) in order to subsequently lift the corporate veil so as to establish the liability of a person/entity that, by then, would already be a party to the arbitration.

Certain legal scholars, however, are more inclined to the use of the disregard doctrine in arbitration. Cândido Rangel Dinamarco identifies a trend toward arbitrations in which the issues involve other members of a group of companies of which the signatory to an arbitration clause is a member.[46] In such cases, he considers that the existence of commingling of assets between group members could serve as grounds for piercing the corporate veil in order to enable the tribunal to require these non-signatories to participate in arbitration proceedings.

Professor Dinamarco makes it clear that the disregard of the legal entity would only be possible if the requirements of Article 50 of the Civil Code have been satisfied. If the prerequisites have been met, the order for disregard could be used to enable the arbitral tribunal to then consider

---

42 Paula B. Cardoso, *Limites subjetivos da convenção de arbitragem*, Master thesis, University of São Paulo, p. 155 (2013).

43 In the same way, *see* Leonardo Melo, Extensão da cláusula compromissória e grupos de sociedades na prática CCI, *Revista de Arbitragem e Mediação*, v. 36, pp. 255-278 (2013).

44 Rafael B. Xavier, A desconsideração na arbitragem? O consentimento atrás do véu, *Revista Brasileira de Arbitragem*, v. XVII, p. 66 (2020).

45 Rafael B. Xavier, A desconsideração na arbitragem? O consentimento atrás do véu, *Revista Brasileira de Arbitragem*, v. XVII, p. 66 (2020).

46 Cândido R. Dinamarco, *A arbitragem na teoria geral do processo*, São Paulo: Malheiros, p. 101 (2013).

whether the conduct of non-signatory members of the business group amounted to implied consent to arbitrate.[47]

Eduardo Secchi Munhoz argues that the disregard doctrine can be seen as a way of attributing implied consent to arbitrate by persons who are hiding behind a legal personality. However, only the objective interpretation of Article 50 of the Brazilian Civil Code could confirm such a statement, regardless of whether Brazilian Corporate Law adopts a model for regulating corporate groups disconnected from their economic reality.[48] It would not be necessary to find abuse of rights, for example (subjective theory of disregard). Thus, Article 50 would serve as a useful tool to attribute reality to what occurs in corporate groups.[49]

Scholars have also examined the issue of piercing the corporate veil through the prism of the effectiveness of the arbitral award. The question that arises is to what extent it might be feasible for the arbitral tribunal itself to ensure the effectiveness of an award by disregarding legal personality so that damages could then be enforced against the assets of third parties who did not participate in the arbitral proceedings.

According to Flávio Yarshell, disregard of legal entity would be a matter to be considered first and foremost by the arbitral tribunal, which has the jurisdiction, under Article 8, Sole Paragraph, of the Brazilian Arbitration Act, to interpret the scope of the arbitration agreement and, therefore, the scope of the arbitration award. As such, applications for disregard should be examined by the arbitrators, and not by a state judge.

The author contends that if the request for lifting the corporate veil is based on the fact that both a signatory and a non-signatory are "debtors" of an obligation, the correct approach would be to hold the arbitration agreement binding on all of them, requiring them to participate in the arbitration and therefore subjecting them to the tribunal's jurisdiction.[50]

Such subjective "expansion" of the arbitration agreement would be for the arbitrators to determine, in line with the application of the principle of competence-competence provided for in Article 8, Single Paragraph of the

47 Cândido R. Dinamarco, *A arbitragem na teoria geral do processo*, São Paulo: Malheiros, p. 102 (2013).

48 Eduardo S. Munhoz, Arbitragem e grupos societários, in Haroldo Verçosa (org), *Aspectos da arbitragem institucional*, São Paulo: Malheiros, p. 179 (2008).

49 Eduardo S. Munhoz, Arbitragem e grupos societários, in Haroldo Verçosa (org), *Aspectos da arbitragem institucional*, São Paulo: Malheiros, p. 180 (2008).

50 Flávio L. Yarshell, Sentença arbitral e desconsideração da personalidade jurídica na fase de cumprimento de sentença, in Adrian Simons et. al. *Estudos em homenagem a Ada Pellegrini Grinover e José Carlos Barbosa Moreira*, São Paulo: Tirant lo Blanch, p. 621 (2019).

Brazilian Arbitration Act. Any interpretation to the contrary would give carte blanche for an interested party to obtain from the Judiciary relief that was within the jurisdiction of the arbitral tribunal to grant, thereby undermining the arbitral process.

In circumstances in which there was resistance in the arbitration to the joinder of non-signatories or a refusal by the arbitral tribunal to include them, then the issue of disregard of the legal entity would clearly be within the remit of state jurisdiction. Professor Yarshell's argument is that the first port of call for "extension" of the effects of the arbitral agreement should be the tribunal, not the Judiciary.[51]

Finally, Carlos Lobo argues that it is perfectly possible for an arbitral tribunal to pierce the corporate veil without violating the subjective and objective limits of the arbitration agreement.[52]

Regarding subjective arbitrability, he contends that non-signatories are bound by the arbitration agreement not because of implied consent but due to the deconstruction of the unlawful concealment of the parent company behind its corporate veil. In this sense, the disregard doctrine would serve as an instrument for the identification and holding accountable of an agent that had committed fraud using the controlled company. Carlos Lobo states that issues arising under Article 50 of the Brazilian Civil Code are within the scope of the "objective" arbitrability and that arbitrators are therefore entitled to make an order on them.

Case Law on the Application of the Disregard Doctrine in Arbitration

The *Continental* case is the most widely known precedent in Brazil on the issue of piercing the corporate veil for the purposes of establishing consent to arbitrate.[53] The dispute in that case arose when the Continental and Serpal companies entered into a civil construction contract to expand Continental's tire plant. Continental alleged that Serpal then breached the contract, leading the parties to refer their dispute to arbitration.

Before filing the arbitration proceedings, Continental sought conservatory relief against Serpal in the State Court of São Paulo in the form of an

51 Flávio L. Yarshell, Sentença arbitral e desconsideração da personalidade jurídica na fase de cumprimento de sentença, in Adrian Simons et. al. *Estudos em homenagem a Ada Pellegrini Grinover e José Carlos Barbosa Moreira*, São Paulo: Tirant lo Blanch, p. 621 (2019).

52 Carlos Lobo, Cláusula compromissória e grupo de sociedades, *Revista de Arbitragem e Mediação*, v. 48, pp. 33-52 (2016).

53 Brazilian Superior Court of Justice, REsp 1.698.730-SP, Justice Bellizze, 3. T. (2018).

order to pierce Serpal's corporate veil and an order for freeze (attachment) of the assets of its controlling shareholder and other members of its business group. The application was filed on the basis that these companies had allegedly fraudulently received assets from Serpal.

Continental argued that the pre-arbitration measure was necessary to secure the effectiveness of a future arbitral award. The first instance court granted the application for disregard, on the grounds that Serpal had dissipated its assets as a means of evading its debts.

Once the arbitral tribunal had been constituted, the state judge sent an official letter to the arbitrators requesting that they issue a decision as to whether or not the provisional remedy granted by the court should be maintained. The arbitral tribunal, however, declined to consider the question, holding that in terms of subjective arbitrability, its jurisdiction was limited to the signatories to the arbitration agreement. Furthermore, in terms of objective arbitrability, the panel held that their jurisdiction did not extend to hearing allegations of abuse of Serpal's legal personality by non-signatory parties, which fell within the jurisdiction of a state court, as a matter pertaining to the enforceability of an arbitral award.

In the light of the arbitrators' response, the state court confirmed the order for conservatory relief, granting Continental's request for attachment of assets. This order was upheld on appeal before the São Paulo State Court of Appeal.

Serpal then lodged an appeal to the Superior Court of Justice, arguing that the state court ruling violated provisions of the Civil Procedure Code and the Civil Code.

In analyzing Serpal's appeal, rapporteur Justice Marco Aurélio Bellizze held that the key issue was whether or not the arbitral tribunal had jurisdiction to hear an application to disregard Serpal's corporate entity.

Justice Bellizze held that the state court should only have granted provisional relief effective until the constitution of the arbitral tribunal and should not then have granted a definitive order. The arbitral tribunal in turn should have analyzed the provisional court order and should have decided whether or not to uphold it. The provisional order dealt with issues that were inherent to the efficacy of the arbitral award, in particular the issue of whether the Serpal's corporate veil should be pierced in order to enable effective enforcement of the future arbitral award. The tribunal was wrong to decline jurisdiction to deal with this issue. Serpal was a signatory to the arbitration agreement, and the fact that the order to disregard the corporate entity of non-signatories did not constitute valid grounds for refusing to rule on the issue.

Justice Bellizze stated that whether a person or entity was bound by said agreement did not depend on how that person was described in a given document but on the substance of the relationships that emerged from the contract in issue. Tacit consent to arbitration existed in circumstances in which an entity abusively exercised powers of control in order to avoid formally signing an arbitration agreement by arranging for another entity to sign the contract, with the controlling-party's intention being to prejudice another party, for example, by dissipating assets and then avoiding liability.

According to Justice Bellizze, to hold that an arbitration agreement was binding only on the actual signatories would enable the misuse of the arbitration process as a shield against the duty to provide redress for loss. The person or entity that was actually responsible for performance of the contractual obligations would be able to avoid the consequences of breach by arranging for the contract containing an arbitration clause to be signed by another member of the business group, safe in the knowledge that such a maneuver could not be challenged by an application to the arbitral tribunal for disregard of corporate personality.

Justice Bellizze concluded his opinion stating that it was open to arbitrators, provided they were formally requested to do so, to make a finding that there had been implicit consent to an arbitration clause by a non-signatory, in circumstances in which the signatory party had acted with abuse of legal personality, fraud, or bad faith. The panel would need to ensure due process and allow the parties (and prospective parties) to present full arguments and call evidence, if necessary. The panel could then issue a ruling to the effect that the non-signatories were to be bound by the arbitration agreement.

In Justice Bellizze's view (obiter dictum), the application for disregard of legal personality in this case, in order to enable future attachment of assets on enforcement, could have been made to the arbitral tribunal, and the arbitrators had full jurisdiction to hear it.

In terms of the practical outcome of the appeal, Justice Bellizze held that since Continental had failed to take any action to challenge the arbitral tribunal's refusal to consider the issue of disregard, and further since Continental had failed to file substantive legal provisions within the stipulated time period following the granting of conservatory relief, Serpal's appeal against provisional attachment was to be granted.

Justice Nancy Andrighi dissented. She argued that it was not open to the arbitral tribunal, in the specific case, to decide on the issue of disregard of Serpal's legal personality, as doing so might amount to violation of the Brazilian Arbitration Act. The main purpose of the disregard application was to preserve the assets of companies (including non-signatory companies) with a view to subsequent enforcement of a future arbitral award. That was not within the scope of the arbitration agreement.

Justice Andrighi made express reference to the importance of party consent as a valid basis for the arbitral tribunal's refusal to examine and decide on the state court's decision to disregard Serpal's legal entity. She emphatically rejected the idea that an arbitral tribunal could rule on a request to lift the corporate veil for the purposes of joinder of parties, and that any such ruling would be a breach of the autonomy (volition) of parties to arbitration.

Justice Paulo de Tarso Sanseverino also dissented, but the vote of the rapporteur prevailed, being followed by Justices Moura Ribeiro and Ricardo Villas Bôas Cueva.

The dispute, however, was not yet finished. Continental prevailed in the arbitration proceedings and then filed for enforcement of the award. Serpal, by that time, had filed for bankruptcy. Continental moved not against Serpal, the original debtor, but against its controlling shareholder and other corporations which had been the subject of the order for disregard of legal entity previously granted by the Judiciary. These parties had not participated in the arbitration.

The respondents to the enforcement based their defense on the argument that there was no enforceable decision against them, as the arbitral award had been rendered only against Serpal. They also argued that the arbitral award was null and void due to failure of service on the trustee of the Serpal Bankruptcy Estate to act in the proceedings in the place of Serpal.

The first instance court granted the challenges to enforcement, holding that the purported judgment debtors did not have standing to be sued, and furthermore that the arbitration award was unenforceable. The court held that it was open to Continental to file proof of credit in the Serpal bankruptcy proceedings and make an application within those proceedings for disregard of the corporate entity of the Bankruptcy Estate, in order to move against the shareholders' private assets. This ruling was subsequently upheld by the São Paulo Court of Appeal.

Conclusion

In Brazilian Law, arbitration relies upon the unequivocal consent of the parties. Nonetheless, there are already both nationally and internationally recognized legal theories that may serve as a basis for construing or implying the consent of parties that are not signatories to a formal arbitration agreement.

These doctrines usually require analysis of the conduct of non-signatories in order to ascertain from their actions an intent to arbitrate. A non-signatory parent company that actively assists the negotiation of a contract that contains an arbitration clause, with the contract being signed by a subsidiary, may be required to participate in the arbitration if the tribunal finds that the parent company's consent can be identified from its behavior during negotiations or during the performance of the contract.

The use of the disregard doctrine as a way to compel a non-signatory to participate in the arbitration proceedings is a substantially different scenario. The disregard of legal entity is a form of sanction applied to the deliberate misuse of legal entities. This characteristic of the disregard doctrine in Brazilian Law makes it difficult to justify application of the measure as a means of establishing a non-signatory's consent to arbitration.

The authors' reservation on the use of the disregard doctrine in arbitration is not based on concerns as to undue "expansion" of the arbitration agreement. Such expansion is admitted in exceptional cases, some of which were indicated in this chapter. The main issue, in the authors' view, is the use of a civil sanction as a means for reaching the conclusion that a certain person or entity has agreed to participate in the arbitration, bearing in mind that this conclusion effectively removes the party's constitutional right to submit a claim to the Judiciary.

We therefore consider that the most appropriate venue for applications for disregard of corporate personality is a state court rather than an arbitration tribunal.

In our view, the dissenting opinion of Justice Andrighi in the Continental case is consistent with the fundamental principles of arbitration. Her opinion held that the application of the disregard doctrine to non-signatories to an arbitration agreement is a matter for state courts. Granting arbitrators the power to decide on the disregard doctrine in such circumstances would therefore amount to a violation of the essential principle that arbitration allows resolution of issues voluntarily submitted by the parties in the free exercise of their volition.

It does not seem to be an appropriate measure to open to an arbitral tribunal the application of the disregard doctrine in order to construe consent to arbitration by a non-signatory, even if the panel considers that there has been fraudulent use of corporate personality (i.e., that the requisites of Article 50 have been met). While we certainly understand the reasoning behind the contrary view held by some legal scholars and we appreciate that allowing arbitrators to make such rulings might be a valuable innovation in combatting misuse of corporate personality to evade arbitration, we do not consider that it has a sound legal basis. In sum, in our view, it is not open to arbitrators to first consider a substantive issue (e.g., alleged fraud) in order to then resolve the preliminary issue of consent to the arbitration agreement on which the proceedings are based.

We do not, however, question the use of the disregard under Article 50 within arbitral proceedings when it is used against parties to the arbitration agreement. Arbitrators can apply Article 50 to disregard the legal entity of a signatory (or of a party held to have impliedly consented to the arbitration) in order to enable enforcement of the award against the assets of another person or company that is also a party to the agreement. If the shareholder is also a party to the arbitration agreement, it is open to the arbitrators to pierce the corporate veil of the respondent company in order to ensure that the award can be enforced directly against the shareholder. Arbitrators have de facto and de jure powers to make findings of fact and decide on the application of the relevant law. In arbitrations governed by Brazilian Law, they can, and should, apply Article 50 in appropriate circumstances.

Arbitrability of Intellectual Property Rights Validity Disputes

Jayems Dhingra
L.L.M. (IP Laws), M.Sc. (Maritime Studies), M.B.A., M. Tech (Knowledge Engineering), B.E. (Electrical), FACICA, FAIADR, MSID, Practicing International Arbitrator, Chartered Arbitrator, Accredited Adjudicator and IP Management Consultant

Introduction

The international arbitration system can perhaps act as a bridge for dealing with multiple jurisdictional issues and provide enforceability of the arbitral awards across 168 countries party to the New York Convention 1958 (NYC),[1] which includes several developing and least developed countries (LDC).[2] Unlike arbitration awards, court judgments and orders for interim protective measures can be tedious to enforce, requiring litigation in courts. However, the fundamental principle of arbitration is party autonomy; thus, an agreement between the parties to refer their disputes to an arbitration forum of their choice is a prerequisite, making it a consensual and a contractual process. Under the current international IP protection framework, invoking arbitration against a non-contractual party, or a claim in tort, is not plausible except through a post-dispute agreement. Furthermore, unlike an action in rem, an arbitral award against one infringer is not binding on other infringers nationwide. The argument is that while the arbitration system falls under Private International Law (PIL), IP Laws are public laws, meaning the two are entirely separate disciplines. IP lawyers take pride in their national and territoriality principles within the context of the international IP system.[3] One may argue that, as private adjudicators appointed by the parties, arbitrators would lack imperium. The issues of dealing with Competition Laws, Antitrust Law, Consumer Protection and

---

1 *See* latest status at: https://uncitral.un.org/en/texts/arbitration/conventions/foreign_arbitral_awards/status2.

2 LDCs are the countries that lack the financial and technical resources to tackle the challenges unaided. *See* at: https://www.un.org/development/desa/dpad/least-developed-country-category/ldcs-at-a-glance.html (last visited February 15, 2021).

3 Paul Torremans, ed. *Intellectual Property and Private International Law*. Cheltenham, UK: An Elgar Research Collection, 2015, at xiii.

Fair-Trading Practices (CPFTA) related laws, which often become intertwined issues to be considered when deciding IP validity and infringement matters, are within the sole jurisdiction of national courts.

There is no doubt that over the last two decades, there has been an increasing trend worldwide of resolving disputes through Alternative Dispute Resolution (ADR) forums, arbitration included, instead of through expensive and long-drawn court litigations.[4] But can challenges against arbitration by IP lawyers and public policy advocates be overcome as a policy decision at an international forum of comity of nations, e.g., the World Trade Organization (WTO) and World Intellectual Property Organization (WIPO)? In the context of 35 U.S.C. §294, Hong Kong Patents (Amendment) Ordinance of 2019 and Intellectual Property (Dispute Resolution) Act 2019 of Singapore, this chapter postulates that by reviewing the Agreement on Trade-Related Aspects of Intellectual Property Rights (TRIPS) or drafting a new IPR Enforceability Convention (IPRE Convention), it would be possible to allow arbitrability of disputes arising out of or related to Intellectual Property Rights (IPR) validity, leaving the public policy issues for the courts of enforcement jurisdiction.

The objective of such a review or an IPRE Convention could be twofold:

(1) At the national level, to make provisions for IPR holders, to have an option to refer the matter to an arbitration forum, by agreement between the parties, whether as contractual clauses or with the consent of third-party infringers, as an alternative to litigation in courts.

(2) At the international level, to harmonize the IPRE regulations by permitting arbitrability of disputes related to the validity and/or invalidity of registrable IPR such as patents, trademarks, industrial designs and utility patents (Industrial Property); and to recognize arbitration agreements and foreign arbitral awards the same as under NYC, thereby not treating IP validity related awards as being against public policy under Article V(2) of NYC.

4 Reported by WIPO at: https://www.wipo.int/amc/en/center/background.html (last visited February 15, 2020).

Deficiencies in Current Status of IPR Protection Forums

The motivation for making ADR methods in general and arbitration in particular accessible forums for IPR validity disputes is to curtail the widespread growth in infringements and enhance the protection of IPR. A 2019 study conducted by the WIPO and Organization for Economic Cooperation and Development (OECD) reported infringements of IPR by international trade worth EUR 121 billion per year in 2016, a sum which has been growing since due to the production of counterfeits, fake goods, and piracy.[5]

A tangible property owner can possibly engage security services to protect its immovable property (*private goods*), or go to national courts for redress, but for an IPR (*public goods but with exclusive rights*) owner to protect its movable intangible IP, traveling across borders at the speed of internet may not be feasible. For an average non-corporate inventor or author, costs of protection of the IPR through court-based litigations could outweigh the investments in its creation and benefits to be gained during the tenure of protection granted. The differentiation in costs of legal protection between the tangible and intangible property (IPR) by virtue of a legal framework may be argued as justifiable for protection of the public interest in IPR. However, if an inventor or a creative artist does not disclose his creation, then the public is deprived of the new or innovative ways of life. A balance must be struck between public interest and effectiveness of IPR protection. The IPR are territorial but the benefits can be reaped cross-borders through global trade. Given the increasing cross-border connectivity enabled by the internet and accordingly easy access to patented technology and products, the number of countries with an underdeveloped legal framework for protection of IPR is a cause of concern for infringement, also identified in the *WIPO 2019 Status Report on Infringement.*[6]

Articles 41-61 of the TRIPS Agreement provide a range of measures for IPR enforcement and protection, as a set of guidelines to be adapted in the respective legislation of each Member State. The unequivocal language of Article 41(1) promotes harmonization in enforcement measures as well as in granting IPR:

---

5 *See* at: https://euipo.europa.eu/ohimportal/en/web/observatory/status-reports-on-ip-infringement (last visited January 25, 2020).

6 *See* at: https://euipo.europa.eu/ohimportal/en/web/observatory/status-reports-on-ip-infringement (last visited January 25, 2020).

> 1. Members shall ensure that enforcement procedures as specified in this Part are available under their law so as to permit effective action against any act of infringement of intellectual property rights covered by this Agreement, *including expeditious remedies to prevent infringements and remedies which constitute a deterrent to further infringements*. These procedures shall be applied in such a manner as *to avoid the creation of barriers to legitimate trade and to provide for safeguards against their abuse*.
>
> (*Emphasis added*)

The IPR protection is the prerogative of the jurisdiction of the State which grants IPR in the first place. The international legislative framework requires an IP owner to register it in multiple States to seek protection in the future. To pursue an infringer operating in multiple States, the IPR owner is expected to initiate multiple parallel litigation suits in those States for the same case. This requires engaging legal counsel and translation of all documents and evidence into the languages of each respective court. There would be an uncertainty of the time span for each of the judgments and whether the decision of each of the courts would be same or irreconcilable with each other. Article 2 of the Paris Convention also provides national treatment for protection of IPR, which may not be the same as in the country of domicile of the IPR owner. However, given the sovereignty of each State and flexibility to develop their respective legal framework as a national policy matter, it cannot be expected that for the same case facts, judgment should be the same in each of the State courts. These conventions aim to harmonize the grant of IPR, but allow flexibility in enforcement of IPR based on the principle of territoriality. It appears that TRIPS Agreement Article 41(1) does not aim for harmonization in the laws for protection and enforcement of IPR.

In certain countries, there are special Courts and Tribunals within the Intellectual Property Offices (IPO) for resolving IP disputes, which has resulted in harmonizing the interpretation of treaties, process of substantive examination, and grant of IPR into Statutes. In the European Union (EU), the preparations for the implementation of the Unitary Patent Protection and Unified Patent Court (UPC) have been underway since 2012. It was expected to be activated by the end of 2020 (which is unlikely to be achieved due to various geopolitical issues and the COVID-19 pandemic). Under the terms of the UPC project, the UPC was expected to provide IP protection across the EU Member States.[7] However, the challenges of enforcing the judgments of such special courts outside the respective States will remain. The time and costs to be incurred for litigation through courts would be some of the basic motivations for invoking international arbitration forums.[8] ADR forums are widely used for international contractual disputes, including patent licensing and technology transfer related disputes. In some states, such as the U.S.A., Hong Kong, and Singapore, even issues of challenging the validity of a patent can also be referred to arbitration, unlike in the EU and the Latin American States, where the national courts have exclusive jurisdiction.[9] According to the WIPO Advisory Committee on Enforcement, "ADR has much to offer in IPR enforcement, as it allows disputes about IP, irrespective of the existence, at least initially, of any underlying agreement, to be resolved in ways in which national court, or other traditional or official enforcement systems cannot, or in ways in which, if they can, they do not necessarily do well."[10]

It is trite that the arbitration rules of most of the international arbitration centers, including the United Nations Commission on International Trade Law (UNCITRAL) Arbitration Rules 2013 and WIPO Arbitration Rules 2020, are premised on an existing or contemporary agreement between the parties to resolve their disputes by submitting it exclusively to arbitration. The agreement to invoke an arbitration forum and not courts can be either a Clause in the contract if it exists or an agreement in a post-dispute situation, without any prior contract.

This concept of arbitration for IPR validity disputes raises three underlying questions: (1) will the development of jurisprudence based on case laws from specialized IP disputes related Courts be marginalized due to privileges of confidentiality and unchallenged arbitral awards on issues of public interest; (2) how the decision on validity of IPR between parties to an arbitration will influence the registration of an IPR with the National *IPO*, which is a matter of public interest and involves other stakeholders; (3) how legislation and arbitral institutions can contribute in the Cluster F

---

7 EU Regulation No. 1257/2012, December 17, 2012, *Agreement on Unified Patent Court* (not in force till date).

8 An ICC report on specialised IP jurisdictions worldwide, *Adjudicating Intellectual Property Disputes*, 2016, at 9.

9 Article 24.4 of Regulation (EU) No. 1215/2012, December 12, 2012 on Jurisdiction and the Recognition and Enforcement of Judgments in Civil and Commercial Matters.

10 Trevor Cook, *Alternative Dispute Resolution (ADR) As A Tool for Intellectual Property (IP) Enforcement*, WIPO ACE/9/3, January 21, 2014, at 3.

Item 45 of the WIPO Development Agenda?[11] In the quest to answer the above questions, three propositions are presented:

(1) Jurisprudence can be developed in tandem by court decisions and arbitral awards collaboratively, for the benefit of world trade, and the development of intellectual property.
(2) Enforcement of IPR through decisions of arbitration and ADR forums can be more effectively rendered as judgments by national courts in underdeveloped jurisdictions,[12] which are pro-arbitration.
(3) Statutory provisions for arbitrability of IPR enforcement proceedings as a prerequisite for development of jurisprudence, for encouraging growth of intellectual property of a State.[13]

The significance of this chapter is in benefits which may be realized by engaging the international arbitral institutions and courts of the Member States to contribute to the Development Agenda Item 45 (Category F) of WIPO, by supporting the enforcement of IPR in the context of Article 7 and Part III of the TRIPS Agreement.[14]

Limitation

The third parties referred to are limited to alleged infringers but rational and responsible entities, engaged in legitimate international commercial trading and/or related production activities, with potential for infringement of IPR; it does not include parties engaged in piracy and counterfeiting. The range of IPRs is much broader, but this chapter is focused on Intellectual Industrial Property, i.e., Patents, Utility Models, Industrial Designs, Integrated Circuits, and Trademarks.

---

11 *See also* Article 7 of TRIPS Agreement.

12 The legal framework is defined as underdeveloped when there are no designated judges or courts or tribunals for IP litigation cases; legal framework for enforcement of IPR and judgments is not defined clearly, or it is older than 35 years and outdated.

13 The jurisdictions where legal framework for grant of IPR and administration of appeals and challenge procedures are non-existent. The enforcement jurisprudence is with limited case precedents, for example, in Africa, South East Asia, and Pacific Island countries.

14 Agreement on Trade-Related Aspects of Intellectual Property Rights (1994) is binding on all members of the WTO by Article 11.2 of the WTO Agreement.

International Laws and Treaties for Enforcement of IPRs and Challenges to Arbitration Forum

The first and foremost treaty in the modern context with a bearing on the foreseeable future is the *Paris Convention.* Article (2) of the *Paris Convention* provides that nationals of any Member State of the Union shall be accorded the same protection against infringement of their IP rights as the nationals of all other country members of the Union, without a requirement for domicile or establishment in the country where protection is sought.[15] However, for Article (2) to be applicable, the relevant IPR must first be acquired within the territory, in compliance with Articles (4) and (5). Thus, IPR is territorial, and claims against infringement can only be pursued after the securing entitlement of such IPR. This is an uphill task for a foreign patent holder endeavoring to claim against a party in a country where the relevant IP is not registered. The counterargument would be that an infringement cannot be alleged unless there was a prior registration. If there is no registration, there is no right. If there is no right, there is no infringement. Thus, by virtue of the IP protection framework, to encourage a healthy public domain and open access, IPR must be acquired first. The challenges in registration of IPR in certain countries are revealed in a biannual piracy and counterfeit goods report: "The duration of patent examination in some countries, such as Brazil and Thailand, is overly long and covers most of the patent term."[16] If registration of an IP takes longer than the expected duration of IPR, then it creates a hairline gap between piracy and territoriality of the IPR grant system in the context of the national policy of balancing IPR with public welfare. Thus, if an IPR is granted in Country-A and the IP owner licenses to a party in Country-B, where the IPR registration is pending in the process, the party from Country-B may not agree to pay royalty, as the IPR in Country-B is not yet granted.

---

15 Article 2(1) and (2) of the Paris Convention for the Protection of Industrial Property of March 1883, as amended on September 28, 1979.

16 European Commission, *Report on the protection and enforcement of intellectual property rights in third countries*, January 8, 2020, at 11-12.

Challenge #1: Lack of Jurisdiction of Arbitral Tribunal to Determine Arbitrability of IPR Validity Issues

The arbitral tribunal has the inherent jurisdiction under the doctrine of "kompetenz-kompetenz" to determine the validity of an arbitration agreement between the parties and the arbitrability of an IPR validity issue, which is to be determined under the arbitration law of the seat of the arbitration. If the issue of the validity of an IPR is submitted to arbitration, then whether the arbitrability of validity of an IPR is to be determined by the law of the seat of arbitration or by the law of the country where IP is registered may become a substantive issue for the tribunal to decide, provided the parties have expressly submitted to the tribunal to assess and determine the validity, according to the applicable law. But it raises a challenge that courts of the State granting such IPR should have the authority to decide the arbitrability, not the tribunal appointed by the parties. According to Cook and Garcia, some authors suggest that "this exercise might require analysis of provisions of general application dealing with public policy as a limitation to party autonomy under applicable law."[17] This issue, even if determined by an arbitral tribunal, can become a ground for the challenge during enforcement of an arbitral award, on the grounds of public policy depending on the laws of the State where IPR is registered and the place of enforcement of the arbitral award. However, as the authors suggested, "In our view, submitting to arbitration all sorts of issues relating to an IP dispute—including issues of invalidity—does not violate international public policy."[18] In contrast, as a matter of domestic policy, it could be a matter of public policy to refer IPR validity disputes exclusively to the jurisdiction of national courts or special IP Tribunals.

International Public Policy

The registration of an Industrial Property in a Convention Country is a prerequisite for pursuing a claim against an infringer in that Member Country. The Berne Convention 1886 is a widely adopted treaty with impact on ubiquitous intellectual properties (except for patents, utility models, trademarks, and marks) with IPR holders. Article 2(6) provides that, "The works mentioned in this Article shall enjoy protection in all

17 Trevor Cook & Alejandro I. Garcia. *International Intellectual Property Arbitration*. The Netherlands: Kluwer Law International B.V., 2010, at 54-58.

18 Trevor Cook & Alejandro I. Garcia. *International Intellectual Property Arbitration*. The Netherlands: Kluwer Law International B.V., 2010, at 54-58.

countries of the Union. This protection shall operate for the benefit of the author and his successors in title." Further, Article 5 guarantees that IPRs outside the country of origin shall not be subject to any formality.[19]

Article 2 of the Berne Convention describes the wide range of subject matter eligible for protection as intellectual properties under this convention. In general, these IPs do not require registrations and/or approvals like Industrial Property in Article 1(2) of the Paris Convention. However, in accordance with Article 15: Right to Enforce Protected Rights and Article 16: Seizure of Infringing Copies, the substantive laws applicable for protection of these IPRs are the domestic laws of the country where action is pursued. The arbitrability of infringement claims of IPs under the Berne Convention is generally permitted.

The most relevant treaty for protection of IPRs and pursuing action against infringements is the WTO Agreement, which, with its 164 members, represents 98 percent of the global trade.[20] The WTO Members are obliged to comply with the TRIPS Agreement, which is not a separate treaty but an integral part of the membership obligations for WTO Members. Article 2 of the TRIPS Agreement by reference incorporates parts of the substantive law in the Paris Convention. Article 9 and Article 10 are integrated with the Berne Convention for protection of Copyrights and Related Rights, including Computer Programs and Compilations of Data. The TRIPS Agreement is the most comprehensive compilation of all prevailing and upcoming conventions and treaties related to IPR. Part III, Articles 41-61, gives detailed provisions that Member States are expected to adopt in their respective national legislation to ensure adequate enforcement of IPRs of nationals of all WTO members. This is in addition to their respective obligations under other IP-related treaties and conventions. The noteworthy provisions from Part II of the TRIPS Agreement are:

a) Members shall ensure that enforcement procedures … permit *effective action against any act of infringement of intellectual property rights covered by this Agreement, including expeditious remedies to prevent infringements and remedies which constitute a deterrent to further infringements* (Article 41(1))
b) Procedures concerning the enforcement of intellectual property rights shall be *fair and equitable* (Article 41(2))

19 *See* Article 5 of the Berne Convention for the Protection of Literary and Artistic Works, as amended on September 28, 1979.
20 *See* at https://www.wto.org/english/thewto_e/thewto_e.htm (last visited April 20, 2020).

c) It is understood that this Part does not create any obligation to put in place *a judicial system for the enforcement of intellectual property rights distinct from that for the enforcement of law in general, nor does it affect the capacity of Members to enforce their law in general* (Article 41(5)).

(Emphasis added)

The TRIPS Agreement Part III did not distinguish the judicial authority from arbitral tribunals, special courts, or general courts, and left it for the State to use the prevailing judicial system for civil matters and criminal matters. The IPR infringement matters, including blatant abuse of IPRs, are generally civil matters, except production of duplicates and pirated copies, which fall under criminal matters in several jurisdictions.[21]

The arbitration forum for dispute resolution as an alternative to courts for civil and commercial claims has been well established since the adoption of *NYC 1958*. Article I(3) and Article II of the NYC 1958 are crucial for overcoming *Challenge #1* in this chapter, providing as follows:

Article I (3)

3. … It may also declare that it will apply the Convention only to differences arising out of legal relationships, *whether contractual or not,* which are considered as *commercial under the national law* of the State making such declaration.

Article II

1. Each Contracting State shall recognize an agreement in writing under which the parties undertake to submit to arbitration all or any differences *which have arisen or which may arise between them in respect of a defined legal relationship, whether contractual or not*, concerning a subject matter capable of settlement by arbitration.
2. The term "agreement in writing" shall include an arbitral clause in a contract *or an arbitration agreement*, signed by the parties or contained in an exchange of letters or telegrams.

(Emphasis added)

In the context of complex multi-jurisdiction IPR infringement disputes, if in the TRIPS Agreement Article 41(5), the meaning of "judicial system" is elaborated as "including ADR forums and arbitration," then the challenge of arbitrability under national laws of many countries could be overcome:

21 *See*, for example, in §260(6) and §261 of Singapore Copyright Act (Cap. 63), 2006; and Article 81 of the Swiss Patent Act.

The 168 States that are signatory to NYC and members of WTO would be able to expand their judicial systems accordingly at no additional costs or legislative burden. This will be just like what Hong Kong and Singapore have clarified through amendments in their respective arbitration laws in 2019.

In countries that have not clearly defined in their legislation the arbitrability of IPR infringement matters, the ambiguity prevails under the pretext of civil and commercial matters, involving an economic interest. For instance, in Austria, §582(2) *Zivilprozessordnung* (ZPO) expressly provides lists of non-arbitrable matters.[22] In the article on Arbitrability of Patent Law Disputes under Austrian Law, the author conducted a comprehensive analysis to expose the deficiency due to this ambiguity. The comparative analysis reflected that Belgian Patents Act §51(1) states that an arbitral tribunal has jurisdiction to annul a patent with *erga omnes* effect; in contrast, the South African Patents Act excludes arbitrability of matters governed by its Patent Act. The article's analysis shows Austria is more of a black box when it comes to arbitrability of patent law disputes. Austria has no specific legal provisions on the arbitrability of patent law disputes, nor is there any jurisprudence providing concrete guidelines.[23]

On the other hand, as per Article 24(4) of EU Regulation 1215/2012, the Courts of the Member State where the IP is registered shall have exclusive jurisdiction over issues related to patents, trademarks, designs, or other similar rights required to be deposited or registered.[24] If an inference is to be drawn from the status of the legislative framework in Austria and in Belgium,[25] the Member State where IP matters are not specifically excluded from arbitrability could be arbitrable. Due to the lack of jurisprudence available on this ambiguity in Austria, Belgium as well as other similar EU Member States, the uncertainty prevails.

Under Portugal Arbitration Law (PAL 63/2011), pharmaceutical patent disputes must be resolved through mandatory arbitration. Whenever the national pharmaceutical agency (*Infarmed*) receives an application for

---

22 Zeiler Gerold & Zojer Alexander, eds. *Resolving IP Disputes*. Austria, Wien: NWV Verlagh GmbH, Graz, 2018, at 121-142.

23 Zeiler Gerold & Zojer Alexander, eds. *Resolving IP Disputes*. Austria, Wien: NWV Verlagh GmbH, Graz, 2018, at 130.

24 Article 24(4) of Regulation (EU) No. 1215/2012 of the European Parliament and of The Council of December 12, 2012 on Jurisdiction and the Recognition and Enforcement of Judgments in Civil and Commercial Matters.

25 *See* Belgian Judicial Code Article 1676 §1. "Any pecuniary claim may be submitted to arbitration. Nonpecuniary claims with regard to which a settlement agreement may be made may also be submitted to arbitration."

approval of a generic pharmaceutical product, it publishes a notice; within thirty days, the innovator can file a request for arbitration (either ad hoc or institutional) if it deems that the generic medicine is in breach of its IP rights. This is one of the special provisions in Portugal only, not in the other EU Member States. In Italy, a similar provision was not allowed, citing reasons that it would be unconstitutional to compel a party with a mandatory arbitration clause.[26]

ADR forums are being given special significance for resolving infringement disputes related to Standard Essential Patents (*SEP*) in the Japan Intellectual Property Arbitration Center (*JIPAC*). JIPAC describes itself as one of the most cost-effective dispute resolution service providers for *SEP*-related disputes between small and medium enterprises (SMEs) and licensing organizations.[27]

In South Korea (referred herein as "Korea"), another IP5 member,[28] the trend toward using the ADR forum for IPR matters is slowly and steadily gaining momentum. In recent years, the court-based litigation system has been simplified by creating designated IP Courts and an appellate court, with a special foreign litigation matters unit for litigation in English. When an alleged infringer chooses to challenge the validity of an IPR as its first line of defense, or as a counterclaim, then the statutory provisions for the exclusive jurisdiction of courts will become applicable. However, the issues of validity or invalidity of a patent cannot be referred to mediation or arbitration but should be referred to the designated IP courts. Including arbitrability of validity issues as a question of the legal jurisdiction of the arbitrator is not permissible, despite representing a possible mechanism for more efficient dispute resolution. The scholars and arbitral community in Asia are hopeful that Korea may soon allow arbitrability of all types of IP disputes.

In China, the number one ranked country for the largest number of patents, industrial designs, trademarks, and plant varieties filed in the last five years, a special IP Court at a national level has been recently established. *The Intellectual Property Court is a standing judicial organ of the Supreme People's Court located in Beijing, which primarily hears cases on*

26 Legal Instruments and Practice of Arbitration in the EU, Directorate General for Internal Policies, Policy Department C: Citizens' Rights and Constitutional Affairs Legal Affairs, 2014, at 153.

27 *See* at https://www.ip-adr.gr.jp/eng/ (last visited March 27, 2020).

28 IP5 is referred to the group of top five IP ownership members, i.e., China, EU, Japan, Korea, and U.S.A.

appeal over patent and other intellectual property rights involving professional technologies throughout the country.[29] In accordance with Article 60 of the Patent Law of China, the IP office can conduct mediation between the parties. Failing mediation, the arbitrability of IPR disputes is not yet an option in the matter of infringement disputes, whether before an arbitral tribunal of IPO or organized under an artificial intelligence (AI).

In Switzerland, like China, the Federal Patent Court established under Federal Patent Court Act 2009 has exclusive jurisdiction (Article 26) in disputes over validity and infringement of patents. Article 177(1) of the Federal Arbitration Law provides that, "Any dispute of financial interest may be the subject of an arbitration." This provision is generally interpreted broadly in Swiss Jurisprudence to include disputes related to antitrust and competition law matters; however, like in Austria, the ambiguity of arbitrability of IP infringement disputes remains. In Belgium, arbitrability of IP disputes is not excluded from the Belgian Judicial Code Part VI. Article 1676(1) states: "Any pecuniary claim may be submitted to arbitration. Nonpecuniary claims with regard to which a settlement agreement may be made may also be submitted to arbitration." This is a clearer text as compared to the Swiss Arbitration Code, as it implies that IPR infringement disputes which result only in a settlement agreement between the parties, without monetary issues, can also be submitted to arbitration. The questions of validity and/or invalidity of a patent, trademark, or industrial design apparently are not within the ambit of the arbitration forum. In order for avoidance of doubt that the arbitral award should not fall within the boundaries of Article V(2)(a) or (b) of the NYC ("the subject-matter of the dispute is not capable of settlement by arbitration"), the international arbitration laws (*under IPRL and IPL*) of the NYC Member States could make an unequivocal expression that an IPR dispute between parties is also capable of settlement through arbitration and shall not be against the public policy of a state.

In the U.K., when part of the EU, the jurisdiction of IP disputes involving validity or invalidity of IPRs is exclusively reserved for the courts under EU Regulation 1215/2012. The Intellectual Property Enterprise Court (IPEC), a specialist court, part of the High Court and Patents Court, resolves disputes of infringement matters related to registered IPR. Thus, arbitrability of such IPR is a matter yet to be considered, when feasible, as an amendment to the Arbitration Act 1996 and U.K. Copyrights, Designs and Patents Act 1988.

---

29 *See* at http://ipc.court.gov.cn/en-us/index.html (last visited March 27, 2020).

In Australia, intellectual property disputes are decided by Federal Courts under the Intellectual Property National Practice Area, which includes patents, trademarks, copyrights, industrial designs, and all other categories of IP. Likewise, in other countries where the jurisdiction for IP matters is entrusted to the State courts, the arbitrability and ADR forums are limited to contractual commercial disputes only.

In view of the above short survey, it is evident that except for a few countries, it is an uphill task for an IPR owner, willing to adopt the ADR route, to seek redress against infringements across borders. In the present well-connected and interdependent economies of the world, the access to justice for inventors, artists, authors, and creative entities remains an expensive and arduous path, besides the initial investment in the development of IP and selection of target countries in which to register an IP. Once the marketability of the product is established, counterfeiters and infringers may soon surface from countries where registration is still pending at IPOs. To overcome such difficulties, a concerted and collective effort by all WTO members can achieve the objectives of Article 7 of the TRIPS Agreement and WIPO Development Agenda #45.

Challenge #2: National Authorities Only Can Adjudicate Public Policy Matters

The traditional viewpoint has been that the IPR is granted by a State, and only a competent authority, designated by the State, can invalidate, revoke or alter such an IPR. Furthermore, IPRs are monopoly rights granted for a specific period, which have an impact on public welfare and consumer rights. The state competition authority usually acts as a watchdog and monitors any collusion between competing parties or price-fixing practices. If arbitrability of IPR issues between parties is allowed, then due to the confidentiality of arbitral decisions, it will be difficult to monitor abuse of dominant position or antitrust and anti-competition behavior.

The counterargument is that for public authorities to monitor and investigate anti-competitive agreements, mergers and acquisitions, abuse of dominant position and consumer protection, authorities like the *Competition and Consumer Commission of Singapore* (CCCS) conduct their own investigations to implement the relevant competition and antitrust laws of the State.[30] The affected parties or members of the public can also directly lodge reports with such authorities. The State does not have to rely

30 *See* at https://www.cccs.gov.sg/about-cccs; (last visited May 16, 2020).

on IP disputes, court judgments, and arbitral decisions to monitor and implement public policy. Second, grant of IPR by a state is to an individual or entity for commercial benefits for a limited period; thus, IP is a commercial matter. In the case of pharmaceutical and public health matters, there are designated authorities and laws of each state to administer public health policies. Therefore, it will be a constricted viewpoint for prohibiting arbitrability of IP issues as a public policy matter. This is further evident from divergent views on public policy across the Member States for arbitrability and enforcement of arbitral awards. To single out only IP matters among various other commercial segments as non-arbitrable is a subjective viewpoint. The two key features of arbitrability are:[31]

> First, arbitration only binds the parties to the proceedings, that is, it has inter-parties' effect only. National law can expressly extend the effect of arbitral awards so that they have *erga omnes* effect, but this is quite exceptional.
> Secondly, international arbitration is developed as a means to resolve conflicts of international trade where parochial views that may limit trans-national commerce have been largely disregarded. As a result, it is increasingly accepted that *international arbitration has its own standard of international public policy, tempered by the necessities of international trade.*
>
> *(Emphasis added)*

Challenge #3: Arbitrators Are Private Adjudicators and Lack Imperium

The argument that arbitral tribunals lack the coercive powers to force a party or impose coercive sanctions upon the disobedient party is now a thing of the past. In the latest edition of Model Arbitration Law and lex arbitri of pro-arbitration jurisdictions, arbitral tribunals are given a wide range of powers, including sanctions, injunctions, and subpoena to compel witnesses to be brought in for giving evidence, if required.[32] Except for contempt of court powers, the tribunal does have the widest latitude, much like high court judges, to sanction non-complying parties. The Parties to an

---

31 Trevor Cook & Alejandro I. Garcia. *International Intellectual Property Arbitration*. The Netherlands: Kluwer Law International B.V., 2010, at 54-58.

32 *See* Article 17, UNCITRAL Model Law on International Commercial Arbitration, 2008.

arbitration need not go to court for interim reliefs; furthermore, in an emergency, arbitrators can be appointed within twenty-four hours for urgent matters.[33]

The argument that arbitral tribunals lack powers on third parties is correct, but the same is also relevant in court litigations, except in criminal offenses. A third party cannot be forced to join litigation between two parties unless a separate writ of summons is taken by a claimant or respondent.

Statutory Provisions for Arbitrability of IPR Disputes

IPRs (patents, trademarks, utility patents, industrial designs, marks) are granted by the IPO of a State, in accordance with administrative legislation and regulations for granting such rights. The initial objections for invalidity or opposition to such grants of IPR are normally made during the pre-grant period by lodging a protest at the relevant IPO.

Challenge #4: Exclusive Jurisdictions for Intellectual Property Disputes

After the grant of an IPR and during its validity period, when disputes arise related to infringement, and if in defense, challenges to its validity and revocation are raised between the parties in dispute, the jurisdiction for deciding such matters as a de facto procedure is the issuing authority of a State. The policymakers of a State have an option to either delegate this jurisdiction to general courts of a State or specialized IP Courts, if prevalent in a country.[34] The disputes of infringements are commercial matters between the parties, to which national legislation for commercial arbitration would be applicable, unless IPR matters are specifically excluded like in the EU Member States.[35]

---

33 *See* Article 17, UNCITRAL Model Law on International Commercial Arbitration, 2008 and Article 26: Interim Measures, UNCITRAL Arbitration Rules 2010 and Article 23 HKIAC Arbitration Rules 2018.

34 *See* latest status at: https://uncitral.un.org/en/texts/arbitration/conventions/foreign_arbitral_awards/status2.

35 Article 24(4) of Regulation (EU) No. 1215/2012 of the European Parliament and ofThe Council of December 12, 2012 on Jurisdiction and the Recognition and Enforcement of Judgments in Civil and Commercial Matters.

However, in many of the advanced and IP5 member countries and industrialized economies in Asia (i.e., Australia, Hong Kong, Malaysia, and Singapore), arbitrability of IPR disputes is well recognized in the legislation as well as in the jurisprudence. There has been an increasing trend for the parties in Technology Media and Telecom (TMT) industries to opt for arbitration as the preferred mode of dispute resolution.[36] A critic might discount the survey reports as not an authentic source for development of new legislation and opinions of scholars and promoters of ADR as being biased. However, one cannot ignore the positive steps taken through amendments in IP legislation of the rising economies of Asia to afford ADR options. The brief review of provisions for arbitration in United States (U.S.) Patent Laws and recent amendments in Hong Kong and Singapore are discussed hereunder.

United States Code Title 35—Patents

§294 of U.S.C. Title 35 recognizes voluntary arbitration agreements between the parties as well as dispute resolution clauses within a contract related to licensing or similar agreements:

> **Voluntary arbitration.**
>
> a) A contract involving a patent or any right under a patent may contain a provision requiring arbitration of any dispute relating to patent validity or infringement arising under the contract. *In the absence of such a provision, the parties to an existing patent validity or infringement dispute may agree in writing to settle such dispute by arbitration.* Any such provision or agreement shall be valid, irrevocable, and enforceable, except on any grounds that exist at law or in equity for revocation of a contract. (*Emphasis added*)

§294(b) provides a clear unequivocal link to the U.S.C. Title 9—Arbitration, and declares jurisdiction of an arbitrator to consider defenses raised by a party pursuant to §282 of the 35 U.S.C. Furthermore, §294(c) makes it clear that the arbitral award shall be final and binding between the parties, without any effect on any other person. There is a provision

---

36 Ignacio de Castro, Leandro Toscano & Andrzej Gadkowski. *An Update on International Trends in Technology, Media and Telecoms Dispute Resolution, Including Intellectual Property Disputes*, Les Nouvelles, Journal of the Licensing Executives Society International, June 2018 at 6 §VI.

allowing a U.S. competent court to modify or amend an award if any court has decided a patent that was the subject matter of an award and from which no further appeal can or has been taken. In addition, there is a mandatory procedural requirement to notify the United States Patent and Trademark Office (USPTO) for any award invalidating a patent.

Thus, effective since September 16, 2012 in the U.S., §294 sets three key precedents for patents: (1) arbitrability of IP disputes; (2) like high courts of common law countries, an arbitration tribunal has the full jurisdiction to render an enforceable and binding arbitral award; (3) parties can enter into an arbitration agreement after the dispute has arisen in case of claims for infringements. This is one of the model Articles related to IPR disputes, worth consideration by other countries to promote arbitrability of IPR validity disputes.

In a recent trademark dispute *Landau v. Rheinold*, the U.S. Court of Appeals for the Second Circuit reaffirmed the arbitral award of a five-member tribunal, which was affirmed by the district court.[37] This case is a good example of the agreement to submit to arbitration after a dispute had arisen. The background is noteworthy where the parties agreed voluntarily to submit the matter to arbitration instead of courts, due to a large number of witnesses, 613 respondents, and the sensitive nature of the religious societies.

The Court of Appeals emphasized its limited jurisdiction to review an arbitral award by referring to the case precedents, writing, "Arbitration awards are subject to very limited review in order to avoid undermining the twin goals of arbitration, namely, settling disputes efficiently and avoiding long and expensive litigation."[38] This proves that arbitral awards can be more effective for enforcement for the winning parties due to limited grounds of appeal, saving the litigants the unnecessary costs and time associated with appeals and counter appeals at various tiers of the judicial courts.

---

37 *Asher Baruch Landau, et al. (Petitioner—Appellees) v. Baruch Eisenberg (Respondent-Appellant) v. Zvi Arye Rheinold, et al. (respondents—Appellees), Yakov Berger, et al. (Respondents)*. Docket No. 17-3963, Decided: May 1, 2019.

38 By referring to the precedents set by cases like *Rich v. Spartis*, 516 F.3d 75, 81 (2d Cir. 2008) and *Nat'l Football League Mgmt. Council v. Nat'l Football League Players Ass'n*, 820 F.3d 527, 536 (2d Cir. 2016).

Hong Kong Arbitration Ordinance Cap 609 Part 11A

The recently amended Arbitration Ordinance of Hong Kong in 2017, effective from January 1, 2018, includes a Part 11(A) dedicated to IPR matters and appears to have set a precedent for the world to follow.[39] It is a comprehensive provision on arbitrability of disputes related to all types of IPR matters, with options available for parties regardless of whether IPR infringement is an issue within or from outside Hong Kong or whether the arbitration agreement is in a contract or made after a dispute. An arbitral award is enforceable in accordance with Article 35 UNCITRAL Model Law and under NYC, with limited grounds for challenges as in any other arbitral award, whether related to IPRs or commercial matters.

The major leap forward toward the future of IPR disputes is in the breadth of IPR matters whether the *locus standi* is in Hong Kong or outside, making it possible that, even when an infringement issue arises in a third country, the parties can still arbitrate the matter in Hong Kong, subject to consent between the parties.

Section 103D unambiguously states: (1) "An IPR dispute is capable of settlement by arbitration as between the parties to the IPR dispute." The list of IPR matters is broad as evident hereunder:

103B. Interpretation: IPR

(1) In this Part, an intellectual property right (*IPR*) means—

...

(j) *a right to protect goodwill by way of passing off or similar action against unfair competition; or*

(k) *any other IPR of whatever nature.*

(2) In this Part, a reference to an IPR is a reference to such an IPR—

(a) *whether or not the IPR is protectible by registration; and*

(b) *whether or not the IPR is registered, or subsists, in Hong Kong.*

(3) In this Part, a reference to an IPR includes an application for the registration of an IPR if the IPR is protectible by registration.

(4) In this section—

registration in relation to an IPR, includes the grant of the IPR.

(Emphasis added)

The foreign arbitral awards related to IPR subject matter can be enforced in Hong Kong.

---

39 *See* Part 11(A) containing 10 sections from 103(A) to (J) in Cap. 609 Arbitration Ordinance of Hong Kong.

Singapore Intellectual Property (Dispute Resolution) Act 2019

The Domestic Arbitration Act (Cap. 10) and International Arbitration Act (Cap. 143A) were amended on August 29, 2019, and effective from November 21, 2019. The amendments are the mirror of the amendments made in the Hong Kong Arbitration Ordinance. The Singapore IP (Dispute Resolution) Act 2019 also provides the details of changes made in other relevant IPR-related Acts, thus setting the stage for harmonious resolution of IPR disputes through arbitration.[40]

Singapore and Hong Kong emerged as the IP hubs where intellectual property disputes of the international cases may be arbitrated and IPR subject matter need not be from within the respective countries. The foreign arbitral awards related to IPR matters can also be entered as a judgment in both Singapore and Hong Kong.

In the case of a multinational corporation (MNC) alleged to be infringing in multiple jurisdictions, the issues can be resolved in a single forum, thus saving time and money by avoiding multiple parallel proceedings in international courts and the legal costs of litigation, which are often prohibitive to the extent that frustrates IPR owners to drop their claims.

Overview of Arbitrability of IPR Disputes in Other Jurisdictions

A brief survey is conducted to identify the countries where IPR validity and infringement tort (voluntary, negligent, and strict liability) related disputes can be arbitrated, so as to overcome the challenge of convincing and educating the IPR holders that litigation in courts is not the only forum to redress their grievances against infringers. The findings show there are five countries in favor of IPR arbitrability, including two IP5 countries (the U.S. and Japan). Discussions are seriously progressing in Korea to promote arbitration for IPR disputes.

Trend of Post Dispute Non-contractual Arbitration Applications

According to the WIPO Case Load Summary published on its website, "the WIPO Centre has assisted parties in over 550 'Good Offices' requests (some of these are followed by WIPO ADR proceedings) based in different

---

40 *See* Singapore *Intellectual Property (Dispute Resolution) Act 2019* (No. 23 of 2019), Part 1 and Part 4.

jurisdictions from all regions of the world."[41] Though most of the disputes administered were based on contractual disputes, 35 percent of these (i.e., 228 cases) were non-contractual, based on the agreement to refer the disputes to WIPO ADR services after a dispute had arisen. This shows that even without a contract or prior arbitration agreement, there are parties that voluntarily opt for ADR forums. With State-supported pro-ADR policies and enhanced awareness of the IPR community, the trend is set to grow. From an economist's perspective, firms are rational, and they will normally take rational decisions in dispute settlement forums as well, provided the legislation of the State does not prohibit enforcement of IP-related arbitral awards or create exclusive jurisdictions of Courts for IPR validity matters.

Incentives and Disadvantages of Intellectual Property Arbitration

Once an IPR Holder discovers that an entity in a certain country is infringing its IPRs, the most probable objectives of an IPR holder would be to stop the entity from infringing further, get compensation for the damages caused or losses suffered, and claim for the royalties on the sales and stocks held. These claims are well within the category of international commercial claims. The actions sought in this process of enforcement of IPRs could be seeking immediate interim injunctions, followed by permanent injunctions, confiscation of infringing materials, orders for destruction of counterfeits, and monetary claims for damages and royalties. The *locus standi* for an IPR holder to enforce its legitimate rights is protected under the International Treaties, International Private Laws (IPL), and National Laws of the infringer's domicile or place where the infringements are occurring or occurred. Therefore, the forum for commencing a legal action would be through national courts and arbitral forums as an alternative to courts.

Incentives and Disadvantages of ADR Forum and Arbitration

(a) *Confidentiality*: Courts are public forums, meaning litigants' names and the details of their disputes freely enter the public domain as a

41 *See* at https://www.wipo.int/amc/en/center/caseload.html (last visited March 15, 2020).

result of litigation. A party must weigh the immediate impacts on its market value of being accused as an infringer, and until after several years of litigation, whether the verdict is against or in favor. By agreeing to ADR forums, parties can avail of the strict confidentiality provisions within the procedural rules of the forum. For instance, Articles 75-78 of WIPO Arbitration Rules ensure confidentiality.[42] IP disputes are invariably technology-intensive with the need for protection of business methods and trade secrets. Thus, confidentiality of the ADR forums and arbitration is the most significant incentive for a contractual as well as a non-contractual party to agree to arbitration.

(b) *Single Forum Covering Multiple Jurisdictions*: In the post-World War II era, the Arbitration Forum is one of the very few neutral forums worldwide for resolving a wide range of issues between commercial entities under a single forum, from jurisdictional challenges, interim reliefs, and protection of property and equipment, to multinational issues and multi-party disputes:

In Japan, refusal to reach a settlement upon the prima facie case of infringement permits IPR holders to commence criminal prosecution action through national authorities, which can lead to imprisonment in addition to fine and damages.[43]

In a country where IP is not registered, the counterargument would be that the ADR forum is not an incentive for a non-contractual party, and an alleged infringer is not bound by national laws to agree to an arbitration, as the courts of the State also may not have jurisdiction either. International treaties do provide flexibilities on the procedure for enforcement of IPRs, provided IPRs are duly registered within the Member State where enforcement action is being pursued.

Under such scenarios, the alleged infringer with international operations, after having received a notice of infringement with an invitation to agree to arbitration as a forum for dispute resolutions, and having ignored the notice or refused to accept the invitation to agree to an ADR forum, is exposed to actions by the IPR holder on multiple fronts. The alleged infringer also has a choice to preempt the accuser of infringement by initiating legal

---

42 WIPO Arbitration Rules 2020 section VII.

43 *See* at https://www.meti.go.jp/policy/ipr/eng/infringe/remedy/remedy04.html (last visited March 7, 2020).

proceedings in national courts for invalidating the IPR. In such a scenario, the ADR option may not be feasible unless the time, reputation, confidentiality, market valuation, and costs of litigation, among other economic factors, are not the major concerns of the parties.

First and foremost, the alleged infringer will carry the label of being an infringer without even a trial in a legal forum. This could be bad for business and future growth. When exporting its products and services to countries where IPR is registered, the risk of confiscation by Customs and Border Control authorities will be heightened. Criminal prosecution may also be permissible if the countries where the alleged infringer conducts its business have ratified the Anti-Counterfeiting Treaty.

(c) *International Enforceability of Arbitral Awards*: Unlike court judgments that can only be enforced within the State or in countries with the treaty on Reciprocal Recognition of Court Judgments, the Arbitral Awards are enforceable simultaneously across 168 countries (NYC States) as per the choice of the winning party, which is normally enforced where the losing party has maximum recoverable capital and stocks. For enforcing foreign courts judgments in a country on an exequatur basis, the time taken to pursue such action besides review of the case in the context of national laws, public policy, and subject matter of dispute would be much longer than enforcement of a foreign arbitral award. It brings to mind the well-known adage that "Justice Delayed is Justice Denied!" Now considering the case of a non-contractual third party accused as an infringer, this is certainly not an incentive to accept the invitation for arbitration. But it is in the best interest of the IPR holder to pursue an ADR Forum and arbitration. Thus, the question arises, why should an infringer voluntarily submit to arbitration?:

There could be three probabilities: (1) the alleged infringer believes not to be an infringer but the claimant's IPRs are invalid or defective; (2) the alleged infringer is unaware of infringement of any IPRs of the claimant and is taken by surprise; (3) the alleged infringer is knowingly and willingly infringing the IPRs for commercial gains as long as feasible.[44] The efficiency and

44 *See* at https://www.meti.go.jp/policy/ipr/eng/infringe/remedy/remedy04.html (last visited March 7, 2020). *Ibid.*, *infra* n. 60.

efficacy of implementation of national laws and international conventions to protect IPRs are dependent on the overall efficiency of the court system in the respective Member States. Therefore, the infringer entities in the third category will always be there irrespective of the nature of property rights, until the full extent of the law is tested. This group is not the potential candidate for voluntary arbitration. However, the categories (1) and (2) have valid commercial reasons to consider and defend themselves against allegations of infringement, although entities in the third category also have an incentive to voluntarily agree to an ADR forum to negotiate for licensing options on favorable terms and avoid the consequences of punitive court orders.

(d) *Time and Cost Advantage*: Unlike actions for breach of contract, the actions related to enforcement of IPRs are against non-contractual parties. The potential for delay tactics in contractual disputes by a party for strategic gains is unlikely to be prevalent in IP disputes. The parties are expected to be rational business entities and would prefer to continue with their production processes without interruptions and the label of infringer for a longer period:

In arbitration, due to party autonomy, the parties are in control of the time frame to resolve all issues without being in a queue of cases in a series of courts and appeal courts, where the outcome is shrouded with uncertainties, and time and costs of litigation continue to rise. Time to get a final binding outcome of an IP dispute is of further significant advantage, especially for high-end technological disputes, drugs, biotechnology, and pharmaceutical industries. Courts, with due respect, do not give special privileges or discrimination to one IP dispute application over another, as the Rules of Court (*ROC*) are equally applicable for all cases, even in specialized IP courts.
In arbitrations through well-recognized Arbitral Institutions (*AIs*), the parties can also adopt expedited arbitration procedures to resolve their issues of infringements within a matter of six months or earlier, depending on the complexity of a case. Such short timelines would not be plausible in terms of court litigations and follow-up appeal processes.

(e) *Decisions by a Tribunal with Subject Matter Expertise:* At times, the disputes of infringement of a technical nature present a hairline difference between infringement and non-infringement. For instance, in patents and industrial designs, the scope of the claim and boundaries of protection create a situation of fence posts versus signposts,[45] which require the intellect of a professional from within the same industry. In an assembly of hundreds of components for electronic or electrical equipment, if one or some of the components are on the boundary line of infringement of a patent owner, the entire assembly can be suspended from further production until the issue of infringement is resolved.[46] The parties cannot decide who will be the judge in a court setting, but in an arbitration forum, the parties have a choice to create a balanced tribunal with both legal acumen and technological expertise:

> As discussed briefly earlier, the example of changing trends for IP Arbitration is evident from the Japan IPO. Since July 2019, the JIPAC and Japan Patent Office (JPO) provide support for ADR forums and arbitration in the SEP matters, by providing independent opinion upon request by the parties and/or the tribunal.[47] JIPAC also supports the infringement matters and disputes related to non-contractual parties through mediation and arbitration forums.

(f) *Options for Expert Determination and Neutral Evaluation*: The parties have an option to resolve their issues of infringement or technical differences through independent experts appointed in accordance with Expert Determination Procedural Rules of ADR service providers and AIs:[48]

> In AIs like the Hong Kong International Arbitration Centre (HKIAC), the International Chamber of Commerce (ICC), the Korean Commercial Arbitration Board (KCAB) (Korean International Arbitration Centre (KIAC)), and the WIPO, specific rules and panels of experts are available to assist the parties in

---

45 Dan L. Burk & Mark A. Lemley, *Fence Posts or Sign Posts? Rethinking Patent Claim Construction*, University of Pennsylvania Law Review, Volume 157: 1743.

46 *Erickson Inc. v. TCL Communication Technology Holdings Ltd.*, CASE NO: SACV 14-341 NS(DFMx) Consolidated with CASE NO: CV 15-2370 NS(DFMx), District Court California, U.S.A.

47 *See* at https://www.meti.go.jp/policy/ipr/eng/infringe/remedy/remedy02.html (last visited March 7, 2020).

48 For example, WIPO, JIPAC, International Litigation Chambers, Korean Commercial Arbitration Board, and other similar AIs.

resolving cross-border disputes, not necessarily contractual. ADR options offered by the WIPO Center are widely recognized as particularly suitable for, but not limited to, cross-border IP disputes. The WIPO ADR Rules are appropriate for all commercial disputes and, additionally, feature provisions addressing specific needs in IP disputes, namely provisions on confidentiality, evidence, experiments, site visits, agreed primers and models, and trade secrets.[49]

(g) *Risk of Punitive Damages Award by Courts in Some Countries*: This is one of the most important sound legal perspectives for all three categories of alleged infringers (as identified in ¶(c) above) to seriously consider voluntarily agreeing to arbitration. More and more courts from international jurisdictions are imposing punitive orders like fines and/or imprisonment in addition to damages. For instance, in the U.S., 35 U.S.C. §284 claimants can claim for enhanced damages up to three times the amount assessed as damages against willful infringers and egregious cases of misconduct.[50] It may be argued that deterrence is a public good produced by court judgments, which may not be served under an ADR forum. So, although punitive damages may incentivize the private parties to opt for ADR, it does so at a cost to society in the form of reduced deterrence for future infringements. However, the award of punitive damages restores the rights of IPR owners and compensates them for their loss without altering the public benefit. On the contrary, taxpayers' and public funds are saved by saving time and cost incurred by the courts:

Similarly, the courts in China, Japan, Korea, and the U.K. have considered imposing exemplary damages as a punitive measure for willful infringers.[51] The Italian approach shows it as a warning for infringers, taking into consideration all the background facts while assessing damages:

49 *See* at https://www.wipo.int/amc/en/center/specific-sectors/ (last visited April 13, 2020).

50 *Calculating Damages for Patent Infringement in Different Jurisdictions*, Special Feature by AIPF Patent Committee, October 7, 2019, at 2 with reference to *Halo Elecs., Inc. v. Pulse Elecs., Inc.*, 136 S. Ct. 1923, 1935 (2016).

51 European Patent Academy, *National Approaches to Damages*, Patent Litigation Block 3 with reference to *Kuddas v. Chief Constable of Leicestershire* [2001] UKHL 29.

> "Innocent infringers" are considered rare, as there is a presumption that all parties know about the existence of the others' patents. Even then, an innocent infringer is liable for the value of a license assessed at a reasonable commercial rate. *If infringers have been negligent, they are likely to be liable for a larger royalty (perhaps at double the usual commercial rate), and if grossly negligent, some proportion of the infringer's profits might also be granted as damages.*[52]
>
> (*Emphasis added*)

The legislation and IP protection framework are certainly not working to curtail infringements. Even if there may be adequate protection in certain emerging and developing economies, it trails behind the developed nations. This is evident from the membership register of WIPO (193 States) and TRIPS Agreement (164 WTO Member States)[53] committed to upholding IPRs.

Thus, the answer to the question, "How the decision on validity of IPR between parties to an arbitration will influence the non-infringement of an IPR," lies in the risk management of the IPR owner and the alleged infringer. The reasons (a) to (g) above provide strong incentives for the alleged infringers and non-contractual parties to voluntarily agree to ADR forums and arbitration for the final resolution of IP-related disputes. The WIPO ADR Caseload report shows that over the last ten years, the "WIPO Center has assisted parties in over 550 'Good Offices' requests based in different jurisdictions from all regions of the world." The growth of such requests is significant in the year 2019.[54]

Disadvantages

There are a number of arguments highlighting the disadvantages of arbitration besides costs and lack of judiciary powers on third parties. The procedural framework for appointment of a tribunal and choice of arbitral institutions is left to the parties to decide, unlike in courts where it is set by

---

52 Agreement on Trade-Related Aspects of Intellectual Property Rights (1994) is binding on all members of the WTO by Article 11.2 of the WTO Agreement.

53 Current Status of Membership published on WIPO website.

54 Available at https://www.wipo.int/amc/en/center/caseload.html (last visited March 8, 2020).

a State. The vested interests of parties, their legal representatives, and arbitral institutions do attract such criticism, which, at times, is a valid reason for not opting for arbitration. However, in general, experienced legal counsel and professionals can improve the situations. Unlike in courts with extensive powers under the Judicature Act of a State, tribunals and arbitral laws of the seat will have to be robust to deal with such instances.

Economists' Perspective of Dispute Resolution Forums

From an economist's perspective, the transaction costs of IP should be kept low to maintain the overall cost of public goods at the optimum level with minimum deadweight loss, thus in favor of public welfare. However, transaction costs of resolving disputes, whether by trial or settlement, are low when liability is certain and damages are easily measured. Cases of disputes related to infringements and validity challenges fall under tort liability and are between the parties. Such costs are internalized because the infringer, if a losing party, will compensate the IPR owner, so such costs are not to be treated as externalities. Thus, any claims for damages and costs incurred by choice of a dispute resolution forum, whether by arbitration or litigation in multiple jurisdictions, will be internalized and should not have an impact on public goods or transaction costs in general.

However, from the perspective of the IPR owner, the costs of enforcing the IPR during its validity period will add to the costs of transactions for licensing and royalty payments, which will have an impact on the cost of public goods and public welfare. "Tort liability is only one of several policy instruments available to internalize externalities created by high transaction costs. Alternative policy instruments include criminal statutes, safety regulations, and tax incentives. Each alternative has its advantages and disadvantages."[55] If the arbitrability of IPR disputes and use of ADR forums results in reduced legal costs for IPR owners, this indirectly creates better-licensing contracts, reducing infringements and ultimately resulting in the reduction of transaction costs and enhancement of public welfare. Thus, as a policy matter, arbitrability of IPR validity disputes will enhance the public welfare by reducing costs and time to be incurred in multi-jurisdictional disputes to settlement under one roof. The downside could be a reduction in public goods in the form of jurisprudence due to the confidentiality of arbitrations, potentially resulting in non-availability of

---

55 Robert Cooter & Thomas Ulen. *Law and Economics,* 6th Edition. Boston: Addison-Wesley, 2006, Chapter 6.

case laws, information about the nature of infringements and/or disputes, and application of IP laws as lessons to be learned. To overcome such a loss of public goods, some arbitral institutions like the ICC, Society of Maritime Arbitrators (SMA) (New York, U.S.A.), Singapore Chamber of Maritime Arbitration (SCMA, Singapore), and KCAB (Korea) are regularly publishing redacted arbitral awards for public information, jurisprudence development, education, and training purposes.

In biotechnological or pharmaceutical sectors, the parties may have a non-commercial interest to pursue court litigation, seeking to establish jurisprudence for future similar cases. Likewise, parties interested in protecting their brand image and trademarks may prefer public forums for their media and publicity, which could discourage other infringers; so, in such cases, ADR may not be an attractive option. These cases often increase the transaction costs and raise the costs of drugs for the consumers with a negative impact on public welfare.

Under a project initiated by the American Law Institute (*ALI*), a set of principles on the jurisdiction, recognition of judgments, and applicable law in transnational IPR disputes are promulgated. These principles recognize the context of the digital age with globally integrated economies dependent on free movement of goods. In general, the promulgated principles express:[56]

> The objectives of international trade may be achieved both through harmonizing substantive intellectual property law and by *facilitating international adjudication*. The free movement of goods propels the free movement of disputes and judgments: emerging conditions call for a mechanism for effective international coordination and recognition of judgments.

This ALI Project explicitly and implicitly supports the theme of this chapter that, by making arbitrability of IPR disputes and supporting ADR forums in the WTO Member States, the objective of international adjudication of disputes will not only serve the interest of IPR owners but also enhance the value of public goods and welfare.

56 The American Law Institute. *Intellectual Property—Principles Governing Jurisdiction, Choice of Law and Judgments in Transnational Disputes*. California: American Law Institute Publishers, 2008, p. 7.

Jurisdictional Challenges in Validity and Infringements of IPR

In countries where arbitrability of IPR enforcement and actions against infringement is not permissible, the IPR holders are faced with the challenge of submitting their claims before a series of courts in multiple jurisdictions. Thus, the principle of territoriality is the weak link in protecting IPR, and it requires IPR owners to have patience and plenty of financial strength to pursue their claims until the end.

Challenge #5: Enforcing IP Rights and Defending Counterclaim of Invalidity of an IPR from Infringers

For a foreign IPR owner, defending and pursuing claims against infringements within the EU are a highly challenging task due to territoriality and exclusive jurisdictions of national courts. The litigation process gets more complex when infringer defendants invoke ancillary EU Regulations like the EU Charter of Human Rights, Unfair Competition, and Treaty for Functioning of European Union (TFEU). The starting point for patent infringement claims in the EU is Article 64(3) of the Convention on the Grant of European Patent 2016 (*EPC*), which provides: "Any infringement of a European patent shall be dealt with by national law." If under the national law, arbitrability of patents and IPR infringements are not permitted or unclear, the cases will have to be referred to litigation in national courts.

In the matter of *Huawei v. Zhongxing Telecommunications Equipment (ZTE)*, there was no issue that ZTE had been infringing the SEP owned by Huawei. The notice of infringement and offer to grant a license on Fair, Reasonable, and Nondiscriminatory (FRAND) terms were given to ZTE and apparently ignored, and/or a counter-proposal was made for cross-licensing, resulting in no agreement.[57] Thus, ZTE continued with the use of the patent of "Long Term Evolution Standard for Telecommunications" without a license and payment of royalties, which became a case of obvious infringement. On April 28, 2011, Huawei initiated the legal action in Düsseldorf (Germany) Court for injunctions against infringements and claims for damages. In March 2013, the Dusseldorf Court referred the

57 *Huawei Technologies Limited v. ZTE Corp. and ZTE Deutschland GmbH*, C-170/13, ECLI:EU:C:2015:477.

matter to the Court of Justice of the European Union (CJEU) for a preliminary ruling on five questions, which were answered in July 2015. The defense raised by alleged infringer ZTE was pursuant to Article 102 of TFEU *inter alia*, citing abuse of dominant position and the prohibitory nature of the injunction sought by Huawei. In the context of the evidence, the Court decided that Huawei neither violated Article 102 of TFEU nor abused its dominant position. The IPR owner spent nearly five years in litigation to get the judgment, and the willful infringer misused or misinterpreted the public policy grounds. No doubt this case has set many precedents for future SEP and FRAND matters and developed the jurisprudence, but from the perspective of inventors and patent owners, it represents a costly and challenging adventure for an IP owner to exploit its IPR, despite having agreed with the authorities to grant SEP licenses on FRAND terms.[58]

The interpretation of the term "Commercial" in UNCITRAL Texts is given a broad meaning without limited prescription, which includes investments, and it is left to the Member States and Courts to give the meaning to the term "Commercial." A U.S. court has similarly held that the notion of "commercial relationship" is broad, noting that its purpose is only "to exclude matrimonial and other domestic relations awards, political awards, and the like."[59] Thus, considering the broad meaning of commercial, if the national laws of a country do not specifically exclude IP validity matters from arbitration laws, then they should be assumed to have provided for arbitrability of IP validity disputes, like in the case of Austria and Belgium.

In *Huawei v. ZTE*, the CJEU did raise the point that the effective judicial protection guaranteed by Article 47 of the Charter may also include the right of access to a tribunal.[60] There is a further reference to an independent third party for resolving disputes on FRAND terms, but it falls short of stating arbitration or ADR forums.[61]

In the U.S.A. for SEPs and FRAND licensing terms, when ordered by the Standards Setting Organization (SSO) and telecommunication or Infocom authorities of a state as part of the Intellectual Property Licensing

58 *Unwired Planet International Ltd v. Huawei Technologies Co. Ltd & Others*, [2017] EWHC 711 (Pat); *Samsung v. EC (Apple Complaints)* Case Comp. AT.39939 April 29, 2014 and *Motorola v. EC (Apple Complaint)* Case Comp AT.39985 April 29, 2014.

59 *Island Territory of Curacao v. Solitron Devices, Inc.*, Court of Appeals, Second Circuit, United States of America, February 14, 1973, 356 F. Supp. 1. Cited in UNCITRAL Secretariat Guide on the Convention on the Recognition and Enforcement of Foreign Arbitral Awards (New York, 1958) 2016 Edition, at 34.

60 *Huawei v. ZTE*, Judgment ¶57.

61 *Huawei v. ZTE*, Judgment ¶68.

Policy, dispute resolution through ADR and arbitration is an essential part of the licensing terms between SEP owners and third parties. In the case of the complaint to the Bureau of Competition, resulting in the investigation against Motorola Mobility LLC and Google Inc., the U.S. Federal Trade Commission issued an order with FRAND terms, including a Binding Arbitration Clause.[62] The ADR forum is not only helpful for the economy and SMEs but also maintains expediency in the functioning system of a State and reduces the burden on the courts.

The costs of licensing, earning royalties, monitoring infringers, and litigating for enforcement all add to the transaction costs of the technology. When there is widespread infringement, and the patent or IP owner is not a large firm, the infringers tend to take the risk of being sued, as they know it will be a long-drawn battle for the pursuer.[63] The comprehensive analysis of such market behavior and the impact on IPR owners are well presented in the appropriately titled article, "Patent Enforcement in an Uncertain World: Widespread Infringement and the Paradox of Value for Patented Technologies." When, alongside international laws, the legislation of the same State that granted the privileges of exclusivity to an inventor becomes its hurdle, should the inventors be encouraged to continue inventing or hold back from public disclosure as trade secrets? The plight of the SME IPR owners is summarized in the words of Akemann et al.:

> Intuitively, patent holders who face the prospect of having to litigate repeatedly against multiple infringers have to be concerned about what might be termed a 'one-way ratchet' effect. If the patent holder wins one case against one infringer, that does not mean that others will agree to take a license; they may believe that the earlier defendant failed to make the best arguments. However, if the patent holder ever loses a case—especially on validity grounds—then there is likely to be a significant adverse effect on the patent holder's ability to gain license revenues from that patent in the future. In effect, the patent holder has to 'win them all,' while the infringers may only have to 'win one.' In this way, widespread infringement can create a situation where a patent holder faces the prospect of serial litigation against many infringers/licensees, and significant

62 *See* the Decision and Order by the Federal Trade Commission ("Commission"), In the Matter of Motorola Mobility LLC and Google Inc., Docket No. C-4410 issued on July 23, 2013.

63 Michael P. Akemann, John A. Blair & David J. Teece, *Patent Enforcement in an Uncertain World: Widespread Infringement and the Paradox of Value for Patented Technologies,* September 28, 2016.

> flow-on risks associated with a single loss (e.g., on validity) on the future stream of potential licensees (and hence royalties), and transactions costs and/or enforcement problem, could lead to a set of rates in the marketplace that are significantly depressed relative to actual value.

Besides the transaction costs, the legislation does create additional hurdles for IPR owners as compared to lawsuits of non-IP commercial matters, which can freely opt for ADR forums.

Legal Framework for Development of Jurisprudence

Proponents of exclusive jurisdiction of courts will likely contend that the development of jurisprudence based on case law from specialized IP Courts will be marginalized due to the greater scope for confidentiality in arbitration and arbitral awards only subject to limited review determining issues of public interest. This question to some extent conflicts with the objectives of the TRIPS Agreement (Article 7) to reap the major benefits for the Member States, stay committed to the development of technological innovations, and not focus solely on the development of jurisprudence. Second, Apex Courts of Member States do have the supervisory powers to monitor and support international commercial arbitration. Arbitral awards are confidential, but sanitized versions are being published by several arbitral institutions to reflect and encourage uniformity in application of international laws. The arbitral awards that are challenged on grounds of public policy in State Courts further contribute qualitatively to the development of jurisprudence.

Challenge #6: Upholding Arbitral Awards Versus Development of Jurisprudence

The case in point is *Oracle America v. Myriad Group A.G.*, which related to the interpretation of Oracle's Community License and alleged infringement of its IPR by continued use of Java trademarks by Myriad.[64] The key issue was whether the parties could submit a dispute involving the determination of arbitrability of the claims to arbitrators, or whether courts have

64 *Oracle America, Inc. v. Myriad Group A.G.*, United States Court of Appeal for the Ninth Circuit, No. 11-17186, D.C. No.: 4:10-cv-05604-SBA, July 26, 2013.

the exclusive jurisdiction to determine arbitrability of IPR claims. Myriad, under a Community Source License from Oracle in 2002 and a separate Java Specification Participation Agreement (JSPA), considered that its license included the right to use Java language and testing protocols without payment of royalties. Oracle disagreed and filed a suit in 2011 for copyright infringement and unfair competition under California law in the Northern District Court of California. Myriad applied to compel arbitration based on an arbitration clause in the Source License. The District Court Judge allowed arbitration only for contract claims but denied for all other claims, leading to an appeal by Myriad. The Court of Appeals considered the jurisprudence of the Federal Arbitration Law and a series of case laws with carve-out arbitration clauses, as well as narrowly worded arbitration agreements. In the context of the UNCITRAL Arbitration Rules, AAA Arbitration Rules, and decisions of the past references, the Court of Appeals reaffirmed the principle of "kompetenz-kompetenz" and authority of the arbitrator to determine arbitrability of claims submitted by the parties in accordance with their arbitration agreement. In conclusion, Morgan Christen J stated that "Incorporation of the UNCITRAL arbitration rules into the parties' commercial contract constitutes clear and unmistakable evidence that the parties agreed to arbitrate arbitrability." Thus, under the principle of party autonomy, parties can decide in their arbitration agreement which disputes and/or claims will be submitted to the arbitral tribunal, and courts will not intervene to determine the arbitrability of the claims. The arbitration agreement was upheld by the Courts.

In its 1971 version, the Hague Convention on the Recognition and Enforcement of Foreign Judgments in Civil or Commercial Matters (not yet in force) did not exclude IP matters, but in the latest version, it has categorically excluded Article 1 that this Convention shall not apply to intellectual property. The WIPO Advisory Committee on Enforcement had identified the lacuna in its 2014 report and made a proposal.[65]

The Hague Convention 2019 could not achieve the recognition of the judgment of national courts in commercial matters, and despite a series of conferences between Member States for the last 20 years, it is very unlikely that there could be any consensus for recognition of judgments on IP matters, whether as exequatur or otherwise. The only plausible alternative is for the WTO Member States to develop a Convention in the context of TRIPS Agreement Part II: Enforcement of Intellectual Property Rights (Articles 41-61), NYC 1958 and UNCITRAL Model Law on International

65 Trevor Cook, *Alternative Dispute Resolution (ADR) As a Tool for Intellectual Property (IP) Enforcement*. WIPO/ACE/9/3, January 21, 2014, ¶33.

Commercial Arbitration, and the reforms introduced by Hong Kong Arbitration (Amendment) Ordinance, §103 in 2017 and 2019, and the Singapore Intellectual Property (Dispute Resolution) Act 2019. In the context of developing countries and LDCs, such a convention will help alleviate the caseload on their courts and is likely to enhance the potential for technology transfer opportunities, and foreign direct investments (FDI) by IPR owners, without fear of an inadequate legal enforcement system.

Conclusion and Recommendations

The theme of this chapter is to encourage the development of policies at national and international levels to make arbitrability feasible for IPR disputes, including issues of validity and/or invalidity. Second, it has endeavored to expose the challenges of ownership of IPRs with respect to guarding and protection costs of legitimate rights. Third, the case law examples and availability of cost-effective ADR forums showcase that it is in the best interest of all involved to opt for a confidential and cost-effective forum.

Once an IPR is granted and the IPR owners are setting out the monetization strategies, the issues related to infringements or defense against infringement by invoking the validity or invalidity of the grant of an IPR by a State are the subject matter of dispute resolution systems. The territoriality principle was not meant to extend the involvement of the State in commercial risks, IPR (infringements), and licensing deals of the IPR owners.

Article 7 of the TRIPS Agreement could not have been clearer: "The protection and enforcement of intellectual property rights should contribute to the promotion of technological innovation and to the transfer of dissemination of technology, to the mutual advantage of producers and users of technical knowledge and in a manner conducive to social and economic welfare, and to balance of rights and obligations." Article 7 implies in an unequivocal manner that the cost of protection and enforcement should not deter technological innovation and its dissemination. It should not be to the disadvantage of producers of technology, while also maintaining a balance with social and economic welfare. Economic welfare also encompasses protecting the interests of competitors, consumers, and public research institutions. Protection of IPR and efficient dispute resolution mechanisms at affordable costs encourage more innovation, FDI, and trade, which drives economies for both developed and less developed countries (LDCs). The supportive legislative framework for private entities is indirectly for the benefit of the country. Thus, it is imperative that the WTO Member States review their respective legislative frameworks to allow for the arbitrability of the IPR disputes, including validity challenges. In the EU, the current situation is unsatisfactory, and it lacks legal certainty. If properly regulated, commercial arbitration can become an important instrument functional to the EU market efficiency.[66] The examples set by Hong Kong and Singapore legislators are indeed commendable for their promotion of technological innovations, laying the groundwork for engaging intentional infringers due to the efficiency of the ADR forums and the supervisory Courts in these countries.

The two most illustrious treaties ratified since World War II are NYC 1958 and TRIPS Agreement 1994. Global trade could not have reached the present levels but for NYC 1958. Likewise, the growth of innovation and industrial development in underdeveloped countries over the last two decades would not have been possible without the TRIPS Agreement.[67] Now, to keep the momentum of growth and with an objective of developing the LDC, the bottleneck on the path of enforcement of IPR needs to be removed by a new Convention, enabling arbitrability of all types of issues related to intellectual property disputes, including validity. Such a convention can set the template for Member States to adopt into their national legal system for harmonization of IPR enforcement laws.

Finally, the development of jurisprudence is only feasible by the reduction in duration of IPR litigations and expansion of ADR forums. Jurisprudence is worthwhile if it is an enabler of an economy and not a hurdle. The current pattern of IP litigation, ranging from 5 to 15 years in the modern digital age, is certainly not laudable. This further adds to the discontent when an IP owner often receives irreconcilable outcomes from different Courts for the same type of infringement claims. International justiciability, judicial efficiency, certainty, timely enforcement, and protection of IPRs will be the drivers of innovation and economy, which is not a new formula but needs renewed invigoration.

66 Trevor Cook, *Alternative Dispute Resolution (ADR) As a Tool for Intellectual Property (IP) Enforcement*. WIPO/ACE/9/3, January 21, 2014, ¶33.

67 WIPO Annual Reports and IP Statistics at: https://www.wipo.int/ipstats/en/ (last visited April 18, 2020).

A New Mediation Act? The Way Forward for Pakistan

Tariq Mahmood
Head of Arbitration & ADR, London, United Kingdom

Mian Sheraz Javaid
B.Sc. (Civil Engineering), L.L.B. (Pb), M.Sc. (Construction Law), PE, FCIArb, FPD, FCInstCES—Unregistered Barrister, MK Consultus Limited, London, England, United Kingdom

Introduction

Alternative dispute resolution (ADR) has been through its own vicissitudes in Pakistan's legal system. Arbitration is known to be the most common method of ADR in Pakistan, as compared to other ADR mechanisms like mediation or conciliation.[1] One of the key reasons for choosing arbitration over other ADR mechanisms is the existing legal framework in Pakistan, which despite being archaic does provide an elaborate mechanism to govern the arbitral process.[2]

In a country such as Pakistan, where the backlog of court cases runs into millions,[3] the use of ADR mechanisms ought to have been promoted since well before recent times. The current and previous government, as well as the judiciary, have been strong proponents for the introduction of ADR-friendly laws. In 2013, the government of Pakistan developed the "Pakistan Vision 2025," pledging that the laws and regulations would be "simplified,

1 Ahsan Zahir Rizvi & Mazhar Bangash, "Pakistan: A Study of the Arbitration Law Regime in Pakistan" (Mondaq, July 5, 2019), https://www.mondaq.com/arbitration-dispute-resolution/822502/a-study-of-the-arbitration-law-regime-in-pakistan accessed 17 May 2021.

2 Arbitration was the only recognized form of ADR governed under the Arbitration 1940 until the enactment of the Punjab Alternate Dispute Resolution Act 2019, the Alternative Dispute Resolution Act 2017 & the Khyber Pakhtunkhwa Alternate Dispute Resolution Act 2020 that mentions mediation besides arbitration.

3 National Judicial Policy Making Committee, *Statement of Cases Pending, Institution and Disposal During the Period from 1-1-2020 to 31-12-2020 in the Superior Courts and District Judiciary of Pakistan*, http://ljcp.gov.pk/nljcp/assets/dist/news_pdf/courts.pdf; more than 2.0 million cases are pending before various courts of law in Pakistan, as per the report by Law and Justice Commission of Pakistan.

updated, modernized, made more transparent, and their discretionary application discouraged regarding the ADR mechanisms."[4]

The Law and Justice Commission of Pakistan held the eighth Judicial Conference in the Supreme Court of Pakistan in 2018. ADR methodologies, deterring factors, strategies for delay reduction, and expeditious disposal of the backlog of cases were discussed in the form of focus groups, and recommendations known as the "Islamabad Declaration 2018" were issued to the government of Pakistan by the Supreme Court of Pakistan.[5]

The Pakistan Vision 2025[6] and the recommendations at the eighth Judicial Conference by the Supreme Court of Pakistan paved the path for the enactment of ADR Acts in various provinces of Pakistan.[7]

While the provision of ADR mechanisms is going through its own process of evolution, there is still a lot to be done before it is accepted by the legal fraternity as well as the public at large. Although the ADR Acts have a mandatory requirement to refer certain types of cases to ADR at the early stage in the proceedings,[8] a clear picture of mandatory ADR is still missing. The accredited ADR centers in Pakistan are yet to be established. The act makes reference to the establishment of accredited ADR centers; however, the accreditation procedures have thus far not been formulated. Pakistan is still yet to be a signatory of the "Singapore Convention."

This chapter aims to explore and review the relevance and importance of mediation in Pakistan and whether the ADR Acts in various provinces of Pakistan have been effective in promoting mediation. The chapter explains the benefits of mediation, including its ability to reduce the substantial backlog of cases and act as an effective dispute resolution method as an alternative to other mechanisms. The authors consider and advocate the benefits of having a bespoke mediation act for Pakistan.

---

4 Planning Commission Ministry of Planning and Development, *Pakistan's Vision 2025*, p. 70, https://www.pc.gov.pk/uploads/vision2025/Pakistan-Vision-2025.pdf

5 National Judicial Policy Making Committee, Islamabad Declaration 2018, pp. 3-4, http://ljcp.gov.pk/nljcp/assets/dist/news_pdf/f0ec2-ljcp-islamabad-declaration-dated-5th-of-may.pdf The Islamabad Declaration 2018 was issued by the Honorable Supreme Court of Pakistan as a result of eighth Supreme judicial conference held in 2018, recommendations of group II.

6 Planning Commission Ministry of Planning and Development, *Pakistan's Vision 2025*, p. 70, https://www.pc.gov.pk/uploads/vision2025/Pakistan-Vision-2025.pdf.

7 The Punjab Alternate Dispute Resolution Act 2019; the Alternative Dispute Resolution Act 2017; the Khyber Pakhtunkhwa Alternate Dispute Resolution Act 2020.

8 Section 3(1) of the Punjab Alternative Dispute Act 2019, http://punjablaws.gov.pk/laws/2739.html

What Is Mediation?

Mediation is a form of neutrally assisted negotiation.[9] The negotiations take place with the help of a neutral third party within a structured process, and in a formal setting during a defined period, all of which will help create an impetus for settlement. The mediator works to facilitate a settlement between the parties, but will not himself impose one or decide the outcome of the dispute.[10] The parties, with the assistance of the mediator, reach a solution that is tailored to their real needs and interests. It is crucial to note that the conclusive result of the mediation is not binding upon the parties, unlike other ADR methods.

In essence, mediation is different from the rest of the ADR methods.[11] Although other methods are distinct *inter se*, the distinction of mediation stands out on two accounts: first, the skill set of mediator; and second, the process of mediation.[12]

Mediation is defined by the Centre for Effective Dispute Resolution (CEDR)[13] as:

> Mediation is a flexible process conducted confidentially in which a neutral person actively assists parties in working towards a negotiated agreement of a dispute or difference, with the parties in ultimate control of the decision to settle and the terms of resolution.

Within mediation, there are different styles and approaches: evaluative, facilitative, and transformative.[14] Multitiered dispute resolution clauses are often found in contracts that prescribe the use of mediation along with other ADR processes such as arbitration, or even traditional court litigation. Where mediation does not work as a method of dispute resolution, it may still be the case that the overall use of what is often called an escalating dispute resolution clause, allowing for "med-arb" or "arb-med," can see a dispute resolved in a quicker time frame than might have happened if the parties had just relied on court litigation.

---

9 Aird & Aird v. Prime Meridian Ltd [2006] BLR 105 [5] (May LJ).

10 Susan Blake, Julie Browne & Stuart Sime, A Practical approach to Alternative Dispute Resolution (OUP, 2018) 225.

11 Stephen J. Ware, Principles of alternative dispute resolution (West Academic, 2007).

12 Lela P. Love & Kimberlee K. Kovach. "ADR: An Eclectic Array of Processes, Rather Than One Eclectic Process" (2000) 2 Journal of Dispute Resolution, p. 295.

13 https://www.cedr.com/commercial/ (accessed April 30, 2021).

14 https://www.pon.harvard.edu/daily/mediation/types-mediation-choose-type-best-suited-conflict/ (accessed April 30, 2021).

Role of Mediators

Mediators play an important role in facilitating discussion between parties. It is not an adjudicative process where the mediator(s) come to a decision. Instead, they employ shuttle diplomacy, enabling the parties to reflect and consider their positions.

The mediation process begins with a joint meeting. The parties then break into private sessions, and the mediator goes back and forth between the parties until they reach an agreement, if possible. It is done on a voluntary basis where no party is compelled. Hence, dealing on a good faith basis is central to the mediation process and often determines its success. In mediation, everyone involved in the dispute sits down together to air their differences and then collaborates on a resolution. In contrast to a trial or arbitration proceeding, the mediation process is inherently non-adversarial. The degree to which the mediator intervenes in the process depends on the style of mediation followed. A direct benefit of this approach is that it ensures parties maintain good relationships, which is often not the case in contentious litigation and arbitration, where parties' commercial relationships are often scathed. It also provides parties with greater control and autonomy.

Another core feature of mediation is its private and confidential nature. This provides parties the assurance to discuss matters openly and with confidence, thus ensuring a greater chance of maintaining relationships and achieving the resolution of their dispute.

Benefits of Mediation

The mediator facilitates the parties in holding difficult conversations in a respectful manner and guides them in finding mutual gains for resolving their disputes. The process of communicating and collaborating is powerful and restorative, and as a result, the parties are often able to resume a relationship after mediation in a way that is a rare occurrence in the highly charged adversarial environment of litigation and arbitration.

Mediation helps parties maintain relationships and goodwill by allowing parties to approach the dispute in a nonadversarial manner and find a mutually agreeable outcome. Mediation is less confrontational and helps prevent relationships from being damaged over a dispute. As businesses are often engaged in long-term relationships with various stakeholders, it is often in their interest to resort to mediation so that their relationships are not compromised as a result of the dispute resolution process. For example, it is more beneficial to maintain a good relationship with your long-term suppliers, as switching suppliers may disrupt the existing business and lead to unnecessary administrative costs as well as the uncertainty of dealing with a new supplier.

The confidential nature of mediation further prevents relationships from being harmed. It is private, unlike litigation, which is often publicly available and can lead to significant challenges. Disputes resolved by the traditional court process may also result in mass media coverage, especially if the company is public and the dispute is newsworthy. As reputation is important to businesses, confidential dispute resolution mechanisms may be more beneficial. Mediation can ensure that business disputes are resolved discreetly, minimizing reputational and associated costs.

The Current Position in Pakistan

The *Panchayat* (Village Council) system in Punjab and the *Jirga* System in Khyber Pakhtunkhwa and Baluchistan have been practiced as an alternate justice system for centuries. The word *Panchayat* means "assembly" (ayat) of five (panch). *Panchayats* are comprised of respected and wise elders accepted by the local people conventionally.[15]

The modern Pakistani legal system has not been able to utilize the undoubted strength of mediation despite having traditional recognition of negotiation and resolution of disputes through the *Panchayat* system.

Mediation has been an effective tool in resolving disputes in the business community throughout the world since at least the time of ancient Greece and ancient Rome.

While some countries have made mediation mandatory, others are on the way to make it mandatory in some form or the other. In April 2002, the European Commission issued a Green Paper[16] on ADR in civil and commercial disputes for the promotion of mediation. Later on, in 2008, the

15 https://odad.org/tr/article/a-comparative-study-of-panchayat-system-and-states-judicial-system-in-punjab-pakistan.

16 Commission of the European Communities, "Green Paper on alternative dispute resolution in civil and commercial law," COM (2002) 196 final, Brussels, April 19, 2002.

European Union issued a directive (2008/52/EC)[17] with regard to implementation of mediation in cross-border disputes but categorically mentioned that the Member States may apply such provisions in local disputes as well. The Directive describes mediation as a means which can:

> provide a cost-effective and quick extra-judicial resolution of disputes in civil and commercial matters through processes tailored to the needs of the parties. Agreements resulting from mediation are more likely to be complied with voluntarily and are more likely to preserve an amicable and sustainable relationship between the parties. These benefits become even more pronounced in situations displaying cross-border elements.

In 2002, the resolution of disputes through mediation and conciliation became part of the statutory law for the first time in Pakistan through the enactment of Ordinance XXXIV of 2002 by inserting section 89-A into the Code of Civil Procedure Code (CPC).[18] The National Judiciary (Policy Making) Committee formulated the National Judiciary Policy in 2009, stating that "[t]he Small Claims and Minor Offences Courts Ordinance 2002 should be applied in earnest."[19]

The ADR Act 2017[20] (applicable in federal territory) requires certain matters to be referred to mediation if the parties agree. Punjab implemented this law by inserting Order IX-B in the CPC as well as by enacting the Punjab ADR Act 2019.[21]

The Lahore High Court as part of certain judicial reforms established a mediation center in 2017 to mainstream "court-annexed mediation," a procedure where judges refer cases to mediators assigned by the Lahore High Court. This started in Lahore and has now spread across all 36 districts of Punjab,[22] where there is a mediation center manned by judges who serve as mediators.

---

17 Available at https://eur-lex.europa.eu/legal-content/EN/TXT/?uri=celex:32008L0052.

18 The Dispute Resolution Review [Thirteenth Edition] available at https://www.lexology.com/indepth/the-dispute-resolution-review/pakistan.

19 National Judicial Policy 2009 [Revised edition 2012] p. 36 available at http://ljcp.gov.pk/nljcp/assets/dist/NJP/njp.pdf.

20 http://www.na.gov.pk/uploads/documents/1486554463_506.pdf.

21 http://punjablaws.gov.pk/laws/2739.html.

22 https://lhc.gov.pk/Adr_Centres.

Since 2017, 30,688 cases had been referred to mediation, out of which 14,239 references had been successfully mediated up until January 2019.[23] Mediation has achieved substantial results through the mediation centers established by the Lahore High Court.[24] Recent amendments to the CPC by the provinces and the federal territory have provided for the mandatory referral of certain disputes to mediation as a preliminary measure.

Enforceability of Mediation Settlement in Pakistan Currently

For thc enforceability of the settlement recorded as a result of successful mediation or conciliation, the recently amended CPC by the provinces and the federal capital territory provides section 89-A subclause (7) that empowers the mediator/conciliator to record the settlement of both the parties[25] which will become part of the award/decision.

Mediation Centers in Pakistan

The CEDR initiated a mediation training program in Pakistan in 2012. Around 150 professionals were trained as mediators by CEDR as a part of a program funded by IFC/World Bank Group's ADR Pakistan Project Phase 1 & 2.[26] This project helped the capacity building of mediators in Pakistan and paved the path for establishing mediation centers.

The biggest national mediation body is the Pakistan Mediation Association (PMA)[27] consisting of more than 100 CEDR accredited mediators. The second-largest mediation body is the Lahore Chamber of Commerce and Industry (LCCI)[28] mediation center located in Lahore, Pakistan, with around 85 CEDR accredited mediators. The first and the oldest mediation center of Pakistan is the Karachi Center of Dispute Resolution (KCDR),

23 https://www.lhc.gov.pk/system/files/Consolidated%20ADR%20till%2001.02.2019.pdf.
24 https://asiafoundation.org/2019/12/18/alternative-dispute-resolution-gains-traction-in-pakistan/.
25 Available at http://www.na.gov.pk/uploads/documents/1448431640_759.pdf.
26 https://www.adrmediate.com/docs/Dispute%20Resolution%20Update%20-%20April%202012.pdf.
27 Pakistan Mediation Association (PMA), http://www.pma.org.pk/about-pma/.
28 https://www.lcci.com.pk/mediation/about_us1.php.

now known as the National Center of Dispute Resolution (NCDR)[29] with around 55 CEDR accredited mediators.

What a New Mediation Law Can Offer Pakistan?

Of course, the outstanding question is if Pakistan passes a new mediation act, what form should it take? We believe that Pakistan can more easily follow the lead given by the *United Nations Convention on the International Settlement Agreements Resulting from Mediation* (the Singapore Convention on Mediation)[30] and should be a signatory to this Convention. An existing framework already exists for Pakistan to emulate, but we need to bear in mind that the Convention is limited in scope, excluding family mediations and consumer mediations, and therefore national legislation need not be so restrictive in its scope. However, we can use the Convention framework to develop and further shape a national law. What the Singapore Convention requires is that the agreements settled through mediation are to be enforceable in the courts of any signatory state, but that although this is to be in accordance with their own rules of procedure, it is to be under the conditions laid down in the Singapore Convention. The effect of this is that such settlements will have international recognition.[31] We would suggest that this is the most obvious source of action for Pakistan, giving it the greatest benefit with the least amount of institutional legal restructuring.

Pakistan should follow the United Kingdom (U.K.) by way of making it compulsory to conduct mediation at the outset in certain cases. There are a number of "Pre-Action Protocols" that are followed in the English Courts and Family Courts, which make it compulsory for the parties to go through the process of mediation before they can proceed with the trial. This is extremely helpful and allows parties to try and reach a settlement at an early stage and avoid substantial court costs. It might be helpful for the Pakistani and English judiciary to engage on this topic and provide workshops and mentoring to enable them to see the benefits of mediation being

29 https://www.ncdr.pk/.

30 The Singapore Convention on Mediation (available at https://treaties.un.org/pages/ViewDetails.aspx?src=TREATY&mtdsg_no=XXII-4&chapter=22&clang=_en, last seen on April 7, 2020).

31 It was on December 20, 2018, that this Convention was adopted, when the Singapore Convention Roundtable was held on August 7, 2019, which led to the signing ceremony of the Singapore Convention on mediation. Available at: https://www.singaporeconvention.org/, last seen on April 7, 2020.

made compulsory pretrial. In our opinion, the pre-action stage for compulsory mediation should be set out in the new mediation act, so that it is loud and clear to all parties the importance that the court is placing on mediation pre-litigation.

Further, Pakistan can benefit tremendously from commercial/family mediation training to ensure that mediators are suitably qualified and equipped to deal with complex commercial/family disputes. There are a number of recognized institutions in the U.K. which provide accredited training and certify individuals as mediators. There is a dire need to have highly specialized mediators trained so that the parties can have confidence in the mediator. There are a number of organizations in Pakistan that are providing mediation training, and recently ADR ODR is offering a six-day course which is recognized by the U.K. Civil Mediation Council (CMS) and certified by the International Mediation Institute (IMI). Since COVID-19, the world has gone through dramatic changes, and the virtual world has brought about the benefits of e-technology, where training organizations are successfully running online mediation courses without any of the parties having to travel outside their home country. We need to embrace this new world and benefit from training organizations that can shape and develop the future mediators of Pakistan.

Specialist training needs to be provided in order to address issues of professional ethics for mediators. Pakistan needs to devise its own policy to ensure that mediators practicing fully comply with a code of conduct to ensure that individuals and businesses have confidence in the process.

Challenges and the Way Forward

One of the obstacles faced by mediation in its fight for an independent existence in Pakistan has been the resistance from the legal fraternity. Lawyers, due to their legal training, find it difficult to adjust to a "client-centred vision of dispute resolution,"[32] which is an essential feature of mediation. Some hold the view that it is a question of public perception—it is important for clients to have had their day in court where justice can be seen to be done. Greater awareness needs to be created regarding mediation and its benefits, which will alter the cultural outlook toward dispute resolution. The results and benefits achieved from the establishment of the

32 Bryan Clark, "Mediation and Scottish Lawyers: Past, Present and Future" (2009) 13 Edinburgh Law Review, p. 252.

mediation centers by the Lahore High Court should be promoted through public awareness campaigns to create a shift toward mediation.

Besides having a traditional history of resolution of disputes through alternate judicial systems of *Panchayat* and *Jirga* Systems over the centuries, we need to address issues owing to which Pakistan has not been able to utilize the mediation mechanism. It is seen that despite the establishment of mediation centers by the Chambers of Commerce and Industry and a few other organizations, the mediation mechanism is unable to mark its place as a preferred ADR mechanism.

There exists a dire need in Pakistan to develop a separate legal framework governing the mediation process and the enforceability of the agreements reached through mediation. An independent mediation act would best serve the purpose of provision of cost-effective and cost-efficient resolution of disputes in Pakistan. Through such legislation, the cases best suited for mediation should be made mandatory as a part of pre-action protocol before the commencement of proceedings. Besides "court-annexed" mediation, justice models for ADR delivery including "court-referred" and "court-connected" mediation may also be developed, and such mediation centers should be established considering the recent ADR Acts for the provision of time- and cost-effective resolution of disputes.

The Punjab Alternative Dispute Resolution Act 2019 (PADRA) requires the prerequisite of being established under the Companies Act 2017 to become an accredited ADR Center. This no doubt will bring regulatory supervision of the Security and Exchange Commission of Pakistan (SECP) as well as transparency in the working of such ADR centers. At the moment, there is no such body available in the country regulating ADR centers and practitioners (other than the bar councils regulating lawyers who are mediators). The rules, regulations, and the procedures for the accreditation of the ADR centers are yet to be created. A regulatory body may be established by the State that should work for the establishment and regulation of private ADR centers. However, a delicate balance must be achieved in such regulation, as ADR by its very nature thrives on party autonomy and flexibility, which excessive regulation inherently curtails.

Collaborations and partnerships may be developed with globally recognized bodies working for the provision of ADR, such as the CEDR and the Chartered Institute of Arbitrators (CIArb).

The use of mediation as an inexpensive and efficient dispute resolution system should be made popular among the public through awareness campaigns at the district level. Seminars may also be conducted among the business community through the regional Chambers of Commerce and

Industry and simplified procedures may be introduced for the business community.

At the global level, the use of mediation is becoming more structured with pre-action protocols in many countries providing that the use of the process should be encouraged or made compulsory. What is relatively little known in the Pakistani context is whether commercial dispute resolution in cross-border transactions or domestic e-transaction disputes can be effectively amenable to an online dispute resolution system. With the global pandemic, the world has been compelled to adapt to a new way of working, where virtual mediations and arbitrations have entered into the mainstream.

Conclusion

The judiciary and government of Pakistan have played a pivotal role in the development of ADR-friendly legislation.[33] The benefits that mediation offers can make it an extremely popular mode of dispute resolution in a country such as Pakistan where the court system is marred with delays. Recent positive developments in the country align with the global push toward mediation, and will inevitably lead to greater recognition and use of this medium. Support from bar councils and the legal fraternity will be crucial in determining how rapidly the mechanism evolves and the shape it takes. The future of mediation in Pakistan does appear to be bright, as long as it continues in the direction it is headed. A mediation act is a must for Pakistan. Pakistan needs to adopt a similar approach to that of the U.K. and work closely with the English judiciary to see how pre-action protocols stipulating mediation at the outset can be adopted effectively into the Pakistani legal system. Individuals interested in developing careers in mediation need to be trained effectively through international organizations that are governed in providing specialist training in mediation. A governing mediation body needs to exist to ensure individuals practicing in mediation follow a code of conduct to ensure mediators act ethically and understand the principles of "conflict of interest" and "confidentiality."

---

33 Derric Yeoh, "Is Online Dispute Resolution the Future of Alternative Dispute Resolution?," Kluwer Arbitration Blog, March 29, 2018. Also available at: http://arbitrationblog.kluwerarbitration.com/2018/03/29/online-dispute-resolution-future-alternative-dispute-resolution, last seen on April 17, 2021.

Taxing Offshore Indirect Transfers in Brazil: Discussions on International Tax Policies and Recommendations for Reform

Juliana Midori Kuteken
Research Assistant and Master's Candidate in International Tax Law and Development at the Brazilian Institute of Tax Law (IBDT)

Introduction

Taxation of the so-called offshore indirect transfers (OITs), i.e., the transfer of property whenever the transferor is a tax resident in any jurisdiction that is different from the one where the underlying asset is located, *and* when there exists at least one interposed entity between such asset and the transferor, has received more attention in the recent years, especially from the perspective of developing countries.

Although not specifically addressed in the Base Erosion and Profit Shifting (BEPS) project, conducted by the joint efforts of the Group of Twenty (G20) and the Organization for Economic Co-Operation and Development (OECD), the issue has received its deserved attention in a recent work developed by the Platform for Collaboration on Tax (PCT).[1] The PCT work has resulted in a toolkit published on June 4, 2020 (PCT Toolkit),[2] which addressed the challenges and possible answers for taxing OITs and was aimed at identifying practicable options.

The key issue regarding the taxation of OITs—which the present chapter intends to discuss—can be summarized as follows. The first question is whether and on which grounds the state where the asset is located[3] should be entitled to tax OITs, given the fact that the state where

1 The PCT comprises the joint efforts of the International Monetary Fund (IMF), the OECD, the United Nations (UN) and the World Bank Group (WBG).

2 PLATFORM FOR COLLABORATION ON TAX. *The Taxation of Offshore Indirect Transfers—A Toolkit.* IMF, OECD, UN, WBG, 2020. Available at: https://www.tax-platform.org/sites/pct/files/publications/PCT_Toolkit_The_Taxation_of_Offshore_Indirect_Transfers.pdf.

3 Hereinafter referred to as the "location state" or the "source state," as a reference to the country where the income or gain is deemed to arise.

the transferor is resident[4] might also claim its powers to tax income from its own residents, which would include income from such transfers. If the answer to such a question is affirmative, the following question is how such taxation could be implemented by the source state.

While the central question above might seem at first quite intuitive,[5] since there is widespread consensus in respect to the taxation of capital gains by the state where the asset in question is located, in practice, there are few countries imposing taxation of OITs, such as, for example, Chile, Peru, and China.

As for the current Brazilian approach, it is worth mentioning that tax legislation in force sets forth a case for the levy of withholding income tax on capital gains earned by non-residents whenever the underlying "goods" giving rise to such gains are located in Brazil. The word "goods" is understood to include shares or immovable property, but the legislation leaves unresolved whether it also encompasses the transfer of "rights," for instance. Such provision, however, is limited to direct transfers and does not entitle the state to claim taxing rights on indirect transfers, and the tax authorities' solution so far has relied on the application of anti-avoidance approaches to exercising its taxing right.

However, relying on anti-avoidance approaches brings two main difficulties. One is that usually it requires a high threshold to be applicable; that is, it is necessary to demonstrate the occurrence of fraud, sham, or the lack of business purpose. The second is that Brazil does not have a clear anti-avoidance rule—it is something that has been developed in the jurisprudence and not applied in a consistent manner.

Against such background, the present chapter deals with some of the common arguments and challenges for taxation of OITs by the source state, aiming to address two selected issues: (i) first, whether taxation of OITs by Brazil would be aligned with the state's policies in respect to international taxation; and, if so, (ii) how to best design such taxation.

The following section presents a definition of OITs and outlines the most common international tax issues that may arise and the main economic principles and tax policies that could shape the taxation of OITs. The subsequent section then presents the current Brazilian approach to the matter, discusses policy reasons on whether to tax, and makes tentative

---

4 Hereinafter referred to as the "residence state."

5 Cui, Wei. "Taxing indirect transfers: improving an instrument for stemming tax and legal base erosion." In: *Virginia Tax Review*. v. 33. n. 4. Charlottesville: University of Virginia School of Law, 2014. Available at: https://ssrn.com/abstract=2274711. p. 656.

reform recommendations. The final section summarizes the discussions and presents the conclusions.

Offshore Indirect Transfers

Definition and Overview of Relevant Tax Issues

Transfers of assets can be either *onshore* or *offshore*. *Onshore transfers* refer to all transfers of assets located in a certain state by a resident in that same state. By its turn, *offshore transfers* refer to all transfers of assets by a non-resident, i.e., where the owner and transferor are not resident in the same state where the disposing asset in question is located.[6]

In addition, a transfer can be either *direct* or *indirect*. *Direct transfers* simply refer to the transfer of an asset by the person who holds direct ownership, whereas *indirect transfers* usually refer to the transfer of an asset by the person who holds indirect ownership; i.e., there is at least one intervening entity between the transferor and the asset.[7]

Bearing such definitions in mind, OITs can be defined as the indirect transfer of an asset where the transferor is resident in a different state than that where the asset in question is located.

The following structure will be deemed as the base scenario for the discussions of the present chapter.[8] Although rather simple, the structure is sufficient to illustrate the relevant discussions on OITs: economic group ABC, whose parent company is C, domiciled in country C, intends to sell certain assets held in country A to company D, also domiciled in country C (Figure 5.1[9]).

6 PCT Toolkit. p. 10.
7 PCT Toolkit. p. 10.
8 The example and illustration presented mirror the one adopted in the PCT Toolkit, with minor adaptations to best suit the purposes of this chapter.
9 Created by the author.

Figure 5.1 Base Structure

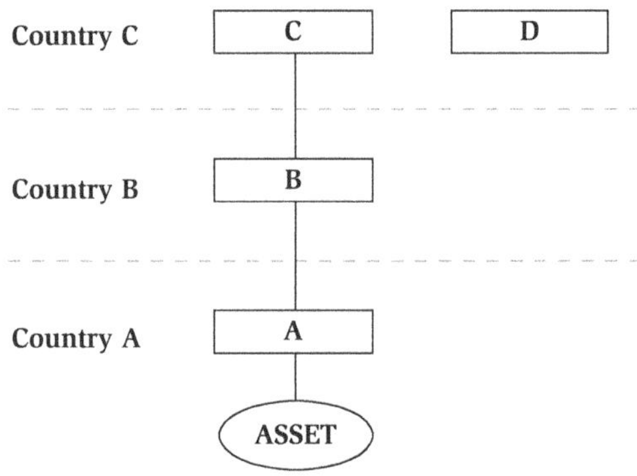

One way to arrange this transaction would consist of company A selling the asset directly to company D, which would be deemed as an onshore direct transfer of the assets and subject to capital gain taxation levied in country A. This transaction could be illustrated as follows (Figure 5.2[10]).

Figure 5.2 Direct Transfer

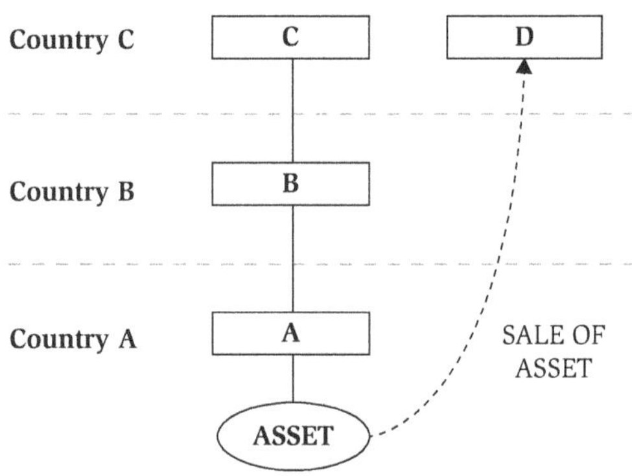

Alternatively, and assuming for the purposes of the present example that country B would have a lower tax rate on the realization of capital gains than country A, the ABC group could consider arranging an offshore transfer, which would consist of having company B selling its interest held in company A to company D. Another possible option would be company C transferring the entities' chain to company D, and the ultimate tax efficiency of such an alternative would depend on the tax treatment of capital

10 Created by the author.

gains in country C. Both options would be characterized as an OIT and could be illustrated as follows (Figure 5.3[11]).

Figure 5.3 Indirect Transfers

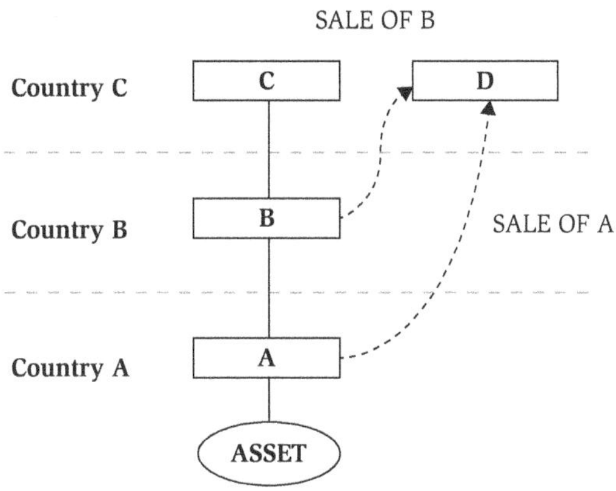

In the previous figure, "sale of A" would consist of not only a direct transfer of A but also an indirect transfer of the asset. By its turn, "sale of B" would consist of not only a direct transfer of B but also an indirect transfer of both the asset and company A.

Tax issues would arise when the state in which the transaction's underlying asset is located (in the example, country A) decides to tax gains realized on such transfers. Such issues would become even more complex if both countries A and B decide to impose taxation on offshore transfers carried out by non-residents. In both scenarios, it is expected that country C also claims its jurisdiction to tax.

Whether or not the state where the underlying asset is located should have jurisdiction to tax and, if so, how should this taxation be imposed are the two central questions this chapter intends to address.

Taxing Indirect Transfers under the OECD and UN Model Tax Conventions

Both the OECD and UN Model Tax Conventions[12] contain provisions on taxing OITs of immovable property by the state where such asset is located.

11 Created by the author.

12 2017 Income and Capital Model Convention (OECD Model) and 2017 United Nations Model Double Taxation Convention between Developed and Developing Countries (UN Model).

The relevant provision is Article 13(4), which since 2017 is identical in both models and reads as follows:

> Article 13(4)
> Gains derived by a resident of a Contracting State from the alienation of shares or comparable interests, such as interests in a partnership or trust, may be taxed in the other Contracting State if, at any time during the 365 days preceding the alienation, these shares or comparable interests derived more than 50 percent of their value directly or indirectly from immovable property, as defined in Article 6, situated in that other State.

However, adoption of such provision is not very popular: Article 13(4) is found in only around 35 percent of all double tax treaties (DTT) and is less likely to be found in DTTs when one party is a low-income but resource-rich state.[13]

Even for the states that do adopt the suggested wording of Article 13(4), it should be noted that the scope of the wording is limited since it only refers to OITs involving immovable property,[14] and allocation of taxing rights to the source state depends on the verification of the time and value thresholds set forth therein.

Regardless of the treaty-level approach, the relevant treatment of taxing OITs will be found at the domestic level. The following sections delve into the common economic and tax policy justifications for the decision of a source state to provide taxation of OITs under domestic law.

Taxation of OITs by the Source State: Justification under Economic Principles and International Tax Competition

Tax Equity or Fairness

Tax equity or fairness is all about imposing equal taxes on taxpayers with equal income or equal ability to pay, without reference to the source or type of income and the legal structures through which the income is derived.[15]

---

13 According to the PCT Toolkit. p. 7.

14 Brazil has presented a reservation to Article 13 of the OECD Model in respect to having the right to tax at source gains from the alienation of property other than those mentioned in the paragraphs 1, 2, 3 and 4.

15 Holmes, Kevin. *International Tax Policy and Double Tax Treaties: An Introduction to Principles and Application*. Amsterdam: IBFD, 2007. p. 2.

The fairness of a tax system, however, relies on legitimate *expectations* as well as redistributive aspects. In this regard, tax changes that impose an unexpected burden on previous expectations can be perceived as unfair—in this sense, imposition of capital gains taxes could reduce the net *expected* capital gain.[16] Thus, the introduction of taxation of OITs, if lacking transparency and grounded exclusively on revenue collection or claims for redistributive justice, could face the risk of being regarded as unfair and even prejudice the state's image in an international tax competition context.

Thus, especially in regard to capital-importing states' position, taxation of OITs should be consistent with legitimate expectations of foreign investors and also with the state's own international tax policies and objectives—that is the key issue that this chapter aims at contributing to.

It is generally accepted that capital gains arising in *onshore* transfers are taxable by the state in which the asset is located. This wide acceptance is due to a combination of economic principles that have helped to reach a certain consensus.

Source taxation is traditionally justified by the *benefit theory*, pursuant to which taxes would be a means of compensation due to the government in consideration for its support granted in the generation of income. Such support would be found in the provision of public services and in the maintenance of an adequate institutional scenario by the *source state*, factors that altogether would entitle the state to share the non-resident's profit generated within (or at least, with the help of) the jurisdiction.

On the other hand, however, the *residence state* could also invoke the benefit theory to justify its jurisdiction to tax the very same transaction, based on the also reasonable assumption that the taxpayer might have benefited from certain public services at the residence, and that the institutional scenario provided by residence state might have enabled the taxpayers to generate income abroad.

These two very reasonable expected reactions from the source and the residence states toward the benefit theory indicate that the theory would be easier to apply at the domestic level than at the international level. At the domestic level, the benefit theory is suitable to deal with the classic dilemma of the fiscal state, that is, to which extent is taxation in the first place *legitimate*, whereas at the international level, the question is which state should have the right to impose taxation and on which grounds. In

16 Mirrlees James; et al. *Tax by Design*. Oxford: Oxford University Press, 2011. Available at: http://www.ifs.org.uk/publications/5353. p. 33.

other words, conflicting visions on the meaning of "benefit" could arise when two sovereign states are counterposed.

This view is supported by Schön, who emphasizes that the traditional features of the benefit principle might not be helpful to determine the allocation of taxing rights between different states. This is not only because the residence state could also claim its application—since the concept of "benefit" is very volatile and subject to different views—but also because, in the context of a competitive globalized economy, it is likely that tax competition constraints push states to reduce tax rates, irrespective of any benefits that could have been enjoyed by the taxpayer.[17]

Application of the benefit theory to taxing OITs would face similar challenges, to the extent that the state of the underlying asset may claim to have contributed to creating a substantial part of the transaction value derived from the asset in question. A counterargument from the residence state would be that its own residents, who ultimately conducted the transaction and earned its results, would have benefited from public services at the residence state as well. The PCT Toolkit admits that the *benefit theory* would not be especially compelling as applied to the taxation of OITs, in that it relies on the relationship between state benefit and gains (or profits), which may be a poor proxy for the benefits received.[18]

If not perfectly justified by the benefit theory, taxation of OITs could be justified by the so-called *economic allegiance theory*, which can be defined as the undeniable genuine link established between the taxable income and the state,[19] in respect to which the right to tax would be largely accepted.

The economic allegiance theory may justify source taxation in several situations, and such rationale is even more evident in the case of immovable property since there is a physical, evident, connection to the land.[20] Application of the economic allegiance theory to capital gains arising from immovable property would imply that the country where the asset is located, i.e., the "*situs* state," has a genuine connection with the origin of wealth and, because of that, there would be little controversy in respect to granting taxation rights to the situs state.

---

17 Schön, Wolfgang. "International Tax Coordination for a Second-Best World (Part I)." In: *World Tax Journal*, v. 1. n. 1. September 2009. Available at: https://ssrn.com/abstract=1577035. pp. 75-78.

18 PCT Toolkit. p. 19.

19 Schön, Wolfgang. "International Tax Coordination for a Second-Best World (Part I)." *Supra* pp. 90-91.

20 Li, Jinyan; Avella, Francesco. "Article 13: Capital Gains." In: *Global Tax Treaty Commentaries*. Amsterdam: IBFD, 2018. Chapter 1.1.2.1.

Following such a conclusion, taxation of OITs could find its grounds in the economic allegiance theory. By setting the location of the asset as the point of reference for the assessment of value creation, indirect transfers would be no different from direct transfers, no matter how many interposed layers of entities could exist between the asset and the transferor.

Taxation of capital gains—whether direct or indirect—by the situs state would encounter further justification in the also existing consensus that the right to tax *income* arising from a certain asset and the right to tax capital gains arising from *alienation* of the same asset should follow the same rationale, what is known as the *principle of symmetry*. In this sense, the principle of symmetry would set out the interaction between Article 13 (distributive rule on capital gains) and other distributive rules on income, such as Articles 6 (immovable property), 7 (business profits), and 8 (international transport), for instance. Under all of these provisions, if taxation over one element of *income* is allocated to one contracting state, then it is expected that taxation over the *capital gains* associated with the alienation of the asset giving rise to that very income is allocated to the same contracting state.[21] In respect to OITs, it could be expected that existing allocation to the source state of certain elements of income should guide the allocation of taxing rights of capital gains as well, even if earned indirectly.

Although there is no perfect symmetry between Articles 10 (dividends) and 13 (capital gains), since Article 10 sets forth *shared* taxing rights for source and residence, while Article 13 sets forth *exclusive* taxing rights either to the source or to the residence as the case may be,[22] this "imperfect" symmetry between dividends and capital gains could at least encompass one common factor: attribution of taxing rights to the source state to a certain extent.

This is the rationale behind the argument that the asset price in a capital gain transaction reflects accumulated and undistributed earnings, which the location state would be entitled to tax at source upon its future

21 Elaboration on the principle of symmetry is made by Pijl, Hans. "Capital Gains: The Principle of Symmetry, the Internal Order of Article 13 and the Dynamic Interpretation of the Changes in the 2010 Commentary on 'Forming Part' and 'Effectively Connected' in Taxation of Companies on Capital Gains under Domestic Law." In: Maisto, Guglielmo. *Taxation of Companies on Capital Gains on Shares under Domestic Law: EU Law and Tax Treaties*. Amsterdam: IBFD, 2013. pp. 1-2.

22 Pijl, Hans. "Capital Gains: The Principle of Symmetry, the Internal Order of Article 13 and the Dynamic Interpretation of the Changes in the 2010 Commentary on 'Forming Part' and 'Effectively Connected' in Taxation of Companies on Capital Gains under Domestic Law." *Supra* p. 2.

distribution in the form of dividends/profits. Yet, this precise rationale has been used as an argument against the taxation of OITs, in the sense that the supposedly enshrined gain would be taxed upon such future distribution of dividends/profits—there is no need to anticipate any taxation.

However, such an argument ignores the fact that the distribution of such corresponding profits may happen only after a certain time or never at all, or there may be a mismatch between the tax rates applicable to capital gains and to profits. In the case of Brazil, the distribution of dividends is currently exempt from tax, while capital gains are not. Policy reasons for the distinction go beyond the scope of this chapter. For the purposes of the present analysis, it is sufficient to assume that Brazil, as the source country, would be *entitled* to tax at source dividends remitted to a beneficiary resident abroad.

Taxing OITs at source, then, would avoid tax deferral of gains retained at the corporate level.[23] If one was to apply the principle of symmetry, taxation of dividends at source—even though not exclusively—should be somewhat symmetrical to taxation of capital gains by the "source," i.e., the state where the asset is located.

While such a rationale might seem appealing, it does not take into consideration the perspective of the residence state, in the sense that the value of the transferred asset may also derive, at least in part, from the expertise and work of its owners/managers and not *solely* from the fact that some asset is located in a certain state. In respect to capital gains in corporate reorganizations, it could be added that, as a result of expected future profits or achievement of synergies, the purchase price may exceed the elements defined in the transaction, resulting in higher capital gains.[24]

In other words, although the economic allegiance theory would grant taxation rights to the situs state based on the assumption that the state would have contributed to the economic value of the asset, it could happen that part of the value-enhancement came from abroad.[25] This would be a counterargument in the sense that the residence state should also be granted jurisdiction to tax.

---

23 For a numeric example of possible tax deferral effects, *see*: Kane, Mitchell A. "Offshore Transfers: Policies and Divergent Views." In: *Bulletin for International Taxation*. v. 72. April-May 2018. Amsterdam: IBFD, 2018. pp. 331-338.

24 Maisto, Guglielmo; Malherbe, Jacques. "Chapter 1: General Report on Taxation of Companies on Capital Gains on Shares under Domestic Law." In: Maisto, Guglielmo. *Taxation of Companies on Capital Gains on Shares under Domestic Law: EU Law and Tax Treaties*. Amsterdam: IBFD, 2013. p. 1.

25 The PCT Toolkit. p. 18.

Establishing to which extent such returns in a capital gain transaction refer to the asset itself (and thus, to the situs state) is not an easy task since contributions from both the location and the efforts employed by its non-resident owners are intrinsically interrelated.

Economic Efficiency

According to the principle of tax neutrality, tax rules should not distort economic agents' decisions unless specifically designed to do so, nor should tax rules treat similar transactions differently. Imposition of tax must seek to be unbiased as between the array of different domestic and foreign investment options made available to the investor.[26]

From such a perspective, taxing OITs would promote *neutrality* between direct and indirect transfers since no incentive to transferring assets by means of interposed entities would be granted.

In addition, by taxing OITs, capital import neutrality would be achieved since residents and non-residents would be treated equally in respect to taxation of capital gains.[27] On the opposite side, the absence of taxation of OITs by the source state would create not only an incentive to non-residents to the detriment of residents, thus in prejudice of such capital import neutrality, but also an opportunity for residents to employ "round-tripping" strategies. Round-tripping would consist of arrangements of chain transactions in which the beginning and end of the chain are in the same state and probably ultimately refer to the same taxpayer, but intermediate transactions take place outside the country.[28]

Lastly, the PCT Toolkit also points out that the immovability of an asset could reflect "location-specific rents."[29] Location-specific rents refer to income uniquely associated with a particular location, such as natural resources. Differently from general rents (whose value or equivalent could be found elsewhere), location-specific rents are a strong indication of value arising significantly from an asset's location—which contributes to the arguments in favor of the taxation by the location country. In respect to the exploitation of natural resources, justifications would go beyond such a rationale to the extent that the location country should be concerned in its

---

26 Holmes, Kevin. *International Tax Policy and Double Tax Treaties*. *Supra* p. 2.
27 Li, Jinyan; Avella, Francesco. "Article 13: Capital Gains." *Supra* Chapter 1.1.2.3.
28 The PCT Toolkit. p. 6.
29 The PCT Toolkit defines location-specific rents as economic returns that exceed the normal level of return that an investor requires. p. 5.

conservation and should need resources to enhance sustainable exploitation. The existence of location-specific rents is of paramount importance to developing countries, and it should be taken into consideration when designing a tax policy on taxation of OITs, as addressed in the following section.

International Tax Competition: Challenges to Taxation of OITs

The traditional conception of states as powerful sovereigns has given place to an interrelated and highly competitive global market. Dagan analyzes how “classic” economic principles such as efficiency and fairness are influenced by international tax competition. The author defines international tax competition with an illustrative example: the states act as recruiters, soliciting investments as well as residents, seeking to offer competitive deals of public goods and services at low prices.[30] In such a context, states’ tax policies aim at shifting both economic activity and taxable revenues into their jurisdictions by attracting residents and investors.

Mirrlees et al. state that optimal taxation should achieve its proposed objectives while satisfying the constraints of international tax competition.[31] Applying such an ideal to the taxation of OITs, source states should be expected to seek to tax such gains as to guarantee taxable basis and revenue collection associated with value creation, but under the constraints imposed by international tax competition, which could have the negative side effect of shifting non-resident investors away.

Under these constraints, the challenge is to determine whether international capital mobility would put pressure on a race-to-the-bottom competition between states regarding taxation of OITs. This is because, on the one hand, it could seem a sensible choice to tax OITs whose underlying asset is relatively immobile, such as location-specific rents associated with scarcity (for instance, natural resources). On the other hand, imposing taxation on OITs whose underlying asset is highly mobile could possibly deter inward investments.[32]

One may curb the impulse to conclude that a source state should tax OITs only in connection to immobile assets, leaving mobile assets and activities aside. Also, it would be premature to conclude that establishing a

30 Dagan, Tsilly. *International Tax Policy: Between Competition and Cooperation (Cambridge Tax Law Series)*. Cambridge: Cambridge University Press, 2018. p. 13.

31 Mirrlees, James. *Tax by design. Supra* p. 36.

32 Mirrlees, James. *Tax by design. Supra* pp. 438-439.

higher tax rate to immobile-related OITs would be efficient since they are less likely to relocate elsewhere. Ring-fencing could not only increase the complexity of the system but could also be deemed as a harmful tax practice and thus should be discouraged.

There are two arguments for this conclusion.

First, in respect to location-specific rents, the assumption that taxation at a high rate would be 100 percent efficient is not entirely accurate. Part of these rents may reflect returns on the efforts and improvements made by non-residents, and taxing them at a high rate might discourage further investments.

Second, in respect to highly mobile activities, the assumption that imposing a certain level of taxation would result in absolute capital flight is also not entirely accurate. In this sense, Griffith et al. observe that even if we assume a non-cooperative tax setting and a highly competitive international scene, capital income taxes do not need to lower beyond an optimal level.[33] In addition, at least in respect to the already invested capital, investors would have to consider costs of the lock-in effect, that is, divestment costs and costs necessary to pursue alternative investments in other jurisdictions.[34]

An efficient answer to taxation of OITs by the source state would rely on finding a balance to contemplate a comprehensive set of possible natures of the underlying asset. Mirrlees et al. suggest that should a single tax rate apply to all companies, the appropriate rate would reflect a trade-off between the desirability of taxing location-specific rents and the danger of taxing mobile rents.[35]

The following section tries to adapt such conclusions to the Brazilian approach.

---

33 The authors regard an "optimal level of taxation" as the minimum required not to decrease welfare. Griffith, Rachel; Hines, James; Sørensen, Peter B. "International Capital Taxation." In: Mirrlees, James. *Dimensions of Tax Design: the Mirrlees Review.* Oxford: Oxford University Press, 2010. Available at: https://ifs.org.uk/uploads/mirrleesreview/dimensions/ch10.pdf. p. 934.

34 Maisto, Guglielmo; Malherbe, Jacques. "Chapter 1: General Report on Taxation of Companies on Capital Gains on Shares under Domestic Law." In: Maisto, Guglielmo. *Taxation of Companies on Capital Gains on Shares under Domestic Law: EU Law and Tax Treaties.* Amsterdam: IBFD, 2013. p. 2.

35 Mirrlees, James. *Tax by Design. Supra* p. 441.

Offshore Indirect Transfers in Brazil

Current Brazilian Approach

Brazilian domestic rules provide for a broad hypothesis of source taxation on capital gains earned by non-residents. Article 26 of Federal Law No. 10,833, of December 29, 2003, sets forth that capital gains earned by non-residents upon sale of goods directly held in Brazil are subject to withholding income tax, to be collected by the buyer, if resident or domiciled in Brazil, or by the buyer's legal representative, whenever a buyer is domiciled abroad:

> The buyer, individual or legal entity resident or domiciled in Brazil, or its legal representative, when the purchaser is resident or domiciled abroad, shall be responsible for withholding and collecting income tax due on the capital gain referred to in Article 18 of Law No. 9,249, of December 26, 1995, earned by the individual or legal entity resident or domiciled abroad who disposes goods located in Brazil.[36]

This provision raises some discussions at the domestic level that may exceed the scope of the present chapter. It is worth mentioning, however, that the Brazilian approach to the taxation of capital gains earned by non-residents is essentially based on an expanded source element of connection. That is, withholding income tax is levied on capital gains earned by non-residents even if both the buyer and seller are located abroad, meaning that there is no source of payment or even any flow of funds within Brazil. Source taxation, in this case, is justified by the concept of a source of production, referring to the relevant asset giving rise to capital gain.[37]

---

36 Original in Portuguese:

> Art. 26. O adquirente, pessoa física ou jurídica residente ou domiciliada no Brasil, ou o procurador, quando o adquirente for residente ou domiciliado no exterior, fica responsável pela retenção e recolhimento do imposto de renda incidente sobre o ganho de capital a que se refere o art. 18 da Lei nº 9.249, de 26 de dezembro de 1995, auferido por pessoa física ou jurídica residente ou domiciliada no exterior que alienar bens localizados no Brasil.

37 Xavier, Alberto. *Direito Tributário Internacional do Brasil.* 8. ed. Rio de Janeiro: Forense, 2015. pp. 518-520.

Such provision only applies to *direct* transfers of Brazilian "goods," which encompasses immovable and movable property pursuant to domestic law—in this sense, real property and shares and other comparable interest are deemed to fall within the scope of the rule—but whether rights such as licenses, grants, and concessions to explore natural resources, for instance, would qualify as "goods" is not clarified by the legislation.

In the example given under "Definition and Overview of Relevant Tax Issues" above, the current domestic provision is sufficient to cover the *direct* transfer of company A, irrespective of the fact that the underlying asset is only *indirectly* transferred, as seen below (Figure 5.4[38]).

Figure 5.4 Indirect Transfer in Brazil

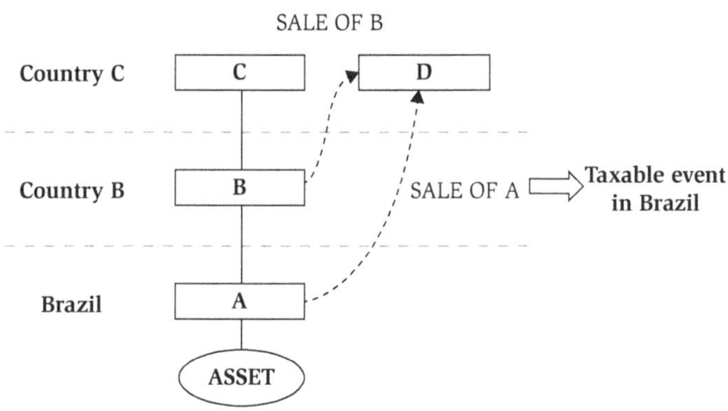

The legislation, however, does not expressly authorize taxation of OITs if the above transaction was carried out at the level of company C. In the absence of a direct element of connection in Brazil, tax authorities have adopted in recent cases a look-through approach to disregard the company B level as to enable the application of Article 26 and to levy withholding income tax on indirect transfers.[39]

However, reliance on anti-avoidance rules to tax OITs faces several challenges. First of all, Brazil does not have a general anti-avoidance rule (GAAR), and the anti-abuse doctrine is mostly based on interpretations

38 Created by the author.

39 A detailed description of relevant recent case law on the matter can be found in Fonseca, Isabel Garcia Calich da. "Taxation of Capital Gains on Indirect Sale of Shares of Brazilian Companies by Non-residents: The Allocation of Taxing Rights or Tax Avoidance Schemes?." In: *Bulletin for International Taxation.* June 2020. Amsterdam: Journals IBFD, 2020. pp. 324-331. And Carvalho, Laura Kurth Marques. "Taxation of Offshore Indirect Transfers in Brazil in Need of Reform." In: *Bulletin for International Taxation.* March 2020. Amsterdam: Journals IBFD, 2020. pp. 123-133.

construed within the jurisprudence. As a civil law country, this brings uncertainty and increases the difficulties of applying the anti-abuse doctrine in a predictable way.

Second, the tax authorities may encounter difficulties in objectively demonstrating the existence of fraud or sham in order to apply such a look-through approach and claim the application of the domestic capital gains rule.

Lastly, this approach is not sufficient to cover all OITs since it is limited to abusive transactions carried out with the specific intention of avoiding capital gains taxation at source. For that reason, the PCT suggests that any GAAR-based approach should be the last resort to taxing OITs.[40]

Whether Brazil Should Impose Taxation on OITs and Tentative Recommendations for Reform

The main objective of this last section is to answer, in the light of the preceding discussions, whether and how Brazil should tax OITs.

The objectives of the current Brazilian international tax policies are quite unclear.[41] While Brazilian tax policies may shift between capital-importing and capital-exporting countries, the country has a strong position in favor of source taxation, which can be observed, for instance, in its DTTs network and in the fact that the domestic legislation provides for a quite comprehensive scenario for levying withholding income tax.

Whenever in the position of a source country, Brazil could benefit from imposing taxation on the gains arising in OITs associated with assets located within its territory.

In this sense, Brazil already taxes at least part of the OIT transactions. As seen in the example given under "Current Brazilian Approach" above, the direct transfer of company A, implying the indirect transfer of the assets, is a taxable transaction pursuant to Brazil's legislation in force. Thus, introducing taxation of indirect transfers would be fully aligned with the already existing tax legislation.

In addition, the introduction of a Brazilian rule of taxation of OITs would not conflict with the current Brazilian network of DTTs. While most of the DTTs in force do not contain specific provisions regarding the taxation of OITs, some of them do expressly provide that *indirect* transfers

40 The PCT Toolkit. p. 37.

41 Schoueri, Luís Eduardo. "Chapter 4: Brazil in BRICS and the Emergence of International Tax Coordination." In: Brauner, Yariv; Pistone, Pasquale (coord.). *BRICS and the Emergence of International Tax Coordination.* Amsterdam: IBFD, 2015. Section 1.1.

are taxable in the source state—that is the case of the treaties with Israel, South Africa, Switzerland, and the United Arab Emirates. Treaties with Finland and France contain a specific provision granting tax powers to the contracting state in which underlying immovable property is located, in respect to capital gains arising from the alienation of shares or any comparable rights held in a legal entity owning such immovable property. The DTT signed with Japan is the only treaty that grants exclusive taxing rights to the residence state in respect to capital gains other than those resulting from alienation of immovable property or pertaining to a permanent establishment.

Some may argue that the introduction of a rule taxing OITs in Brazil would deter highly mobile investments, as argued in the previous sections, but it would be unlikely that reasonable taxation of OITs would result in inward investments vanishing completely. On the contrary, it would be fair to expect that the institution of simple, straightforward and transparent legislation aligned with clear tax policy objectives would contribute to a foreseeable and stable institutional scenario, which might attract investments.

The recent Brazilian approach to OITs has relied on a look-through approach, by means of application of anti-abuse provisions. Although anti-abuse measures could be useful to counter abuse, their scope is limited to abusive transactions, leaving aside potential arbitrary effects and the already mentioned difficulties arising in their application. Thus, the introduction of legislation specifically targeting taxation of OITs would be a welcome reform and would bring more tax certainty when compared to the challenging and controversial application of anti-avoidance approaches.

Brazil is a natural resources-rich state with plenty of investment opportunities related to land, forestry, agriculture, renewable and fossil energy, mineral resources, etc. In addition, the large consumption market represents a relevant share to attract highly mobile activities as well, such as those related to financial, technology, and digital services.

On the one hand, such assets located in Brazil do have their intrinsic value, but on the other hand, it should not be ignored that their value is also enhanced by the foreign investors' expertise, work, and innovation, factors that altogether are expected to be reflected in the determination of an offshore transaction pricing. The design of taxation on OITs should be especially careful not to discourage these kinds of specific and highly aggregated investments since they contribute not only to revenue collection but also, most importantly, to the development of knowledge and technology within Brazil.

In conclusion, it is argued that designing a tax liability rule for OITs in Brazil would not only contribute to raising tax certainty to indirect transactions when compared to the anti-abuse approach but also be aligned with the country's profile as a large economy seeking to provide a sound and predictable scenario to foreign investors. Also, the economic principles addressed under "Taxation of OITs by the Source State: Justification under Economic Principles and International Tax Competition" represent sufficient justification for the country, whenever in a position of a situs state, to claim its taxing rights. The possible key features of such legislation are addressed in the following section.

Designing a Tax Liability Rule for OITs in Brazil

The PCT Toolkit presents two different models for designing a tax liability rule for OITs: (i) taxing the local resident asset-owning entity under a deemed disposal model; and (ii) taxing the non-resident seller.[42]

The first model seeks to tax the local entity that directly owns the asset in question, by deeming that entity as disposing of, and reacquiring, its assets for their market value whenever a change of control (the indirect transfer carried abroad) occurs. The relevant taxpayer under this model is not the seller entity, but rather the entity which actually owns the assets from which the relevant shares derive their value.

The second model seeks to tax the non-resident seller of the relevant shares or comparable interests via a non-resident assessing rule, being supported by a source of income rule, which should provide that a gain is sourced in the location country when the value of the interest disposed of is derived, directly or indirectly, principally from immovable property (and possibly from other assets) located in that country. The PCT Toolkit emphasizes that such a source of income rule may be further supported by a taxable asset rule reflecting some necessary thresholds, such as ownership of minimum interest.

In principle, either model could be considered and possibly a combination of both would fit under Brazil's domestic legislation. The appointment of the local entity as the deemed taxpayer as proposed by Model 1 would be possible, or even a tax liability rule providing for the responsibility of the local entity as the tax would be aligned with the country's practice and the tax legislation. By its turn, the design of a source of income rule as proposed by Model 2 would fit into the existing theories that justify the

42 The PCT Toolkit. pp. 36-41.

capital gains taxation of non-residents by Brazil (Article 26 of Law No. 10,833/2003), even when both seller and buyer are located abroad. That is, as mentioned in the previous sections, taxation in this case is based on an "expanded source" element of connection, meaning that there is no source of payment or even any flow of funds within Brazil. Source taxation, in this case, is justified by the concept of a source of production, referring to the relevant asset giving rise to capital gain—and taxation of OITs could possibly follow such rationale.

Having these objectives in mind, the following features are proposed.

With respect to the scope, ring-fencing different groups of assets would not be efficient and would increase complexity. The current non-resident capital gains rule has a narrow scope since it is restricted to "goods." In view of that, taxation of gains derived from indirect alienation of "assets" could encompass a broader scope, eliminating unnecessary discussions. However, since Article 13(4) of the OECD Model and the UN Model targets immovable property, there might be a legitimate expectation from international players that taxation of OITs by Brazil aims primarily at taxing *immovable property*. Thus, it would be important to establish clear definitions of which kind of assets would trigger withholding income tax in Brazil. In this sense, Cui reminds us that domestic taxation of OITs should not be so broad as to end up taxing more than is necessary.[43]

Despite such suggested broader scope, for reasons of practicability, some thresholds and/or deductions could be introduced, to the extent they do not increase complexity or impose costly compliance obligations. The regime to be introduced by Brazil could encompass thresholds when participation under 10 percent, for instance, of the relevant entity is transferred, such as in portfolio investment. This would avoid unnecessary compliance costs associated with irrelevant tax collection.

Adopting a single general rate (or progressive rates upon certain ranges), irrespective of the nature of the asset, would be easier to understand, thus facilitating compliance and improving the perception of equity and fairness. The design of taxation on OITs in Brazil should refrain from granting special regimes to the targeted groups of investors, but rather foster neutrality. However, a deduction or incentive could be granted if the

43 Cui, Wei. "Taxing Indirect Transfers: Improving an Instrument for Stemming Tax and Legal Base Erosion." In: *Virginia Tax Review.* v. 33. n. 4. Charlottesville: University of Virginia School of Law, 2014. Available at: https://ssrn.com/abstract=2274711. p. 676.

amount resulting from the sale of a capital asset is reinvested in the country.[44]

Lastly, the feasibility of taxing OITs would depend on the capacity of the tax administration to enforce and collect the capital gain tax due.[45] For that purpose, a withholding taxation rule could be designed to impose a levy of withholding income tax upon payments of the purchase price sourced in the country. And if there are no payments sourced in Brazil, the tax liability for the collection of the withholding income tax could still be imposed to the local entity or to the buyer's legal representative—mirroring the current domestic provision of Article 26 of Law No. 10,833/2003 that requires the buyer or its representative to withhold and collect the tax due, even if the transaction is fully completed abroad. Also, regulatory requirements could help to identify indirect transactions. The Brazilian Central Bank currently requires changes of control in foreign direct investments to be informed and updated in the Electronic Registration Statement—Foreign Direct Investment (the "RDE-IED" system), and such information could be used to identify indirect transfers triggering capital gain taxation.

Lastly, Brazil's recent legislative changes regarding disclosure of beneficial owner provisions, country-by-country reporting, and tax information exchange agreements (TIEAs) represent a contribution to international tax cooperation and could help to identify the relevant transactions and to prevent double taxation.

Conclusions

The present chapter aimed at discussing the main international tax policy reasons for a source state to levy taxation on OITs, with a focus on the current Brazilian approach, and attempted to identify which features of such taxation would be desirable.

The chapter pointed out that there may be reasonable economic and tax policy justifications for a source state to claim taxation, based on the

44 Maisto, Guglielmo; Malherbe, Jacques. "Chapter 1: General Report on Taxation of Companies on Capital Gains on Shares under Domestic Law." In: Maisto, Guglielmo. *Taxation of Companies on Capital Gains on Shares under Domestic Law: EU Law and Tax Treaties.* Amsterdam: IBFD, 2013. p. 2.

45 On the role of tax administrations in the operation and implementation of tax systems, *see* Alink, Matthijs; Kommer, Victor van. *Handbook on Tax Administration.* 2 ed. Amsterdam: IBFD, 2016.

traditional concepts of tax equity, fairness, efficiency, and neutrality. It was then recognized that, under constraints of international tax competition, such traditional views may face certain challenges.

The analysis considered the arguments in favor of the idea that taxation of OITs whenever the underlying asset refers to a location-specific rent could be regarded as more efficient than highly mobile activities since the latter would deter inward investments while the former would not. The proposed conclusion is that these arguments for one side and against another cannot be regarded as absolute, and a balance should be achieved. The conclusion of the second section was that while there may be efficiency arguments *not* to impose taxation on foreign investments if one does not want them to be deterred, it does not follow, however, that developing countries should completely refrain from taxing OITs.

The goal of the last section was to provide ideas to enhance further discussion on the taxation of OITs in Brazil. Brazil adopts a source expansion approach to direct transfers, while tax authorities have recently engaged in a look-through approach to disregard interposed entities and achieve taxation of OITs. While this may be appropriate to counter abusive practices, the chapter concluded that a country should not rely exclusively on anti-abuse rules to tax OITs. In this sense, a design of a rule to tax OITs in Brazil would be recommended. As for the characteristics of such a rule, the chapter suggested that neutrality and simplicity would create a sound institutional environment for the attraction of foreign investments.

Back to the Future: Looking for a European Tax System

Olivier Péjout
Legal Clerk, General Court of the European Union (Luxembourg), Former Lecturer, Université de Nantes, Former Research Fellow at the University of Bordeaux, Qualified Lawyer in France

Introduction

The 2020 lockdown crisis took the world by surprise. Grim economic predictions are spreading rapidly. States' responses lie in stimulus packages involving a large amount of public spending. Conversely, they are in a worse financial situation than they were back in the 2008 financial crisis. High public debt levels are plaguing governments as they try to fund unprecedented recovery plans. States are in desperate need to secure as much revenue as they can. Meanwhile, increased digitalization, with its groundbreaking innovations, is profoundly changing our societies. A new breed of the firm has come to the forefront of the digital revolution in the last decade. They were praised for their innovations and criticized for their tax optimization. Those examples have raised concerns about effective taxation of such new activities, and the ongoing crisis gives a greater sense of urgency to this long-standing question.

The digital economy has been "characterized by an unparalleled reliance on intangible assets, the massive use of data (notably personal data), the widespread adoption of multi-sided business models capturing value from externalities generated by free products, and the difficulty of determining the jurisdiction in which value creation occurs."[1] Therefore, it has exacerbated underlying problems of tax avoidance.[2] The international community has been grappling with what they see as a major change and have attempted to update their tax systems accordingly. This chapter will

---

1 OECD. Action Plan on Base Erosion and Profit Shifting, OECD Publishing: Paris, 2013, rec. 10.

2 C. Marchgraber. Avoidance of Double Non-taxation in Double Tax Treaty Law: A Critical Analysis of the Subject-to-Tax Clause Recommended by the European Commission, EC Tax Review, 2014, vol. 23, Issue 5, pp. 293-302; P. Schwarz. Tax-Avoidance Strategies of American Multinationals: An Empirical Analysis, Managerial and Decision Economics, 2019, vol. 30, pp. 539-549.

try to give a European Union (EU) perspective to this subject. Indeed, the EU took part in the discussion with debatable proposals but mostly used the momentum to revive the debate on tax harmonization. From the establishment of the European Economic Community (EEC) in 1957 to the creation of the European Monetary Union (EMU), there has been a constant discussion on the need for cooperation in tax law matters. The EU has always been torn between two scenarios, one providing only limited assistance and the other organizing high-level coordination through the enforcement of the same rules.

In this context, on March 23, 2018, the Commission presented a package of three texts aimed at ensuring that all companies pay their "fair share"[3] of taxes in the EU. Also known as the GAFA[4] package, it consists of two directives and a recommendation. The first proposal for a Directive[5] "aims to reform corporate tax rules so that profits are registered and taxed where businesses have significant interaction with users through digital channels."[6] The second proposal for a Directive[7] provides "an interim tax which covers the main digital activities that currently escape tax altogether in the EU."[8] In addition, there is a proposal for a recommendation[9] that encourages the Member States to reform double taxation treaties signed with third countries to include the concept of significant digital presence.

The GAFA package should be seen as a strong political stance, and not simply a technical proposal, in the search for a solution to the digital tax challenge.[10] The EU wants to convince its Member States that they can

---

3 G7 Biarritz 2019. Chair's summary: G7 Finance ministers and central bank governors' meeting, Chantilly, July 17, 18, 2019, available at: https://www.tresor.economie.gouv.fr/Articles/5f8c26f2-a2cd-4685-ba82-fa9e4d4e5d67/files/e1bfda0e-c9f5-4375-a716-2d1cf42675d6 [accessed on January 18, 2021].

4 Named after several American digital companies: Google, Apple, Facebook, and Amazon.

5 Proposal for a Council Directive laying down rules relating to the corporate taxation of a significant digital presence, COM(2018) 147 final.

6 European Commission—Press release: Digital Taxation: Commission proposes new measures to ensure that all companies pay fair tax in the EU, Brussels, March 21, 2018. Available at: https://ec.europa.eu/commission/presscorner/detail/en/IP_18_2041 [accessed on August 7, 2020].

7 Proposal for a Council Directive on the common system of a digital services tax on revenues resulting from the provision of certain digital services, COM(2018) 148 final.

8 Proposal for a Council Directive on the common system of a digital services tax on revenues resulting from the provision of certain digital services, COM(2018) 148 final.

9 Commission Recommendation relating to the corporate taxation of a significant digital presence, COM(2018) 1650 final.

10 P. Genschel. Globalization and the Transformation of the Tax State. In: Leibfried S. & Zürn M. (eds.). Transformations of the State? Cambridge: Cambridge University Press, 2005, pp. 53-72; T. Falcão, B. Michel. Assessing the Tax Challenges of the Digital

only guarantee their income on a global scale by uniting.[11] This chapter reflects on how the GAFA package has shed new light on the underlying problems raised by tax harmonization in the EU. In fact, the EU is taking advantage of the current debate surrounding taxation of digital companies to ramp up its long-standing plea for a real common tax system in the internal market. Furthermore, the 2020-2021 lockdown crisis bolsters the Commission's endeavor to ensure effective fiscal revenue to support public finances put under severe strain. The EU is the most integrated economic area in the world, but it still lacks a genuine fiscal policy to strengthen it. Even if the GAFA package has its flaws,[12] it serves a much wider EU agenda. Put differently, if tax harmonization is gaining momentum within the Member States, the real issue for the EU's integration is not to devise the best possible solution but rather to ascertain whether it is conceivable to add complementary legal provisions or carry out a complete overhaul of the decision-making process regarding tax law in the Treaty on the Functioning of the European Union (TFEU). This chapter will therefore use the GAFA package as a pretext to carry out an analysis of the challenges of fiscal integration and what success would mean at both the EU and the international levels. If the EU recovery plan was a historic moment because the EU decided to borrow in its name on the market, then fiscal integration could be even more important for Member States' sovereignty.[13]

This chapter intends to take a different perspective on the issue of corporate income taxation.[14] It delves into the complexity of the EU's

---

Economy: An Eye-Opening Case Study, Intertax, 2014, Vol. 42, Issue 5, pp. 317-324; G. Stuart. The Corporate Tax Challenges of the Digital Economy—An Update, Taxes: The Tax Magazine, 2018, vol. 96, Issue 10, pp. 17-20; D. Pinto. Options to Address the Direct Tax Challenges Raised by the Digital Economy—A Critical Analysis, Canadian Tax Journal, 2017, vol. 65, n° 2, pp. 291-332; OCDE. BEPS Project Explanatory Statement: 2015 Final Reports, OECD/G20 Base Erosion and Profit Shifting Project, OCDE Publishing: Paris, 2016; D. Kleist. The Multilateral Convention to Implement Tax Treaty Related Measures to Prevent BEPS—Some Thoughts on Complexity and Uncertainty, Nordic Tax Journal, 2018, n° 1, pp. 31-48.

11 EU Economic and Financial Affairs Council, November 6, 2018. Outcome of the Council meeting. Available at: https://www.consilium.europa.eu/media/37381/st13872-en18-vf.pdf [accessed on August 7, 2020].

12 L. Spinosa, V. Chand. A Long-Term Solution for Taxing Digitalized Business Models: Should the Permanent Establishment Definition Be Modified to Resolve the Issue or Should the Focus Be on a Shared Taxing Rights Mechanism?, Intertax, 2018, vol. 46, Issue 6 & 7, pp. 476-494; E. C.C.M. Kemmeren. Should the Taxation of the Digital Economy Really Be Different?, EC Tax Review, 2018, n°2, pp. 72-73.

13 J. Brunsden, S. Fleming, M. Khan. EU Recovery Fund: How the Plan Will Work, Financial Times, July 21, 2020.

14 L. A. Sheppard. Digital Permanent Establishment and Digital Equalization Taxes, Bulletin for International Taxation, 2018, vol. 72, n° 4a.

policy and decision-making to highlight the key characteristics of these proposals and their consequences for the EU's integration. The chapter will look at the essential element of the current context, which is momentum ("In Search of a European Tax Impetus"). In other words, due to the combination of various events ranging from economic crises to leaks of confidential data on tax evasion, public opinion is exerting increasing pressure to tax digital companies. The GAFA package is not deemed the best solution, but the Commission tried to spur fundamental changes to the current legal framework by fostering debate between the Member States. It has done so through the digital services tax (DST). The chapter will then investigate a second element for a real EU systemic reform, an effective solution able to build consensus, the concept of significant digital presence (SDP) ("Devising an Effective European Fiscal Integration"). The GAFA package is as much a proposal to tax the digital companies as it recaptures the impulse for change to boost a stalling EU while reasserting its role at the international level.

In Search of a European Tax Impetus

The DST, an Imperfect Solution for a Consensus

The DST's Controversial Characteristics

With the DST, the Commission wishes to improve the EU's fiscal coherence while symbolically marking the beginning of a move toward a genuine European tax system. It echoes actions taken by some Member States[15] and constitutes a major step toward the EU's fiscal integration because it forms the most advanced plan for European taxation since the value-added tax (VAT).[16] The EU DST's core provisions are extremely controversial[17] and entail many implementation difficulties[18] while the Commission tries to gather consensus around the proposal.

15 S. Geringer. National Digital Taxes—Lessons from Europe, South African Journal of Accounting Research, 2020, vol. 35, Issue 1, p. 1.

16 G. Kofler, J. Sinnig. Equalization Taxes and the EU's "Digital Services Tax," Intertax, 2019, vol. 47, Issue 2, pp. 176-200.

17 P. A. Hernández González-Barreda. A Historical Analysis of the BEPS Action Plan: Old Acquaintances, New Friends and the Need for a New Approach, Intertax, 2018, vol. 46, Issue 4, pp. 278-295.

18 G. Kofler, J. Sinnig. Equalization Taxes and the EU's "Digital Services Tax," Intertax, 2019, vol. 47, Issue 2, pp. 176-200.

EU's Choice to Ring-Fence Digital Activities

The identification of taxable services is the Commission's core proposal. Originally, there were three key proposals: targeted advertising on a digital interface,[19] the provision of a multisided digital interface, i.e., digital intermediation services,[20] and the collection of data on user activities on these interfaces.[21] The Commission's determination did not reach a consensus among the Member States. Indeed, in desperation, the Council proposed to reduce it to digital advertising only.[22] This alternative has been adopted by India, which applies an equalization levy of 6 percent aimed at taxing business-to-business transactions in the digital advertising space.[23]

With this proposal, the EU was affirming itself as a fiscal activist worldwide. The Commission opened the door to discussion on the opportunity to enact a new targeted tax on highly digitalized businesses (HDB)[24] at a regional scale, that of the EU. The DST is perfectly in line with the definition of the digital economy established by the Organisation for Economic Co-operation and Development's (OECD's) Task Force on Digital Economy (hereinafter TDFE)[25] in 2018, which is: (1) the ability to scale up to large commercial activities "without any, or any significant, physical presence," (2) their reliance on intellectual property and intangible assets, and (3) the crucial role of data and user participation.[26] The EU DST considers that HDB characteristics are so peculiar that they can form the basis of new taxation at least as a defensive interim measure. Therefore, it

19 Proposal for a Council Directive on the common system of a digital services tax on revenues resulting from the provision of certain digital services, COM(2018) 148 final. Article 3 paragraph 1 a).

20 Proposal for a Council Directive on the common system of a digital services tax on revenues resulting from the provision of certain digital services, COM(2018) 148 final. Article 3 paragraph 1 b).

21 Proposal for a Council Directive on the common system of a digital services tax on revenues resulting from the provision of certain digital services, COM(2018) 148 final. Article 3 paragraph 1 c).

22 Council of the European Union. Proposal for a Council Directive on the common system of a digital services tax on revenues resulting from the provision of certain digital services, 2018/0073(CNS).

23 G. Rajgopalan. Taxing Digital Economy—Applicability of Non-discrimination Rules in International Agreements, Background Paper for New Delhi Conference of the International Fiscal Association, April 2018.

24 M. P. Devereux, J. Vella. Taxing the Digitalised Economy: Targeted or System-Wide Reform?, British Tax Review, 2018, n° 4, pp. 387-406.

25 Task Force on Digital Economy; OCDE (2018). Tax Challenges Arising from Digitalisation—Interim Report 2018: Inclusive Framework on BEPS, OECD/G20 Base Erosion and Profit Shifting Project, Éditions OCDE, Paris, paragraphs 32-35.

26 L. V. Faulhaber. Taxing Tech: The Future of Digital Taxation, Virginia Tax Review, vol. 39, n° 2, Winter 2019, p. 151.

is aimed exclusively at activities which the current corporate income tax rules are unable to fully capture, i.e., those heavily reliant on intangible assets.

The EU DST attempts to give substance to the idea of taxing user's value creation through the encounter between the user who owns the resource and the targeted service's provision that monetizes it.[27] If it does not focus on the place of production, the DST has not completely freed itself from the place of consumption to concentrate on the supply side, as VAT has done.[28] It is an in-between example of the gradual transformation of tax systems under the influence of digitalization. The key concept of the EU's DST proposal is deeply entwined with the idea that such services are based on the concept of freemium services.[29] Therefore, for the purpose of determining the location of the revenues derived from those activities, the DST is relying on the notion of "user" rather than the "customer."[30] This contributes to the unidentified nature of this tax proposal, not only borrowing ideas from the supply-side and the demand-side theories of income generation. The misalignment between payment and value creation becomes acute within the reasoning of the DST. While emphasizing that nothing comes for free in life, and those supposedly "free" services involve trade-offs, the EU DST is trying to re-characterize the presumably free relation, or barter, in a pecuniary relationship by reviewing the idea of value creation.[31] However, by doing so, the EU may give too much weight to an issue that preexisted the digital revolution—the problem of two-sided platforms.[32]

Furthermore, the DST is a tax on companies of significant size, mostly multinational enterprises (MNE). Thus, to minimize collateral damage, the proposal uses the threshold technique. It leaves start-ups aside, thanks to a first required minimum of EUR 50 million of the total taxable income

27 G. Marraud des Grottes. Fiscalité du numérique, un enjeu à 5 milliards, Actualités du droit, March 23, 2018.
28 J.-C. Bouchard, F. Locatelli, A.-S. de Bechade. Économie numérique: vers une taxation sans frontières?, Les Nouvelles Fiscales, n° 1224, juin, 15 2018.
29 X. Gu, P. K. Kannan, L. Ma. How Companies Can Get the Most Out of a Freemium Business Model, Harvard Business Review, March 20, 2019.
30 M. Nieminen. The Scope of the Commission's Digital Tax Proposals, Bulletin for International Taxation, 2018, vol. 11, pp. 664-675; A. P. Dourado. Digital Taxation Opens the Pandora Box: The OECD Interim Report and the European Commission Proposals, Intertax, 2018, vol. 46, Issue 6 & 7, pp. 565-572.
31 N. Fishbien. Digital Service Tax, Consumption Tax and the Reverse Application of the Step Transaction Doctrine, International Tax Journal, September-October 2019.
32 A. Hagiu. Two-sided platforms: Product variety and pricing structures, Journal of Economics & Management Strategy, 2009, vol. 18, n° 4, pp. 1011-1043.

generated by the entity in the EU.[33] At the same time, the DST is inspired by the proposed common consolidated corporation tax base (CCCTB)[34] reform with the minimum of EUR 750 million for the total amount of worldwide income reported by the entity.[35] However, threshold effects could hamper the development of certain European companies, the so-called scale-ups, i.e., intermediate-sized entities attached to larger groups for their growth. Consideration should therefore be given to the advisability of establishing a form of tax neutrality for the DST. It will be even more relevant in view of the many initiatives taken by the Member States. In concrete terms, the DST targets companies that are large enough to support its implementation. However, the DST is not a GAFA tax because it does not target all large digital companies. While Google, Facebook, Booking, Uber, Airbnb, and Amazon Marketplace are largely concerned, others are excluded. For example, Amazon in its e-commerce business, Apple, and Netflix are not affected. The DST is not a discriminatory tax either; activities of some European companies are also potentially affected, such as AccorHotels, Solocal, Deezer, and Spotify.[36] Nonetheless, the multiplication of national DSTs, with varying rates and scope of application, could hamper the economic growth of the EU in the field of digital services.

The Location Conundrum for the DST

The place of taxation is a key technical problem. The intangible nature of taxable services makes their location even more difficult. Yet, the Commission's proposal has an essential territorial component. It applies to the proceeds of taxable services as soon as the user is located within the EU. The user's location is the connecting factor required to establish the taxable product in the territory of a Member State.[37] The DST, therefore, moots a major technical issue. The geographical location of the device used for the transaction or consultation is the central element determining the place of

---

33 Proposal for a Council Directive on the common system of a digital services tax on revenues resulting from the provision of certain digital services, COM(2018) 148 final. Article 4 paragraph 1 b).

34 *See* below.

35 *Ibid.*, Article 4 paragraph 1 a).

36 A. Harpaz. Taxation of the Digital Economy: Adapting a Twentieth-Century Tax System to a Twenty-First Century Economy (August 31, 2020), Yale Journal of International Law, Forthcoming, Available at SSRN: https://ssrn.com/abstract=3593936 [accessed on January 18, 2021].

37 Proposal for a Council Directive on the common system of a digital services tax on revenues resulting from the provision of certain digital services, COM(2018) 148 final. Article 5 paragraph 1.

taxation.[38] The proposal for a Directive therefore chooses the Internet Protocol (IP) address of the device as the geo-localization tool. Although this is a straightforward solution, as IP addresses assign a numerical label to each device connected to a computer network that uses the Internet Protocol for communication providing a sort of electronic address, it is not free from troubles. This is not the most reliable way to geo-localize a computer. These shortcomings could give rise to inaccuracies, bias the overall outcome, and distort taxing rights allocation. Moreover, tracking the location of a user and keeping relevant data in files for taxation and control is likely to pose practical problems. This requirement will involve the constitution of impressive data logs and will entail technical costs to generate and maintain as well as administrative expenses to manage allocation of taxing rights.

This is because the proposal leaves the taxable person free to use any other more precise method.[39] The Commission gives a default option but does not impose a specific procedure. It remains to be seen whether such a situation will give taxpayers room for maneuver to reduce the tax base. At the very least, a disparity in geo-localization techniques could arise. However, it is not possible to say in advance whether this will be sufficient to have a significant impact on revenue. The main difficulty could arise at the control stage by a Member State. Indeed, in the absence of uniformity, how can cross-checks be carried out? If several methods coexist, they are likely to produce different results and entail disputes. Will taxpayers be required to keep records of users' location records collected by different methods? In any case, how can public authorities be able to carry out effective control on the sole basis of the taxpayer's records? Solutions will have to be organized to ease *ex post* controls. The use of arbitration could be one such solution. Nevertheless, there is no legal framework for this so far. Furthermore, location-based taxation raises the issue of privacy, as companies will have to keep registers containing IP addresses to be able to determine whether they are liable to pay the tax. This solution creates a surprisingly new risk for a personal data breach at a time when Internet

38 Proposal for a Council Directive on the common system of a digital services tax on revenues resulting from the provision of certain digital services, COM(2018) 148 final. Article 5 paragraph 2.

39 Proposal for a Council Directive on the common system of a digital services tax on revenues resulting from the provision of certain digital services, COM(2018) 148 final. Article 5 paragraph 5.

privacy is increasingly protected, notably within the EU through the General Data Protection Regulation.[40]

The DST's Rate, a Delicate Balance

The primary concern when considering the creation of any new tax always leads to the same question: how much will it cost? In other words, what rate will be applied? For the DST, a single base of 3 percent has been chosen.[41] The reasoning behind it lacks the clarity expected from a Commission's draft. Similar national proposals have selected the same rate[42] or a different rate.[43] The debate on this particularly important parameter has not been commensurate with the stakes. In its impact assessment, the Commission recalls the two important parameters to evaluate: the tax revenue potential and the level of additional tax imposed on companies. Accordingly, it estimates that the fiscal revenue will be rather moderate, amounting to an extra 1.5 percent of the corporate income tax revenue for those firms.[44] Thus, the DST will not put an end to tax inequalities between companies. In fact, "traditional international business models are burdened with an average effective tax rate of 23.2%, whereas international digital business models are taxed at an average rate of only 10.1% (B2C models) and 8.9% (B2B models)."[45] Furthermore, the Commission's proposal rules out any solution based on a mechanism of progressivity according to the size of the turnover achieved. This alternative would, however, have made it possible to further reduce the fiscal imbalance between hegemonic companies in the digital economy and others. However, the preference given to the

---

40 Regulation (EU) 2016/679 of the European Parliament and of the Council of April 27, 2016 on the protection of natural persons with regard to the processing of personal data and on the free movement of such data, and repealing Directive 95/46/EC (General Data Protection Regulation), OJ L 119, May 4, 2016, pp. 1-88.

41 Proposal for a Council Directive on the common system of a digital services tax on revenues resulting from the provision of certain digital services, COM(2018) 148 final. Article 8.

42 Spain's DST Act: Ley 4/2020, de 15 de octubre, del Impuesto sobre Determinados Servicios Digitales, Available at: https://www.boe.es/eli/es/l/2020/10/15/4 [accessed on January 18, 2021].

43 U.K. Finance Act 2020, section 39. Available at: https://services.parliament.uk/bills/2019-21/finance.html [accessed on January 18, 2021].

44 Commission staff working document Impact assessment. Accompanying the document Proposal for a Council Directive laying down rules relating to the corporate taxation of a significant digital presence and Proposal for a Council Directive on the common system of a digital services tax on revenues resulting from the provision of certain digital services, SWD/2018/081 final, p. 69.

45 S. Geringer. National Digital Taxes—Lessons from Europe, South African Journal of Accounting Research, 2020, p. 1.

uniform rate is justified by the concern to avoid giving rise to a discrimination complaint against the United States (U.S.) companies.[46] Nevertheless, even if the tax applies at a consistent rate, based on its effects and not its object, it will in fact affect more U.S. undertakings given Silicon Valley giants' overwhelming dominance in this sector.

The DST's Puzzling Nature

At first sight, the EU's DST has all the main characteristics of a tax on turnover. Its justification is straightforward. This has to do with the strengths and weaknesses of such a measure from a tax policy perspective. On the one hand, taxes on turnover are easy to devise and simple to apply and control. They encompass broad nexus rules focused on the destination of the supplies and apply to both local and foreign-based enterprises. They have the great advantage of restoring a level playing field between resident and nonresident taxpayers. On the other hand, the EU DST's scope could amplify turnover taxes' perverse effects. As the OECD acknowledges, such a measure can have an adverse effect on investment, innovation growth, and welfare, the possibility of overtaxation, a false "interim" nature.[47] They can also be burdensome as they entail important administrative and compliance steps, particularly in relation to collecting tax from foreign-based entities. Besides all of those issues, the most undesirable one relates to the DST's cascading effect (i.e., double taxation). In practice, when a tax is levied on a commodity or a service more than once, it passes on various stages of the production-distribution chain. As a result, the amount of taxes swells, increasing its financial burden for each economic agent, including the end consumer.[48] Not all turnover taxes are plagued with this problem, but as the DST is as much a sales tax as an inputs tax, it may eventually produce this unwanted side effect.[49] Within the business model of digital

46 Commission staff working document Impact assessment. Accompanying the document Proposal for a Council Directive laying down rules relating to the corporate taxation of a significant digital presence and Proposal for a Council Directive on the common system of a digital services tax on revenues resulting from the provision of certain digital services, SWD/2018/081 final, p. 69.

47 OECD. Tax Challenges Arising from Digitalisation—Interim Report 2018: Inclusive Framework on BEPS, OECD/G20 Base Erosion and Profit Shifting Project, OECD Publishing: Paris, 2018, paragraphs 178-179.

48 S. Parthasarathi (ed.). Tax Policy Handbook, USA: International Monetary Fund, 1995, pp. 75 et seq.

49 J. F. Due. The Choice Between a Value-Added Tax and a Retail Sales Tax, Report of Proceedings of the Thirty-Seventh Tax Conference, Toronto: Canadian Tax Foundation, 1985, pp. 16:1-16:10.

companies, it could become an existential threat for some. The Commission explicitly refers in its draft to the issue for online advertising[50] only, without any stand-alone provision to curtail the risk. Consequently, as a turnover tax has a broader base than a profit tax and can induce undesirable side-effects, its rate will necessarily have to be lower to mitigate those consequences. Its effect is even more symbolic, although an increase in tax revenue, in the years to come, is easily foreseeable, given the growing weight of the digital economy.[51]

However, the EU DST's main characteristics equally embody elements of a consumption tax, more precisely, a supply-demand approach.[52] The DST redefines the source of income theory by a technically bold approach. It recalls a simple economic principle that value creation occurs when supply meets demand, in other words, that the user is part of the equation.[53] By focusing on the location of the user/customer, the DST is leaning toward the location of the customer in the same way that a consumption tax does. Therefore, it can be qualified as a "hybrid tax" targeting revenues gained from "value creation" in each Member State, determined by the consumer's involvement in the transaction and the amount of which is likely to be passed on to him.

As a result of this double nature, the DST is totally independent of corporate taxation, whereas it constitutes an additional burden for some companies. Consequently, this tax's impact on their profitability could be significant. The Commission's proposal only indirectly addresses the issue by mentioning the need to provide for the deductibility of the DST paid as a cost from the corporate tax base in their territory. In their own versions of the GAFA levy, several Member States[54] have taken up this idea. Another option, more favorable to taxpayers, would be to deduct this amount from

---

50 Proposal for a Council Directive on the common system of a digital services tax on revenues resulting from the provision of certain digital services, COM(2018) 148 final. Article 3 paragraph 3.

51 Commission staff working document Impact assessment. Accompanying the document Proposal for a Council Directive laying down rules relating to the corporate taxation of a significant digital presence and Proposal for a Council Directive on the common system of a digital services tax on revenues resulting from the provision of certain digital services, SWD/2018/081 final, p. 69. Article 8.

52 D. Pinto. Options to Address the Direct Tax Challenges Raised by the Digital Economy—A Critical Analysis, Canadian Tax Journal, 2017. Vol. 65, n° 2, pp. 291-332.

53 P. Hongler, P. Pistone. IBFD—Blueprints for a New PE Nexus to Tax Business Income in the Era of the Digital Economy, Working Paper January 20, 2015.

54 France: LOI n° 2019-759 du 24 juillet 2019 portant création d'une taxe sur les services numériques et modification de la trajectoire de baisse de l'impôt sur les sociétés, JORF n°0171 du 25 juillet 2019; United Kingdom: For the details of the bill:

the corporation tax itself to reduce the overall tax burden, especially for European companies already more heavily taxed.[55] In the absence of any solution, the consumer will bear the brunt of the new tax, whether it originated from one country or the EU, such as Amazon announced when France enacted its own version of the DST.[56]

The EU's DST proposal seems to equate to a form of access fee digital companies should pay for a user community located in the Member State's territory. The DST may have the effect of monetizing access to users/ citizens in an EU Member State. Indeed, the company is deriving profits from users' participation on a platform, or their use of a service, without generating any taxable profit in this country.[57] From this vantage point, the user generates content, called data, which are valuable under new business models.[58] The user is in fact as much an input as a customer for digital companies. Even in complex two-sided platforms where traditional services and products are mixed with more innovative ones, users remain at the center of value creation. In this example, the company will price below marginal cost on one side (such as for free), increasing the number of its users, and make good the loss on the other side by asking for a higher price. As a result, users on the first side are central to the undertaking's business model and create value. By focusing on revenues generated by users' interaction, the DST creates a form of user fee payable by digital undertakings.

To allocate taxing rights, the user is put at the heart of the new nexus and not the profit. As a result, the EU's DST falls outside the common income tax framework. Therefore, some academics argue that such "DST can be analogized to a variety of taxes […] that are […] imposed on location-specific business profits, such as royalties and resource rent taxes on

---

https://assets.publishing.service.gov.uk/government/uploads/system/uploads/attachment_data/file/816361/Digital_services_tax.pdf [accessed on August 7, 2020]; for other examples: *see* S. Geringer. National Digital Taxes—Lessons from Europe, South African Journal of Accounting Research, 2020, p. 1.

55 G. Kofler, J. Sinnig. Equalization Taxes and the EU's Digital Services Tax, Intertax, 2019, vol. 47, Issue 2, pp. 176-200.

56 B. Cassel, M. Pelloli, A. Laratte. Taxe Gafa: Amazon va faire payer les Français, Le Parisien, August 1, 2019.

57 W. Cui. The Digital Services Tax on the Verge of Implementation, Canadian Tax Journal, 2019, vol. 67, n° 4, pp. 1135-1152.

58 G. W. Voss. Internet, New Technologies, and Value: Taking Share of Economic Surveillance, University of Illinois Journal of Law, Technology & Policy, Fall 2017, vol. 2017, n° 2, pp. 469-486.

natural resource extraction."[59] Strong arguments are pleading in favor of this approach. A location-specific rent (LSR) captures revenues arising from rents earned by digital platforms where they arise. As such, it does not ring-fence the digital economy. The EU DST's nature leans toward an LSR because it focuses on the user's location and not the company's establishment. Thus, if the user located in a Member State is brought to the forefront, the digital services affected by the DST are to be considered a secondary question. The EU's DST could be designed as an LSR tax, although the Commission is not advocating publicly on this issue. Nevertheless, behind the legal definition is lurking the debate on the opportunity to reroute the target of the international tax law from mobile to immobile assets. For the moment, the EU's DST is merely a policy proposal to value the EU's demographic power in the data-driven economy. In other words, the bloc is gradually focusing on new resources that are deeply embedded in its territory.

Value Creation, a Contested Guiding Principle

The EU initiative to create a new turnover tax on digital services is deeply rooted in a broader debate about the desirability and the feasibility of an international tax law reform.[60] Most of the main components of the actual tax systems of OECD countries were developed in another era where sovereignty was an enforceable concept through high tariffs.[61] Modernization of the international tax system had already occurred between the end of the nineteenth and the beginning of the twentieth century. Today, the world faces a moment of reckoning. The profound transformation of the economy induced by digitalization and trans-nationalization needs to be

59 W. Cui, The Superiority of the Digital Services Tax over Significant Digital Presence Proposals, National Tax Journal, December 2019, vol. 72, n° 4, p. 849.

60 L. V. Faulhaber. Taxing Tech: The Future of Digital Taxation, Virginia Tax Review, Winter 2019, vol. 39, n° 2, p. 151.

61 P. Genschel. Globalization and the Transformation of the Tax State. In Leibfried S. & Zürn M. (eds.). Transformations of the State? Cambridge: Cambridge University Press, 2005, pp. 53-72; T. Falcão, B. Michel. Assessing the Tax Challenges of the Digital Economy: An Eye-Opening Case Study Intertax, 2014, vol. 42, Issue 5, pp. 317-324; G. Stuart. The Corporate Tax Challenges of the Digital Economy—An Update, Taxes: The Tax Magazine, 2018, vol. 96, Issue 10, pp. 17-20; D. Pinto. Options to Address the Direct Tax Challenges Raised by the Digital Economy—A Critical Analysis, Canadian Tax Journal, vol. 65, n° 2, 2017, pp. 291-332; OCDE. BEPS Project Explanatory Statement: 2015 Final Reports, OECD/G20 Base Erosion and Profit Shifting Project, OCDE Publishing: Paris, 2016; D. Kleist. The Multilateral Convention to Implement Tax Treaty Related Measures to Prevent BEPS—Some Thoughts on Complexity and Uncertainty, Nordic Tax Journal, 2018, n° 1, pp. 31-48.

better reflected in the tax system.[62] The longtime assumption that all taxable activities had a well identifiable geographical location has disappeared. This legal fiction has never been so unworkable. Thus, the EU's DST proposal is part of a broader trend questioning the current system and pushing for new solutions to emerge.

The international tax system in force was designed in accordance with the principle of economic allegiance based on the benefit theory.[63] According to its advocates, the benefits derived by the undertaking from the public community should be repaid by taxes. It is on this idea that the underlying logic of the system of distribution of tax rights between residence and source has been organized. This system favored exporting countries with strong industrial networks and less so the countries buying those products.[64] Because the economic allegiance relies on the idea of an economic counterpart to the taxing rights, it depended on the physical presence of the undertaking as an allocation technique. Now the latter is not as essential as it was previously to conduct business. New economic models are disrupting the traditional understanding of the relationship between the seller and the buyer. As a result, international tax law has lost some of its effectiveness.

The entire rationale behind the political endorsement of the value creation principle lies in this context where tax fairness is gaining ground.[65] It has the advantage of being polysemous.[66] Certainly, this concept perfectly underlines that taxation in the twenty-first century is sailing in uncharted territories. This principle is now used as a beacon to guide innovative thinking. Indirectly, this could revisit the residence versus source dilemma through the back door while being sufficiently vague to encompass all the possible directions for a reform and foster consensus.[67] Some argue that it lacks the precision and technicality required to form the

62 J. M. Vazquez. Indirect Taxation of Digital Services after BEPS: A Multilateral Instrument to Achieve Harmonization and Effective Enforcement, International Tax Journal, 2017, vol. 43, n°5, pp. 19-34.

63 P. Hongler, P. Pistone. IBFD—Blueprints for a New PE Nexus to Tax Business Income in the Era of the Digital Economy, Working Paper January 20, 2015.

64 D. Paolini, P. Pistone, G. Pulina et al. Tax Treaties with Developing Countries and the Allocation of Taxing Rights, European Journal of Law and Economics, 2016, vol. 42, pp. 383-404.

65 T. Pogge, K. Mehta. Global Tax Fairness, Oxford: Oxford University Press, 2016, p. 366.

66 M. P. Devereux, J. Vella. Taxing the Digitalised Economy: Targeted or System-Wide Reform?, British Tax Review, 2018, n° 4, pp. 387-406.

67 A. Turina. Which "Source Taxation" for the Digital Economy?, Intertax, 2018, vol. 46, n° 6-7, p. 499.

foundation of a reform. But is reform really the objective? As the EU DST puts it, the value creation principle provides direction, but it leaves a wide margin of appreciation to invent a practical solution.

Even if it entails a lot of uncertainties about its real meaning, the EU DST created an impetus to reevaluate the current tax system with new lenses. The groundswell is more about carrying out an overhaul and establishing new examination criteria, rather than considering the value creation as a working principle on its own. The value creation principle emphasizes the central role of geography in international tax law. Since there is no supranational entity collecting taxes, each State is responsible for its own taxes. Therefore, any reform must match tax geography with economic geography. The legal nexus must become more concrete. In fact, the concept is concerned about the growing misalignment between where the value is generated and profit is taxed. The EU DST's proposal is a tribute to this new approach. Whether it is its best translation is another issue.[68] While the EU did not seem to have deeply mulled this connection, the whole DST is a manifestation of this debate.

The DST, a Divisive Solution for an EU Emergency Response

A Divided International Fiscal Community

The ongoing international debate highlights the difficulty of reaching any form of consensus on possible international tax reform in a digitalized era, even though the shortcomings of national tax systems have clearly been emphasized,[69] leading to revenue losses for State budgets.[70] In 2012, this grim observation spurred the OECD to start the Base Erosion and Profit Shifting (BEPS) project.[71] It resulted a year later in the 15 points of the

---

68 I. Grinberg. User Participation in Value Creation, British Tax Review, 2018, n° 4, pp. 407-421.

69 M. Graetz. Taxing International Income: Inadequate Principles, Outdated Concepts, and Unsatisfactory Policies, Tax Law Review, 2001, n° 54, pp. 261-336; A. Ting. iTax—Apple's International Tax Structure and the Double Non-taxation Issue, British Tax Review, 2014, n°1, pp. 40-71.

70 European Commission. Communication from the Commission to the European Parliament and the Council. A Fair and Efficient Tax System in the European Union for the Digital Single Market, COM(2017) 547 final, Brussels, September 21, 2017.

71 Å. Johansson, Ø. Bieltvedt Skeie, S. Sorbe. Anti-avoidance Rules Against International Tax Planning: A classification, OECD Economics Department Working Papers, 2017, n° 1356, OECD Publishing: Paris.

Action Plan on BEPS[72] aimed at preventing legal tax avoidance by multinational firms. Owing to the importance of the stakes, the G20 and the OECD created the Inclusive Framework (IF) in 2016 to engage any country willing to implement the BEPS minimum standards.[73] As of today, 137 countries have implemented the BEPS, a record for an OECD initiative.[74] The strong momentum to reform the international tax law led up to several signs of progress, notably the 2018 Interim Report[75] and its follow-ups[76] such as the January 2020 agreement reached by the IF.[77] The latter stressed the importance that any consensus-based agreement must include a commitment to withdraw relevant unilateral actions such as national or regional DSTs. Unfortunately, this led the international community into a stalemate on June 12, 2020, when the U.S., through the then-Secretary of the Treasury Stephen Mnuchin, asked for a pause in the negotiation while threatening "appropriate commensurate measures" against countries that adopt unilateral DSTs.[78] Since 2018, DSTs have gained momentum, and the U.S. is trying to thwart their development while delaying a long-term solution. The context has changed drastically since the EU rolled out its first proposal. The stalling discussions at the international level may revive the thrust to enact such an EU-wide DST, putting the bloc at risk of a direct confrontation with the U.S.

A Pressing Context to Reach Unanimity at the EU Level

With the DST, the EU was responding to a call for action. The public demand for an overhaul of the current international tax system has never been so high. Better taxation of companies is favored by public opinion

---

72 OECD. Action Plan on Base Erosion and Profit Shifting, OECD Publishing: Paris, 2013, rec. 10.

73 OECD. Inclusive Framework on BEPS—Progress report July 2016/July 2017, OECD Publishing: Paris, 2017.

74 OECD's list of members of the Inclusive Framework, last updated on December 2019. Available at: https://www.oecd.org/tax/beps/inclusive-framework-on-beps-composition.pdf [accessed on August 1, 2020].

75 OECD, *supra* n. 47.

76 OECD. OECD/G20 Inclusive Framework on BEPS—Progress report July 2019-July 2020, OECD Publishing: Paris, 2020.

77 OECD. Statement by the OECD/G20 Inclusive Framework on BEPS on the Two-Pillar Approach to Address the Tax Challenges Arising from the Digitalisation of the Economy—January 2020, OECD/G20 Inclusive Framework on BEPS, OECD Publishing: Paris, 2020; OECD (2020). OECD Secretary-General Tax Report to G20 Finance Ministers and Central Bank Governors—July 2020, OECD Publishing: Paris, 2020.

78 J. Vander Wolk. INSIGHT: OECD/Inclusive Framework—Pillar 1 Impasse Puts the Spotlight on Pillar 2, Bloomberg Tax, June 23, 2020.

because the GAFA have become symbols of recent excesses of harmful tax avoidance.[79] Back in 2008, States invested a vast amount of funds to support the financial sector and the real economy. As a result, public finances were put under severe strain all over the world and particularly in EU countries. This resulted in a budgetary crisis and the implementation of austerity policies by the Member States.[80] Public spending cuts and tax increases have been necessary to halt the rise of national debts.[81] Amid this, a series of revelations, including Lux Leaks[82] and Panama Papers,[83] highlighted the complex tax optimization strategies of companies and individuals to reduce their overall taxation. The disclosure of such information raised political awareness, as European citizens have massively borne the increase in tax pressure. Consequently, these tax avoidance methods have become unbearable for public opinion, resulting in pressure on governments and leaving the field open for such EU-style initiatives.

Astoundingly, an unexpected event could turn upside down the long-standing mistrust of Member States toward any real EU proposal to devise taxes. The COVID-19 pandemic has struck the whole world by surprise. Governments are grappling with health issues as well as plunging markets. As it became clear that heavily indebted Member States would not be able to borrow much more from the markets to support their economies, and that the pandemic was jeopardizing the foundations of the internal market, the EU took a particularly important posture.

At a marathon summit, EU leaders agreed on a EUR 750 billion recovery plan called "Next Generation EU," consisting of EUR 390 billion in grants and the remainder in the form of loans. Strikingly, those funds will be raised using a common borrowing mechanism. This is a historic expansion of EU financial capacities. Nevertheless, debt will have to be repaid. Generally, the EU budget is mainly funded by annual contributions from its Member States and little contributions of its own. As of now, the lack of any room for maneuver threatens future EU budgets as well as national ones. To avoid increasing national taxes or deepening national

---

79 A. Ting, S.J. Gray. The Rise of the Digital Economy: Rethinking the Taxation of Multinational Enterprises, Journal of International Business Studies, 2019, vol. 50, pp. 1656-1667.

80 D. Furceri, A. Zdzienicka. The Consequences of Banking Crises for Public Debt, OECD Economics Department Working Papers, 2010, n° 801, OECD Publishing: Paris.

81 D. Furceri, A. Mourougane. Financial Crises: Past Lessons and Policy Implications, OECD Economics Department Working Papers, 2009, n° 668, OECD Publishing: Paris.

82 https://www.icij.org/investigations/luxembourg-leaks/ [accessed on August 7, 2020].

83 https://www.icij.org/investigations/panama-papers/ [accessed on August 7, 2020].

indebtedness, the Commission has mulled that new revenues will be needed.[84] The EU envisions expanding its "own resources" with new taxes on nonrecycled plastic waste, a carbon border adjustment mechanism, a digital levy, a revised Emissions Trading System (ETS), and longer-term plans for a financial transaction tax (FTT).

Therefore, the DST's initial version could end up being a rehearsal for what will happen in the coming years. As the EU is looking for long-term sustainable revenues to finance its recovery, Member States could be financially compelled to approve a substantial enhancement of fiscal provisions within the EU and therefore transfer more competence. For now, there are few details about real plans for a DST 2.0. The only information drawn from the European Council conclusions resulting from the July 17-21, 2020 meeting is a general timeline for tax proposals including a digital levy.[85] According to this document, a draft is envisaged for the first semester of 2021 and a planned introduction by January 1, 2023.[86] Given the stalled negotiations at the G20/OECD level, the EU ambition in fiscal policy could deliver a new DST version before any consensus is attained at the international level.[87]

The EU DST as an Attempt to Preserve the Internal Market

The proposal for digital services taxation is primarily intended to protect the internal market cohesion in the face of abundant national initiatives. Indeed, DST is envisioned as a unified response to a problem shared by all Member States.

The Commission is emphasizing tax harmonization added value where activities are highly transnational in nature. DST is the EU's emergency solution to the proven or planned introduction of unilateral measures

---

84 European Commission. Speech by President Von der Leyen at the European Parliament Plenary on the EU Recovery package, May 27, 2020.

85 European Council. Special meeting of the European Council (July 17, 18, 19, 20, and 21, 2020), General Secretariat of the Council, July 21, 2020, Available at: https://www.consilium.europa.eu/media/45109/210720-euco-final-conclusions-en.pdf. [accessed on August 1, 2020].

86 European Council. Special meeting of the European Council (July 17, 18, 19, 20, and 21, 2020), General Secretariat of the Council, July 21, 2020, Available at: https://www.consilium.europa.eu/media/45109/210720-euco-final-conclusions-en.pdf. [accessed on August 1, 2020].

87 P. Gentiloni. An EU Tax Crackdown Is Essential for Sustainable Growth, Financial Times, July 14, 2020.

against digital companies by ten or so Member States.[88] With it, the Commission wanted to avoid fiscal confusion and thus protect the level playing field within the internal market. Furthermore, DST would make it possible to reduce the significant competitive tax disadvantage that has been established between U.S. digital undertakings and their European competitors. The Commission is looking for ways to counterbalance the trend toward hegemonic market structures, of which GAFAM[89] are symbols.[90]

DST is also a manifestation of the EU's industrial policy concerns for the digital economy. The EU lags behind other countries, mostly the U.S., in terms of digital innovations, while digitalization has become the cornerstone of modern economies. In 2015, the Commission drafted a strategy for a Digital Single Market on three pillars:[91] (1) better access for consumers and businesses to online goods and services across Europe, (2) creating the right conditions for digital networks and services to flourish, (3) maximizing the growth potential of our European Digital Economy. In this context, the perspective of uncoordinated unilateral measures taken by the Member States could jeopardize the Digital Single Market strategy by amplifying the negative effects of such turnover taxes.[92] The EU was compelled to act to rein in divergent positions. Therefore, the DST is as much the expression of the Commission's free will as it is the result of political pressures threatening the EU's cohesion. To boost its competitiveness in the digital economy, the EU must provide an effective taxation framework fostering start-ups, allowing them to grow at the international level while taking advantage of the EU's market scale. However, is the DST the best tool to achieve this? Nothing is less certain because it does not really address the problem's causes but rather its consequences. The DST is

---

88 Commission staff working document Impact assessment. Accompanying the document Proposal for a Council Directive laying down rules relating to the corporate taxation of a significant digital presence and Proposal for a Council Directive on the common system of a digital services tax on revenues resulting from the provision of certain digital services, SWD/2018/081 final, pp. 53-55.

89 Acronym for Google, Apple, Facebook, Amazon, and Microsoft.

90 Proposal for a Council Directive on the common system of a digital services tax on revenues resulting from the provision of certain digital services, COM(2018) 148 final. Paragraph 2 and paragraph 6.

91 Communication from the Commission to the European Parliament, the Council, the European economic and social committee and the Committee of the regions. A Digital Single Market Strategy for Europe, COM/2015/0192 final, Brussels, May 6, 2015.

92 W. J. G. Paardekooper, M. van der Ven, A. van Esdonk, Y. C. Cattel. Tax Considerations for the European Union's Digital Single Market Strategy, Intertax, 2016, vol. 44, n° 6-7, pp. 513-524.

an original construction to tax the new vectors of value creation while avoiding the question of companies' profits subject to it.[93]

At the same time, the main limitation of the DST is its short-term approach. Indeed, it is expressly described as an interim solution,[94] a quick response, rather defensive, to a contentious topic. It is intrinsically a political act of reappropriation of an area largely falling outside Member States' finances. The Commission's project is not pursuing the root of tax erosion. It is rather a symbolic action on the sources of revenue in the digital economy.

Although temporary, there is only a brief reference to its transitory nature. The DST's provisions do not mention either its lifespan or a clause defining its modalities of extinction. Many national DSTs share a similar approach. For most, the prospect of a technical agreement at the international level should be their natural term.[95] However, the OECD's approach does not appear to be able to fully tackle the same concerns as the DST intends to.[96] Moreover, there is no end in sight for an OECD proposal. Therefore, this interim solution could become definitive. Several examples have already shown that a transitory tax solution tends to become definitive for various reasons which are rarely anticipated at the time of its creation. In France, this was the case of the levy for the reimbursement of the social security debt (also known as CRDS),[97] created in 1996, whose disappearance has been postponed several times. As for the DST, its shortcomings would become the digital single market's definitive problem, taking into consideration the difficulties to gather twice unanimity for its enactment and any subsequent amendments. In its proposal, the Commission did not pay much attention to this issue, even though it insisted on the merits of a graduated response, combining interim measures and long-term action. So, one must question this omission. Is it voluntary? During the discussions, the Council's proposal ended up including a specific term: "the entry

---

93 F. van Horzen, A. van Esdonk. Proposed 3% Digital Services Tax, International Transfer Pricing Journal, 2018, July/August, pp. 267-272.

94 Proposal for a Council Directive on the common system of a digital services tax on revenues resulting from the provision of certain digital services, COM(2018) 148 final, rec. 7.

95 Proposal for a Council Directive on the common system of a digital services tax on revenues resulting from the provision of certain digital services, COM(2018) 148 final, rec. 6; Council of the European Union. Proposal for a Council Directive on the common system of a digital services tax on revenues resulting from the provision of certain digital services, 2018/0073(CNS), Article 24, paragraph 4.

96 OECD. OECD/G20 Inclusive Framework on BEPS—Progress report July 2019-July 2020, OECD Publishing: Paris, 2020.

97 In French : « Contribution pour le remboursement de la dette sociale ».

into application of the revisions to the international corporate tax standards to address the challenges arising from digitalisation agreed at OECD level […].”[98] However, it narrowed its scope considerably by limiting it to online advertising only.[99] In the end, there is no logical end date for a DST because it depends on the rationale behind its adoption. Furthermore, the lack of foreseeable consensus at the OECD level is another reason to be pessimistic about the temporary nature of any EU DST. This raises the question of the tax burden on digital companies within the EU in the long term.

Finally, the EU DST is seeking to prevent the adoption of unilateral measures in several Member States' tax systems.[100] The DST has taken on the great challenge of translating into practice the notion of value in the digital era. The Commission must gain credit for such a pioneering approach to taxing "big data" profits.[101] However, alone it cannot solve the underlying problems of international taxation. Thus, the EU considered another solution for the long term, intended to yield a closer union between the Member States.

Devising an Effective European Fiscal Integration

The SDP, the EU's Latest Major Effort to Reform Corporate Income Taxation

The Current State of Play

The EU SDP proposal is a significant contribution to the recent debate surrounding the international tax law disruption. The Commission

98 Council of the European Union. Proposal for a Council Directive on the common system of a digital services tax on revenues resulting from the provision of certain digital services, 2018/0073(CNS). Paragraph 4.

99 Council of the European Union. Proposal for a Council Directive on the common system of a digital services tax on revenues resulting from the provision of certain digital services, 2018/0073(CNS). Article 3.

100 C. Dimitropoulou. The Digital Service Tax: An Anti-protectionist and Anti-restriction Appraisal under EU Primary Law, Intertax, 2019, vol. 47, Issue 2, pp. 210-218; S. Parthasarathi (ed.). Tax Policy Handbook, USA: International Monetary Fund, 1995, pp. 75-85.

101 P. M. Hartmann, M. Zaki, N. Feldmann, A. Neely. Capturing Value from Big Data—A Taxonomy of Data-Driven Business Models used by Start-up Firms, International Journal of Operations & Production Management, 2016, vol. 36, n° 10, pp. 1382-1406; L. Chiehyeon, K. Ki-Hun, K. Min-Jun, H. Jun-Yeon, K. Kwang-Jae, P. P. Maglio. From Data to Value: A Nine-Factor Framework for Data-Based Value Creation in Information-Intensive Services, International Journal of Information Management, vol. 39, April 2018, pp. 121-135.

conceived it as a comprehensive long-term solution. This is based on the simple ascertainment that the Permanent establishment concept is so entrenched in international tax that the simplest way to update the legal framework is to refine existing principles rather than replace them.[102]

The fiscal upheaval initiated recently requires a return to the fundamentals of the PE to understand its logic and limitations. The historical approach is based on the doctrine of economic allegiance. It attempts to reflect the concern for dual equity between citizens and States. It has "to be regarded as a compromise that strikes a fair balance between the exclusive taxation of the state of residence of the enterprise and the right of the market country to have a fair share of taxes in respect of business activities that are stably located on its territory."[103] The current interpretation of PE is based on a supply-side approach, although many adaptations have taken place over time and crises. The digital revolution calls into question its relevance.

As a result, there has been much debate on what improvements could be made to stop tax base erosion.[104] The OECD shows a preference for targeted short-term actions such as modifying the definition of preparatory or auxiliary activities, the notion of a dependent agent, and anti-abuse clauses.[105] However, the SDP proves that another way is possible. While it follows the traditional idea that establishment requires some sort of persistent continuity or stability in the source state, it assesses the intensity of this permanence through a new criterion related to the guiding principle of value creation.[106] It intends to strike a new balance, focusing more on demand than supply to locate the company's fiscal presence. The SDP is an

102 J. Li, J. Bao; H. C. Li, Value Creation: A Constant Principle in a Changing World of International Taxation, Canadian Tax Journal, 2019, vol. 67, n° 4, pp. 1107-1134.

103 P. Hongler, P. Pistone. IBFD—Blueprints for a New PE Nexus to Tax Business Income in the Era of the Digital Economy, Working Paper January 20, 2015, p. 15.

104 A. P. Dourado. The Priorities for EU Tax Policy, Intertax, 2019, Vol. 47, Issue 10, pp. 808-810; M. Aujean. Tax Competition and Tax Planning: What Solution for the EU, EC Tax Review, 2014, vol. 23, Issue 2, pp. 62-63; C. Oner. Comparative Analysis of the General Anti-abuse Rule of the Anti-Tax Avoidance Directive: An Effective Tool to Tackle Tax Avoidance, EC Tax Review, 2020, Vol. 29, Issue 1, pp. 38-52; G. Ginevra. The EU Anti-tax Avoidance Directive and the Base Erosion and Profit Shifting (BEPS) Action Plan: Necessity and Adequacy of the Measures at EU Level, Intertax, 2017, vol. 45, Issue 2, pp. 120-137; W. Bongaerts, I. Ijzerman. EC Anti-Tax Avoidance Package: Responses from European Tax Practices, ABA Tax Times, 2016, vol. 35, no. 3, pp. 26-34.

105 OECD. Are the Current Treaty Rules for Taxing Business Profits Appropriate for E-Commerce?, OECD Publishing: Paris, 2004; OECD, *supra* n. 47.

106 J. Li, J. Bao; H. C. Li, Value Creation: A Constant Principle in a Changing World of International Taxation, Canadian Tax Journal, 2019, vol. 67, n° 4, pp. 1107-1134.

attempt to strengthen a tangible economic nexus for the twenty-first century, instead of the current overly legalistic one. This solution has many opponents because it implies an overhaul of the almost customary rules governing taxation at the international level.[107] Above all, the SDP highlights that new forms of economic activity significantly blur the distinction between the two methods based on supply or the interaction between supply and demand. The SDP demonstrates a long-term logic not universally accepted, on which it is difficult to reach unanimity even at the EU level alone. In another way, under this approach, residence and source are not the only bases for taxing jurisdiction.[108] A dematerialized economy is profoundly changing how income taxation is apprehended. The Commission's proposal on SDP only acknowledges it and proposes an evolution of the reading grid. It would not be the first to bear witness to the eternal confrontation around the search for a balance between residence and source. Indeed, activities' structure of digital undertakings tends to concentrate all revenues in one place, whereas their origin is global. The SDP could make the EU a testing ground for a new digital tax and spur the OECD to act more boldly.[109] In any case, this must be done with due regard for the European digital companies' interests, which should not be adversely affected.

The Commission's approach is not lacking in originality and ambition for such a contentious issue. This is lively proof of its increased assertiveness in tax matters. Besides, it meddles in a lively international context. Indeed, the Commission is not a forerunner in the debate on the creation of a virtual PE concept. Since the 2015 BEPS Action Plan, the OECD has been trying to provide workable solutions. Therefore, the OECD has chosen a more consensual approach than the Commission.[110] It considered the task too burdensome. More precisely, a foreseeable compromise of the international tax community on the subject was out of reach. The OECD's BEPS Action 7 Final Report took a more limited scope, providing only

107 R. Mason. The Transformation of International Tax, American Journal of International Law, 2020, vol. 114, n° 3, pp. 353-402.

108 L. V. Faulhaber. Taxing Tech: The Future of Digital Taxation, Virginia Tax Review, Winter 2019, vol. 39, n° 2, p. 181.

109 V. Dhuldhoya. The Future of the Permanent Establishment Concept, Bulletin for International Taxation, 2018, vol. 72, n° 4a.

110 M. Olbert, C. Spengel. International Taxation in the Digital Economy: Challenge Accepted?, World Tax Journal, 2017, vol. 9, n° 1, pp. 3-46; R. Collier, J. Vella. Five Core Problems in the Attribution of Profits to Permanent Establishments, World Tax Journal, 2019, vol. 11, n° 2, pp. 159-187; S. Gadžo, Š. Jozipović. International Corporate Tax Regime Post-BEPS: A Regulatory Perspective, Intertax, 2020, vol. 48, n°4, pp. 432-445.

general recommendations to combat tax avoidance practices.[111] Multilateral Convention to Implement Tax Treaty Related Measures to Prevent Base Erosion and Profit Shifting (also known as "Multilateral Instrument" or MLI) has been used as an implementing tool.[112] However, these solutions remained optional and have not been widely backed by signatory States.[113] Now, with the endorsement of the G20, the OECD is reeling in all of the goodwill. It is leading the international community into uncharted territories, but the recent developments are stalling.[114] The intergovernmental economic organization with thirty-seven members has been gathering 137 countries under the IF initiative on updating the international tax law. Although important, the OECD's approach lacks the prevailing early ambition.[115] It is looking to introduce a revised profit allocation rule applicable to multinational enterprises.[116]

Therefore, the initial results of the BEPS Action Plan and its continuation do not seem to be able to provide adequate solutions to the current challenges.[117] The MLI adopted in 2017 only makes one-off corrections without any overall redefinition.[118] The EU's SDP proposal, resulting from the GAFA package, picks up where the tax community left off. In this, the EU, despite its limited competence, acquires a new dimension—that of an international tax reformer. Notwithstanding its decision-making constraints, the Commission asserts itself as a policy entrepreneur projecting influence outward. Only time will tell whether this initiative will spark a breakthrough or be ignored, but the current results are rather disappointing.

---

111 OECD. Preventing the Artificial Avoidance of Permanent Establishment Status, Action 7—2015 Final Report, OECD/G20 Base Erosion and Profit Shifting Project, OECD Publishing: Paris, 2015.

112 S. Tandon. Challenges to Multilateralism in International Taxation: A Tale of Two Measures, British Tax Review, 2019, n° 4, pp. 568-580.

113 OECD. Inclusive Framework on BEPS—Progress report July 2016/July 2017, OECD Publishing: Paris, 2017, p. 20.

114 Y. Brauner. Lost in Construction: What Is the Direction of the Work on the Taxation of the Digital Economy?, Intertax, 2020, vol. 48, Issue 3, pp. 270-272.

115 M. Herzfeld. The Case Against BEPS: Lessons for Tax Coordination, Florida Tax Review, 2017, vol. 21, n°1.

116 OECD. Programme of Work to Develop a Consensus Solution to the Tax Challenges Arising from the Digitalisation of the Economy, OECD/G20 Inclusive Framework on BEPS, OECD Publishing: Paris, 2019.

117 D. Kleist. The Multilateral Convention to Implement Tax Treaty Related Measures to Prevent BEPS—Some Thoughts on Complexity and Uncertainty, Nordic Tax Journal, 2018, n° 1, pp. 31-48.

118 OECD. Multilateral Convention to Implement Tax Treaty Related Measures to Prevent BEPS, Articles 6-11.

For the moment, all Member States should beforehand agree on a solution to give the SDP proposal a future beyond the EU's borders.

The SDP, a Bold New Vision of an Old Concept

The digital economy has brought the international corporate tax debate to the forefront of the political agenda under public pressure. This movement to revise aging rules has entailed the greatest venture of international tax law of the century.[119] Under the combined effect of globalization and digitalization, the perennial idea of national fiscal sovereignty based on economic allegiance must be adapted to a new reality.[120] Given the PE concept has been the nexus for the allocation of taxing rights, it has become the logical target of reform proposals to upgrade it to encompass modern situations.[121]

Within this context, the Commission wishes to introduce a new idea in the tax field: the significant digital presence. In concrete terms, this would allow, "for the purposes of corporate tax,"[122] the presence of a permanent establishment to be considered "if a significant digital presence exists through which a business is wholly or partly carried on,"[123] i.e., if the latter consists "wholly or partly of the supply of digital services through a digital interface."[124] Thus, the Commission is looking for a remedy to the lack of physical presence of digital services that presents a challenge for the PE.[125] This idea does not lead to a revolution in the way corporate profits are taxed. On the contrary, PE remains a pivotal concept. In fact, it is just amended to make it more effective considering the recent changes in the economy. The SDP is only a new threshold to strike a balance between taxing jurisdictions.[126] Through this innovation, the Commission hopes to better grasp the economic activities based on indirect revenues at the heart of wealth creation in digital businesses. This additional nexus is therefore enhancing tax efficiency by modernizing essential tax concepts that preceded the advent of the Internet.

---

119 OECD/G20 Base Erosion and Profit Shifting Project, 2015 Final Reports: Information Brief.
120 J. Li, J. Bao, H. C. Li, *supra* n. 102.
121 P. Hongler, P. Pistone, *supra* n. 53.
122 COM(2018) 147 final, *supra* n. 5, Article 4 paragraph 1.
123 *Ibid.*, Article 4 paragraph 1.
124 *Ibid.*, Article 4 paragraph 3.
125 J. A. Requena, G. Saturnina Moreno. Adapting the Concept of Permanent Establishment to the Context of Digital Commerce: From Fixity to Significant Digital Economic Presence, Intertax, 2017, vol. 45, Issue 11, pp. 732-741.
126 P. Hongler, P. Pistone, *supra* n. 53, p. 9.

The SDP baseline is that a digital interface can become a virtual PE. The rationale for a broader definition of the nexus relies on the assumption that the modern business environment carries out large commercial operations in a given jurisdiction without a physical presence.[127] Thus, the SDP has been conceived as a more appropriate indicator of permanence in a market jurisdiction to allocate taxing rights. However, the EU's SDP proposal is only intended to be an adjunct to the PE concept and not to replace it. This approach considers that digital services' provision equates to an economic presence, i.e., a stream of activity, in a State because of the customer's presence. The EU's proposal is not free from interrogation mostly on definitional aspects of the notion of "digital services through a digital interface."

Furthermore, the Commission is aware that such an approach could lead to an increase in the number of PEs, without this translating into significant revenues for the Member States. Similarly, the cost and administrative burden for the companies concerned could prove unbearable. Tackling the problem, three alternative thresholds thus complete the definition of SDP: EUR 7 million of turnover resulting from the provision of digital services, 100,000 users, 3,000 commercial contracts for the provision of such digital services.[128] These conditions show perfectly how the great diversity of digital activities makes the creation of an effective taxation tool extremely challenging. With such a limitation, the Commission gives a little more emphasis to the idea of significant presence. It is not enough that few people use a digital service, whether free or expensive; rather, a certain level of usage must be ascertained to demonstrate economic presence. Setting the bar sufficiently high ensures that compliance costs will be covered by substantial benefits generated in the new PEs. However, although very inclusive, the chosen solution is not free of circumvention possibilities. One cannot exclude that some companies may seek to fragment their activities to stay below the thresholds.

Issues Unsolved by the SDP

The SDP development is justified by an economic context where digital businesses are increasingly exempt from taxation.[129] The EU's SDP proposal relates more to a rough outline of a working solution rather than a

127 D. Pinto, *supra* n. 10, p. 316.

128 COM(2018) 147 final, *supra* n. 5, Article 4 paragraph 3.

129 W. Peng. Multinational Tax Base Erosion Problem of the Digital Economy, Modern Economy, 2016, n° 7, pp. 345-352; P. Kavelaars. EU and OECD: Fighting Against Tax

complete answer, reducing the probability of its adoption by the Council under the special legislative procedure requiring unanimity. This idea provides only a new administrative threshold on which to apply existing rules. Neither the valuation of intangibles assets nor the role of customers/users in adding value for the corporation is taken into consideration.[130] This issue sheds light on the real extent of such a reform and its shortcomings.

The quantification of benefits attributable to the SDP is done through a functional approach. In other words, the Commission considers that "in order to determine the functions of, and attribute the economic ownership of assets and risks to, the significant digital presence, the economically significant activities performed by such presence through a digital interface shall be taken into account."[131] In addition, it draws up a nonexhaustive list of activities which would be considered as "economically significant activities"[132] for "determining the attributable profits."[133] In other words, profit allocation is made through "economic activity generated by the interaction between customers of that country and a web site of that enterprise."[134] The user then becomes the key to the distribution of profits. As a result, smaller Member States may see their taxable profit base stagnate or even be diminished in favor of the more populous ones. Indeed, the SDP grants a bonus to large Member States, whereas the current system gives smaller States an incentive to accommodate undertakings looking for advantageous international tax planning. There is a risk that those affected in terms of tax revenues would not agree and block the proposal because of the unanimity requirement in tax matters at the EU level.

Furthermore, regarding the contractual allocation of income between entities of large multinational enterprises, the EU's SDP concept does

Avoidance, Intertax, 2013, vol. 41, Issue 10, pp. 507-515; OCDE, Addressing Base Erosion and Profit Shifting, Éditions OCDE: Paris, 2013.

130 J. Li, J. Bao; H. C. Li, Value Creation: A Constant Principle in a Changing World of International Taxation, Canadian Tax Journal, 2019, vol. 67, n° 4, p. 1124.

131 Proposal for a Council Directive laying down rules relating to the corporate taxation of a significant digital presence, COM(2018) 147 final. Article 5 paragraph 3.

132 Proposal for a Council Directive laying down rules relating to the corporate taxation of a significant digital presence, COM(2018) 147 final. Article 5 paragraph 4.

133 Proposal for a Council Directive laying down rules relating to the corporate taxation of a significant digital presence, COM(2018) 147 final. Article 5 paragraph 5.

134 OECD. Are the Current Treaty Rules for Taxing Business Profits Appropriate for E-Commerce?, OECD Publishing: Paris, 2004, paragraph 326.

nothing to cope with the tax planning opportunities offered by the arm's-length principle.[135] This proposal is built on a two-step procedure. As of the first, the SDP is really rolling out an interesting solution to attribute profit by targeting users. On the contrary, the second part of the reasoning is less innovative because profits are determined for these new activities as if they were carried out by a third-party business independent of the rest of the enterprise.[136] The new nexus ambitions seem to be constrained by the legalistic fiction of arm's-length transactions among internal divisions. Therefore, the existing transfer pricing guidelines remain an unsolved major concern for profit shifting in the SDP proposal, reducing its appeal for the Member States.[137]

The vision of a European tax system that would drive tax innovation at the international level remains a dream for the time being. This is regrettable while the EU is looking for a new impetus. Nevertheless, the SDP forms the basis of a long-term plan advertising to the international community that the EU intends to participate in the debate as much as it wishes to strengthen its own fiscal competence.

The EU's New Frontier: The Struggle for Tax Law Harmonization

The EU's Fiscal (In)Competence

The ongoing debate surrounding corporate income taxation and digital services taxation has a special significance when viewed from an EU perspective. For centuries, taxes were linked to some sort of royal prerogative. The person entitled to raise them was the holder of the power to enforce. Nowadays, taxes are the main resource of governments. According to Schumpeter, the modern state is a "tax state";[138] in other words, it can claim sovereignty because it has tax revenues. Public finances are the pivotal element for nations, and within democracies, citizens must consent

---

135 J. Li, J. Bao, H. C. Li, Value Creation: A Constant Principle in a Changing World of International Taxation, Canadian Tax Journal, 2019, vol. 67, n° 4, p. 1124.

136 W. Cui, The Superiority of the Digital Services Tax over Significant Digital Presence Proposals, National Tax Journal, December 2019, vol. 72, n° 4, p. 843.

137 P. Hongler, P. Pistone. IBFD—Blueprints for a New PE Nexus to Tax Business Income in the Era of the Digital Economy, Working Paper January 20, 2015.

138 J. Schumpeter. Die Krise des Steuerstaats, Graz: Leuschner & Lubensky, 1918; K. H. Schmidt. Schumpeter and the Crisis of the Tax State. In: Backhaus J. (eds.). Joseph Alois Schumpeter. The European Heritage in Economics and the Social Sciences, vol 1. Springer: Boston, MA, 2003; R. A. Musgrave. Schumpeter's Crisis of the Tax State: An Essay in Fiscal Sociology, Journal of Evolutionary Economics, 1992, vol. 2, pp. 89-113.

to taxes through their parliaments. Taxation is essential for state independence, which translates into a freedom to conduct its own public policies. Therefore, the mere fact of devising tax rules at the supranational level threatens the core element of modern States and could bring the EU closer to a federation.

This backdrop explains why Member States have been so reluctant to give up their power in fiscal matters to the EU since 1957.[139] As a result, the founding treaties avoided setting tax law objectives. Neither Article 2 nor Article 3 of the TEU nor Article 3 TFEU confers any direct competence on this topic. Moreover, because of the principle of conferral enshrined in Article 4 of the TEU, and its corollaries the principles of subsidiarity and proportionality, there is no prospect for the EU to acquire them indirectly. It is deprived of any legal basis to impose its own fiscal policy on the Member States. Nevertheless, the EU is not completely helpless in front of the challenges raised by divergent tax systems within it.

The achievement of the EU internal market, and the European project as a whole,[140] requires the elimination of tax barriers resulting from the exercise of Member States' sovereignty. Besides, in 1957, the treaty establishing the EEC provided legal bases for these objectives. Owing to this approach, the EU's tax policy was exclusively focused on the integration of national fiscal laws based on three goals.[141] The first was to remove trade barriers to the internal market. The second consisted of finding ways to prevent distortions to competition. The third was to avoid double taxation within the internal market to promote trade. The EU designed its interventions in tax matters according to two methods. At the beginning of the European construction, it focused further on negative integration to gradually remove economic frontiers between its members to operate like a single entity.[142] This approach was particularly relevant from 1957 onward to complete the internal market. As EU integration deepened, it moved toward positive integration, relying on the creation of an institutional

139 F. Wasserfallen. Political and Economic Integration in the EU: The Case of Failed Tax Harmonization, Journal of Common Market Studies, 2014, vol. 52, n° 2, pp. 420-435.

140 R. Beetsma, M. Giuliodori, F. Klaassen. Trade Spill-overs of Fiscal Policy in the European Union: A Panel Analysis. Economic Policy, 2006, vol. 21, Issue 48, pp. 640-687.

141 A. Maitrot de la Motte. Droit fiscal de l'Union européenne, Bruxelles, Bruylant, 2016, p. 867.

142 B. A. Balassa, The Theory of Economic Integration, London: Allen & Urwin, 1961, p. 304.

framework for common policies to allow those integrated economies to operate on equal terms.[143]

The EU has always been restrained in its action on tax law matters by the absence of any direct legal basis. Nevertheless, it has extended its reach to tax issues indirectly through sectoral actions related to the main goal of the EU: the internal market. Thus, each EU tax initiative was associated with its competences based on the latter. In fact, national fiscal rules were subject to European constraints in a triple way.

First, EU law prohibits state aid through any form of public expenditure such as tax aid under Article 107 of the TFEU. A Member State must apply to the Commission for authorization to grant any fiscal advantage to an undertaking. State aid law has always been a tool for negative tax harmonization, but this is no longer sufficient today in an internal market where trade between the Member States has become extremely easy.

Second, in the perspective of the achievement of the internal market, every trade barrier had to be removed. The EU targeted direct and indirect discriminatory taxation established by the Member States in their national tax systems. Based on Articles 30,[144] 34 and 110 of the TFEU, a general prohibition of custom duties, charges having an effect equivalent to customs duties and discriminatory internal taxation against imported goods or protective of domestic goods have been created. These legal provisions are supplemented by Articles 111 and 112 of the TFEU, which ensure fiscal neutrality on exports and imports within the EU. Although useful to remove hindrances to the internal market, this approach is only concerned with leveling the playing field through prohibitions. It is a good substitute for tax harmonization but not a panacea.

Third, the Member States were aware of the difficulties begotten by tax issues in the context of economic integration such as that of the European construction. Hence, they gave an ersatz tax competence to approximate, nay harmonize, tax law regarding some very restricted circumstances. Under Article 113 of the TFEU, the EU can adopt legal provisions concerning indirect taxation (i.e., turnover taxes, excise duties) "to the extent that such harmonization is necessary to ensure the establishment and the functioning of the internal market and to avoid distortion of competition."

143 B. A. Balassa, The Theory of Economic Integration, London, Allen & Urwin, 1961, p. 304.

144 J. Tudor. Discriminatory Internal Taxation in the European Union: The Power of the European Court of Justice to Limit the Tax Sovereignty of Member-States under Article 110 of the TFEU, Willamette Journal of International Law and Dispute Resolution, 2015, vol. 23, n° 1, pp. 141-186.

In addition to this, Articles 114 and 115 of the TFEU give the EU the possibility to enact directives for the approximation of direct taxation[145] whenever they "directly affect the establishment or functioning of the internal market."[146] As much to say, the probability of such a contingency occurring is exceptionally low. However, there is another practically insurmountable obstacle for any approximation or harmonization of tax law. Since Member States have kept tax competence in their hands, they only delegated little fragments provided that a special decision-making process is required, that of unanimity. In other words, even when the EU is deemed to have real power, it turns out to be exceedingly difficult to apply.

Consequently, the EU tax competence remains a myth. As of today, the main objective of the EU in this area is to allow interplay between EU law and national fiscal law. The EU wants to reconcile the divergent interests that sometimes compete within the EU. The economic pressure is mounting, and public demand is growing on the Member States to design a more efficient, fair, and neutral tax system. This should be the long-awaited momentum for achieving substantive tax progress in the EU.

Opportunities for the EU's Internal Fiscal Policy

Company taxation issues in the EU have not arisen with the growth of the digital economy. Difficulties linked to the limited or even nonexistent tax harmonization have always polluted relations between the Member States.[147] This has been the breeding ground for institutional tax competition between them, which has only accentuated tax disadvantages among companies. Over and above the many attempts to approximate national legislation in a positive way, the Commission has had to resort to using other tools to limit the harmful effects of this toxic race.

State aid law has been the Commission's main alternative for many years.[148] These legal provisions combat distortions of competition resulting from the granting of preferential treatment to an undertaking by a Member State. It has even gained legitimacy recently with the actions

---

145 Article 114, paragraph 2 TFEU.

146 Article 115 TFEU.

147 F. Wasserfallen, *supra* n. 139; A. Trandafir. Tax Harmonization Measures at EU Level in the Corporate Tax Field, Contemporary Readings in Law and Social Justice, 2013, vol. 5, n° 2, pp. 647-655.

148 P. Nicolaides. Fiscal State Aid in the EU: The Limits of Tax Autonomy, World Competition, 2004, vol. 27, Issue 3, pp. 365-396; J. Kavanagh, N. Robins. Corporate Tax Arrangements under EU State Aid Scrutiny, European State Aid Law Quarterly, 2015, vol. 14, n° 3, pp. 358-370.

taken against tax rulings established to the benefit of historic companies such as Fiat[149] or Starbucks[150] with mixed results. Digital companies like Amazon[151] and Apple[152] were not spared by the Commission, but the outcomes are more disappointing. The latest judgment rendered by the General Court in the *Apple* case[153] was a blow to the Commission's fresh strategy to tackle aggressive international tax avoidance. Even though the judges were not saying that the Commission was wrong to use state aid law, they concluded that it failed to show to the requisite legal standard that there was an advantage for the purposes of Article 107(1) TFEU and annulled its decision.

Thus, the Commission has tried to interfere in an area where it does not have direct powers to reduce as far as possible selective tax dumping. However, given the most recent case law, it cannot do everything. Its economic-based approach of competition between undertakings does not make it possible to prohibit institutional rivalry between the Member States in the field of taxation. As soon as the conduct becomes a general policy, it can no longer be quashed with this tool. State aid law is insufficient as a tax instrument in an internal market where movement of goods, services, persons, and capital between the Member States has become extremely straightforward and has been intensified by competition for tax systems. A genuine positive tax harmonization policy must be set in motion.[154] The measures planned under the GAFA package are therefore essential to support the approximation process of national tax systems. In the long term, the cohesion of the internal market is at stake and, more broadly, that of the EU. The SDP is therefore a necessary but not sufficient element to address all problems.

The project to broaden the PE definition to include the concept of SDP is not an isolated action of the EU. It is part of the context of legal

149 General Court, September 24, 2019, *Grand Duchy of Luxembourg and Fiat Chrysler Finance Europe v. European Commission*, T-755/15 and T-759/15, ECLI:EU:T:2019:670.

150 General Court, September 24, 2019, *Kingdom of the Netherlands and Others v. European Commission*, T-760/15 and T-636/16, ECLI:EU:T:2019:669.

151 Commission Decision (EU) 2018/859 of 4 October 2017 on State aid SA.38944 implemented by Luxembourg to Amazon, OJ L 153, June 15, 2018, pp. 1-142; General Court, T-816/17 and T-318/18, cases in progress.

152 Commission Decision (EU) 2017/1283 of August 30, 2016 on State aid SA.38373 implemented by Ireland to Apple, OJ L 187 du July 19, 2017, pp. 1-110.

153 General Court, July 15, 2020, *Ireland and Others v. European Commission*, T-778/16 and T-892/16, ECLI:EU:T:2020:338.

154 L. V. Faulhaber, *supra* n. 26; T. Baskaran, M. Lopes da Fonseca. The Economics and Empirics of Tax Competition: A Survey and Lessons for the EU, Erasmus Law Review, 2014, vol. 7, n° 1, pp. 3-12.

innovation. Following the adoption of anti-avoidance rules with the Anti Tax Avoidance Directive (ATAD) Directive,[155] the Commission has relaunched the project of a European-wide corporation tax through the Common Corporate Tax Base (CCTB)[156] and CCCTB.[157] The GAFA package thus complements them as regards the effective taxation of digital company profits at the EU level. Although the chosen solution allows the scope of the SDP to be extended beyond that of the CCCTB, the dynamics surrounding it are extremely favorable, but resistance should not be underestimated. Moreover, beyond the idea itself, its implementation remains complex.

The initiative to reform the PE concept by incorporating the idea of SDP leads to reflection on corporate profits taxation effectiveness in the EU, whether they come from the digital economy or not. The latter have not invented aggressive tax optimization. Their activities have only lent themselves to it more easily, but the habit has always existed. The Commission was aware of the GAFA package's limits from the moment it was presented. It insisted on the added value of close collaboration between national, European, and international players to meet "the challenges of taxation of profits of the digital economy."[158] In this context, the proposal for an SDP Directive must be put into perspective with the relaunch of the CCCTB project in 2016. With the CCCTB, the Commission wishes to see a truly harmonized and consolidated taxation system at the EU level for undertakings. This would be a significant step forward in tax harmonization, an area currently ignored by EU law, and put an end to aggressive tax optimization within it. Above all, this would result in the deterritorialization of taxation, relying on a supranational dimension, a kind of supraterritoriality.[159] However, the Member States are reluctant in this perspective. They do not want to give up their sovereignty over a direct tax, even in an extremely limited way, and they are concerned about the consequences

155 Council Directive (EU) 2016/1164 of July 12, 2016 laying down rules against tax avoidance practices that directly affect the functioning of the internal market, OJ L 193, July 19, 2016, pp. 1-14; W. Bongaerts, I. Ijzerman, *supra* n. 104.

156 Proposal for a Council Directive on a Common Corporate Tax Base (CCTB), COM(2016) 685 final, Strasbourg, October 25, 2016.

157 Proposal for a Council Directive on a Common Consolidated Corporate Tax Base (CCCTB), COM(2016) 683 final, Strasbourg, October 25, 2016.

158 Proposal for a Council Directive laying down rules relating to the corporate taxation of a significant digital presence, COM(2018) 147 final, paragraph 4.

159 M. Isenbaert. The Contemporary Meaning of "Sovereignty" in the Supranational Context of the EC as Applied to the Income Tax Case Law of the ECJ, EC Tax Review, 2009, vol. 18, n° 6, pp. 264-278.

of tax revenue distribution.[160] The CCCTB's lack of neutrality for public finances within the EU has become a central issue for corporate income taxation harmonization. Still, the SDP presented itself as a new key for revenue allocation. The debate is likely to be lengthy and the chances of success uncertain, given the unanimity requirement. Thus, the question arises, what would happen, in fiscal terms, if the EU remains midstream, i.e., with the SDP but without the CCCTB? Is the Commission's graduated response the right solution because of the uncertainties surrounding the complementary steps? Even more problematic is the question of whether, without either step forward, the CCCTB will still have a future. Indeed, the CCCTB is not the ultimate solution to end tax competition between the Member States. Moreover, the rate issue has not been addressed, even though it is the central element of any taxation. Without a minimum framework, as in the case of VAT, there is a risk of slippage, which would be detrimental to fiscal coherence within the internal market.

EU tax initiatives like the CCCTB, the DST, and the SDP seem to be stalling due to the absence of unanimity between the Member States. Therefore, one could think there is no hope for any groundbreaking change. Even if the EU is struggling to pass legislative proposals on tax matters, its institutions remain committed to shoving the current boundaries. There is a strong political will at the EU level to convince the Member States that this is the moment to make a bold move.

One year after the GAFA package, in 2019, the Commission published a communication entitled "Towards a more efficient and democratic decision making in EU tax policy."[161] According to this publication, "new challenges that have emerged, in the EU and globally, have exposed the limits of unanimity in tax policy at both EU and national levels."[162] The need for unanimity makes progress difficult and cumbersome, limits EU tax policy potential to the lowest common denominator, and gives rise to bargaining on unrelated issues. For the Commission, this goes against a

160 C. Cottarelli, M. Guerguil (eds.). Designing a European Fiscal Union, London: Routledge, 2014, p. 270; P. Pistone. European Tax Integration Law, Policy and Politics. Amsterdam: IBFD, 2018, p. 710.

161 Communication from the Commission to the European Parliament, the European Council and the Council. Towards a more efficient and democratic decision making in EU tax policy, COM/2019/8 final, Strasbourg, January 15, 2019.

162 Communication from the Commission to the European Parliament, the European Council and the Council. Towards a more efficient and democratic decision making in EU tax policy, COM/2019/8 final, Strasbourg, January 15, 2019, p. 1.

well-functioning internal market.[163] Accordingly, it presented a plan to move progressively from unanimity voting to the ordinary legislative procedure by using the "*passerelle*" clauses in the Treaties. Under the general *passerelle* clause, Article 48(7) TEU, the EU could introduce qualified majority voting. As a complement, the specific *passerelle* clause of Article 192(2) TFEU could be used to induce the same change regarding environmental tax policy. It is likely that this proposal will end up nowhere, but it demonstrates that any political inclination to reform taxation and its decision-making process has not disappeared. For example, the Commission is considering a general reform of the Energy Tax Directive (ETD) by mid-2021 using the special *passerelle* clause. On another aspect, there is an ongoing proposal for enhanced cooperation since 2013 in financial transaction tax, but negotiations are stalling.

Soft Power and the EU's External Fiscal Agenda

The EU legal framework is noticeably clear on the fact that there is no legal basis on which a tax policy can be carried out from the European perspective. Its weak elements of competence in this area are all oriented internally toward creating a fully functional internal market. The outside world is not in the EU's reach for tax purposes. Notwithstanding, one must not forget that of the thirty-seven OECD member countries, twenty-one are the EU Member States. Moreover, the Union has a special participant status and a permanent delegation in the OECD.[164] Therefore, the EU is concerned about the policy decisions taken at the OECD level. The GAFA package must be seen through this lens. Even if it can be puzzling, some elements of the SDP proposal are clearly directed at the international community and, more precisely, the OECD members.[165]

Indeed, reflection on the evolution of the basic concepts for company taxation requires questioning their implementation in the international

---

163 Communication from the Commission to the European Parliament, the European Council and the Council. Towards a more efficient and democratic decision making in EU tax policy, COM/2019/8 final, Strasbourg, January 15, 2019, p. 1.

164 Supplementary Protocol No. 1 to the Convention on the OECD.

165 W. Lips. The EU Commission's Digital Tax Proposals and Its Cross-Platform Impact in the EU and the OECD, Journal of European Integration, 2020, vol. 42, Issue 7; A. Turina. The Progressive Policy Shift in the Debate on the International Tax Challenges of the Digital Economy: A "Pretext" for Overhaul of the International Tax Regime?, Computer Law & Security Review, 2020, vol. 36, p. 105382.

context.[166] If the problems are important inside the EU, they are even more so when it comes to potential relations with third countries. The main limitation to all the EU solutions put forward remains the international double taxation treaties that Member States have signed with the rest of the world.[167] These conventions can neutralize the SDP effects on the PE concept. Indeed, they already use their own definition of the latter, mostly the OECD one, which does not recognize SDP or other forms of virtual PE. Recent advances in the BEPS Action Plan have not changed this. The SDP would be rendered ineffective if profits taxation were to entail the implementation of such conventions. The Commission is aware of the situation but remains powerless in an area of exclusive competence of the Member States. Nevertheless, to alert them on overall consistency in the mechanism which it would like to see created, the GAFA package also included a recommendation on this subject. It "puts forward a proposal for adaptations to the double tax conventions of Member States with non-Union jurisdictions in order, first, to extend the concept of a permanent establishment so as to include a significant digital presence […], and, second, to include rules for attributing profits to or in respect of a significant digital presence."[168] The modalities are the same as the proposed SDP Directive about the concept's definition, the thresholds, and the leasing of user data.[169] However, unlike the Directive, which is limited in scope to the EU or beyond, in the absence of international conventions,[170] this text covers external tax relations.

The GAFA package is an opportunity to broadly discuss tax concepts and powers needed for this purpose. In fact, the EU SDP proposal is not only intended to apply within the EU. With the proposal for a recommendation, the Commission wishes to play a role in the field of worldwide taxation as well. This initiative reflects on the advisability of conferring the EU a genuine autonomous tax competence both internally and externally.[171] Domestic actions taken to protect the internal market will inevitably have an impact on Member States' relations with non-EU countries.

---

166 M. Sapirie. Permanent Establishment and the Digital Economy, Bulletin for International Taxation, 2018, vol. 72, n° 4a.

167 M. P. Devereux, J. Vella. Taxing the Digitalised Economy: Targeted or System-Wide Reform?, British Tax Review, 2018, n° 4, 387-406.

168 C(2018) 1650 final, *supra*, Article 1.

169 C(2018) 1650 final, *supra*, Article 2.

170 Proposal for a Council Directive laying down rules relating to the corporate taxation of a significant digital presence, COM(2018) 147 final, Article 2.

171 J. Scott. Extraterritoriality and Territorial Extension in EU Law, The American Journal of Comparative Law, 2014, vol. 62, n° 1, pp. 87-125; to draw a parallel: A. R. Young.

As things stand, the founding treaties do not leave the Commission any real room for maneuver.[172] On the contrary, Member States made sure that they would remain in charge of fiscal policy. This initial position, which has been confirmed time and again, now appears to have been overtaken by the challenges raised by digital economy taxation. However, no revolution in this area is conceivable in today's overly sensitive political context.

The SDP proposal cannot be merely envisaged as an interesting long-term solution at the EU level. The timing gives a lot of indications about its hidden outer objective. On March 16, 2018, the OECD released its IF Interim Report.[173] On March 23, 2018, the Commission published what has since been called the GAFA package, i.e., a plan for two directives on the DST and SDP and a recommendation on the latter. This well-timed initiative was designed to build on the momentum created by the OECD's Interim Report while incentivizing the laggard Member States to engage in a constructive debate on corporate income taxation in the twenty-first century. The Commission was not challenging the OECD as the leading institution in international tax standard setting but was publicly emphasizing its participation in the debate. At the EU level, Member States immediately formed camps and engaged in discussions on a common position. Furthermore, the move was intended to build cohesiveness among EU members who wanted to unilaterally introduce defensive interim measures to tax digital undertakings. This was a hand held out to the OECD for a global consensus. At the same time, it puts pressure on the U.S. to commit itself to finding a common solution at the international level. Even though the EU's endeavor did not pay off for the moment, it gave a concrete example of its lasting commitment to developing tax proposals in the hope one day one of them will translate into legislation. The EU's consciousness of the relevance of tax policy is patent. It has taken another dimension lately on July 6, 2020, when the European Commission launched a call for proposals for the creation of an EU tax observatory.[174] Overall, the EU SDP concept enshrined in the proposal for a Directive and a recommendation was a worthy example of EU soft power over global tax governance.

Europe as a Global Regulator? The Limits of EU Influence in International Food Safety Standards, Journal of European Public Policy, 2014, vol. 21, n° 6, pp. 904-922.

172 D. Jancic. National Parliaments and EU Fiscal Integration, European Law Journal, 2016, vol. 22, n° 2, pp. 225-249; L. Poro. Fiscal Union v Individual National Sovereignty of EU Members States: A Conceptual Battle, Journal of International Banking Law and Regulation, 2015, vol. 30, n°2, pp. 68-81.

173 OECD, *supra* n. 47.

174 https://ec.europa.eu/taxation_customs/news/call-proposals-%E2%80%93-will-you-set-eu-tax-observatory_en [accessed on August 6, 2020].

Whereas the fate of the package was pending on the unanimity requirement, making it less likely to pass, its overarching influence at the international level was genuine.

As a result, the EU Commission engaged in "cross-platform policy entrepreneurship";[175] in other words, it used its limited capacities on internal tax matters to advance its policy viewpoint at the external level. In fact, it used its stance to bias the EU Member States' positions in a converging way. Even if the EU has limited competence in tax matters, it can play a leading role in updating tax concepts.

The Commission's initiative to modernize the PE's concept attests to its forward-thinking approach on tax matters. Given the EU's market size and its supranational nature, it could be the next laboratory for fiscal policy endeavors.

The EU had already been at the forefront of fiscal innovation several decades ago. To better assess the scope of its soft power on global tax governance, one must recall the most important tax legislation ever enacted by the bloc in the 1970s: the VAT directives.[176] While the world is undergoing an immense revision of international principles for corporate taxation of multinationals, fostered by the symbolic issue of taxing the digital economy, it is essential to look back in history to recall previous examples. The VAT's origins are a good topical starting point. This new tax originated presumably in the work of two persons: a German businessman Wilhelm Von Siemens in 1918 and an American economist Thomas S. Adams between 1910 and 1921.[177] The VAT was viewed as a technical innovation to the turnover taxes and possibly for Adams an alternative to the business income tax.[178] Even if France was the first country to adopt

175 W. Lips. The EU Commission's Digital Tax Proposals and Its Cross-Platform Impact in the EU and the OECD, Journal of European Integration, 2020, vol. 42, Issue 7.

176 First Council Directive 67/227/EEC of April 11, 1967 on the harmonization of legislation of Member States concerning turnover taxes, OJ 71, April 14, 1967, pp. 1301-1303; Second Council Directive 67/228/CEE of April 11, 1967 on the harmonisation of legislation of Member States concerning turnover taxes—Structure and procedures for application of the common system of value added tax, OJ 71, April 14, 1967, pp. 1303-1312; Sixth Council Directive 77/388/EEC of May 17, 1977 on the harmonization of the laws of the Member States relating to turnover taxes—Common system of value added tax: uniform basis of assessment, OJ L 145, June 13, 1977, pp. 1-40.

177 J. Kathryn. Exploring the Origins and Global Rise of VAT, The VAT Reader (Tax Analysts), 2011, pp. 15-22; L. P. Ebrill, M. Keen, J.-P. Bodin, V. Summers. The Modern Vat, Washington, D.C.: International Monetary Fund, 2001, p. 223.

178 J. Kathryn. Exploring the Origins and Global Rise of VAT, The VAT Reader (Tax Analysts), 2011, pp. 15-22; L. P. Ebrill, M. Keen, J.-P. Bodin, V. Summers. The Modern Vat, Washington, D.C.: International Monetary Fund, 2001, p. 223.

this tax in 1954, its real rise occurred when the EU adopted the well-known VAT directives in the 1970s. Since then, the rest of the world has followed, and VAT has now been adopted by more than 160 countries.[179] Thus, the EU's role in tax matters should never be underestimated.

Within this context of a high-level influence game, the SDP proposal can be understood as a more fundamental challenge to the relevance of corporation tax in its current form. The complexity of the mechanism and the immense difficulties of any reform attempt, both because of the deep differences of opinion and of the vast number of texts to be amended, cast doubt on a possible evolution. In the absence of any progress to new methods of taxation, its long-term obsolescence is to be feared. Corporate tax criteria remain fundamentally tangible, while the digital economy is almost entirely intangible.[180] Recent developments at the OECD level do not seem to change anything profoundly regarding this rationale.[181]

Similarly, while actions such as the SDP are laudable, they may only be a step toward a new conception of territoriality. A debate has gradually emerged on this criterion. If for a long time physical presence dominated, today truly innovative proposals tend toward another solution, that of profit localization, i.e., a criterion of territoriality based on the State where the company's income originates. The SDP proposal is a small step in this direction. However, establishing the residence of an undertaking in a State is easier than reforming other related issues. The possibilities of intragroup consolidation and, with it, the issue of transfer pricing are also elements that must be considered to ensure a fair allocation of taxing rights between States.[182] At present, these concerns are currently far from being settled.

As a result, this never-ending process of adaptation fosters an opinionated stream advocating for a complete overhaul of the paradigm. The

179 *Source*: IMF. Available at: https://www.imf.org/external/np/fad/tpaf/pages/vat.htm [accessed on August 7, 2020].

180 M. F. de Wilde. Comparing Tax Policy Responses for the Digitalizing Economy: Fold or All-in, Intertax, 2018, vol. 46, n° 6, pp. 466-475; P. Hongler, P. Pistone. IBFD—Blueprints for a New PE Nexus to Tax Business Income in the Era of the Digital Economy, Working Paper January 20, 2015.

181 H. Förster, S. Greil, A. Hilse. Taxing the Digital Economy—The OECD Secretariat's New Transfer Pricing A-B-C and Alternative Courses of Action, International Transfer Pricing Journal, 2020, vol. 27, n° 1; D. Kleist. The Multilateral Convention to Implement Tax Treaty Related Measures to Prevent BEPS—Some Thoughts on Complexity and Uncertainty, Nordic Tax Journal, 2018, n° 1, pp. 31-48.

182 R. Petruzzi, S. Buriak. Addressing the Tax Challenges of the Digitalization of the Economy—A Possible Answer in the Proper Application of the Transfer Pricing Rules?, Bulletin for International Taxation, 2018, vol. 72, n° 4a.

digital economy has only exacerbated already existing problems. Furthermore, the overriding difficulties of adjusting to this new challenge stem from a fundamentally flawed framework. Therefore, some argue that a system-wide reform must lead to a new founding theory moving from taxing companies' income according to the location of their mobile factors toward "a system that seeks to tax companies' profit where more immobile factors are located."[183] Under such a paradigm, establishing a company in a country would be determined by its actual economic presence in that country, which should be characterized by its consumers.[184] This would lead to a destination-based mechanism through either a destination-based cash flow taxation[185] or a residual profit allocation system.[186] This system has the merit of having a wider scope of application and being less avoidable and less complicated than the virtual PE or the SDP, neither of which fully answered the question of profit allocation entirely between tax jurisdictions. At the EU level, this endeavor could prove to be effective given the number of Member States and undertakings concerned. Moreover, the focus on immobile factors to locate the company's profits would be particularly relevant in an integrated market of around 447.7 million inhabitants[187] when the free movement of goods, services, persons, and capital has never been so easy, but it could prove unworkable with relation to third countries in the absence of an agreement of the OECD level.

Conclusion

Faced with the international community's slowness to support a modernization of the rules governing corporate profits taxation in the context of the digital economy, unilateralism is mounting. The multiplication of

183 M. P. Devereux, J. Vella. Taxing the Digitalised Economy: Targeted or System-Wide Reform?, British Tax Review, 2018, n° 4, 387-406, p. 404.

184 M. Lamensch. European Value Added Tax in the Digital Era, IBFD Doctoral Series, 2015, vol. 36; G. Beretta. European VAT and the Sharing Economy, Kluwer Law International BV, 2019, p. 413.

185 A.J. Auerbach, M.P. Devereux, M. Keen and J. Vella, Destination Based Cash Flow Taxation, Oxford University. Centre for Business Taxation Working Paper, 2017, WP17/01.

186 M.P. Devereux, A. J. Auerbach, M. Keen, P. Oosterhuis, W. Schön, J. Vella. Residual Profit Allocation by Income, Oxford University Centre for Business Taxation Working Paper, 2019, WP19/01.

187 *Source*: Eurostat. Available at: https://ec.europa.eu/eurostat/statistics-explained/index.php/Population_and_population_change_statistics [accessed on August 7, 2020].

schemes is likely to create fiscal confusion without solving the underlying problems. The GAFA package was the EU's opportunistic answer to advocate for tax harmonization.

The DST proposal showed clearly that the EU was not shying away from the confrontation. On the contrary, it gave a working example of a defensive interim measure targeted at digital companies, especially U.S.-based ones. The DST is much more than just a hovering idea. It is based on strong bolsters and follows a shared impetus despite having its own flaws weakening its probability of being enacted. More importantly, while unilateralism was gaining ground, this proposal is a clear remnant of multilateralism. Cooperation continues to be an effective technique when devising solutions to reform international taxation and put all undertakings, including digital ones, on an equal footing.

The SDP proposal followed the same steps. As a long-term solution, it emphasized the Commission's will to revive the corporate income taxation reform at the EU level while using the pretext of the OECD debate. The SDP delivered a workable solution, shedding light on the limits of such a politically oriented solution when looking to reach a consensus while leaving aside the underlying issues of profit valuation and allocation between tax jurisdictions. The SDP could have been the start of real transnational tax law, a laboratory for new reforms at the international level.

In the end, the OECD's inertia should be an opportunity for the EU, but the question remains of whether the EU will be willing to seize it. The Commission has a clear understanding of the EU's strategic position and its potential leading role. The EU's attempt could be a solid basis to reinterpret company tax rules at a wider level. Indeed, the GAFA package is a bold statement for an entity that lacks a legal basis for an independent tax policy at the supranational level. Nevertheless, these proposals will remain a good example of EU soft power on global governance. They served as a leveraging tool to advocate for a coordinated change. Given the EU's economic and fiscal weight and the number of its consumers, it is a key market for every company in the world. Therefore, it would have been normal to take its opinion seriously. This was the case in some ways. Member States DSTs were inspired by the EU proposal to a certain extent, somewhat dampening fiscal confusion within the internal market.

The main contribution of the GAFA package concerns the EU's integration. The Commission exploits this opportunity to stimulate once again the discussion on the future of the most integrated economic area in the world, where some members are even sharing the same currency, and policies ought to be coordinated. Their fate is so deeply entwined that the

COVID-19 crisis could only be dealt with through an EU-wide recovery fund and the first-ever EU debt. The DST and the SDP proposals were premonitory of the resource problem now facing the EU. In fact, the Commission in "Next-Generation EU"[188] is once again trying to spur the Member States to tie the knot by devising the same tax solutions again and again. Even with the recent events, doubts persist as to whether any new attempt to create a truly innovative European tax system will succeed. At least, especially important questions have already been asked. The EU is perhaps becoming accustomed to missed opportunities as far as taxation is concerned; it seems to be caught in a time loop.

188 O. Picek. Spillover Effects From Next Generation EU, *Intereconomics,* 2020, 55, pp. 325-331.

Private Equity's Arrival in American Sports Leagues

Tanner Schenewark
J.D. 2021 at BYU Law School, Provo, Utah, and Transactional Associate at Clifford Chance, New York, United States

Introduction

The year 2020 will stand out for many reasons in the world of American sports, but one of the most impactful developments may also be one of the least discussed: the arrival of private equity into the United States' (U.S.'s) major sports leagues. For decades, private equity firms have been barred from taking equity stakes of any kind—minority or majority—in most of the top-tier leagues. The few exceptions to this rule have been just that. Now, rule changes to several leagues' bylaws allow for a new influx of private equity capital with more changes likely on the horizon.

This chapter makes the case for why U.S. sports leagues should not only welcome the current inflow of private equity investment but also make additional permanent changes to league bylaws in order to encourage and expand future investment. Specifically, leagues should give private equity opportunities for majority ownership. Welcoming private equity into American sports promises a number of broad benefits to current franchise owners and league executives: First, competition for teams' minority ownership stakes will increase as bidding on those stakes is opened up to the significantly larger pool of buyers represented by private equity funds. This, in turn, will lead to higher team and league valuations, benefitting current owners. Second, broadening the pool of potential owners ensures that those allowed to buy in will be better fits with the franchises they join. Third, increased involvement with private equity funds will lead to innovation in deal structures, creating value in a historically inefficient industry. Fourth, private equity's involvement will improve organizational governance and structure across sports. And, lastly, opening doors wide to private equity will reduce the threat that funds interested in sports might decide to compete directly with existing organizations. There are, of course, potential downsides to increasing funds' involvement in sports. Most probable is a public backlash against fund-led ownership groups, with the public likely to perceive funds as being involved solely for the money as opposed to being driven by a love of the game (and certainly, funds will be in the game with a focus on profits). This backlash could lead to increased calls for financial disclosures from the team and league stakeholders. However, for reasons this chapter discusses, increased disclosure as a result of public ownership and trading of franchises seems likely to be in the cards regardless of whether private equity has a seat at the table.

The chapter is organized into three main sections. Following this introduction, the chapter begins by exploring how private equity has both interacted with and been perceived by sports leagues in the U.S. prior to current developments. It then details the specific ways leagues' recent organizational changes are inviting private equity investment and how managers of private capital have sprung into action to take advantage of these relaxed regulations. The role of the COVID-19 pandemic in hastening and necessitating these changes is also briefly explored. "Private Equity's Investment in European Sports" illustrates how private equity's much more active involvement in European sports provides specific evidence that it is a positive development for sports leagues and teams generally. Finally, the chapter concludes by laying out how private equity developments in the European market, as discussed in "Private Equity's Investment in European Sports," are a basis both for predicting future changes to American sports leagues and for arguing why American leagues ought to allow for expanded participation by private equity firms.

The Development of Private Equity in American Sports

American Perception of Private Equity in Sports

In the past, private equity interest in owning a sports franchise has perturbed team stakeholders—that is, teams' fans and local communities—even when it came to a minority stake that had no decision-making control.[1] Tom Gores' 2011 purchase of the Detroit Pistons—the highest-profile purchase of a professional team by a private equity group to

---

1 *See,* e.g., Peter Lattman, *The Detroit Pistons' New Private Equity Driver*, N.Y. TIMES (April 14, 2011, 1:12 PM), https://dealbook.nytimes.com/2011/04/14/the-detroit-pistons-new-private-equity-driver/.

date[2]—illustrates the stereotypical response that has often followed, or even preceded, such an acquisition.[3] Gores made his money running the private equity firm Platinum Equity, which has a long track record of operating primarily through leveraged buyouts (LBO).[4] The public backlash to Gores' purchase was immediate: Dan Primack, a writer at *Fortune*, rashly concluded that actually Gores' *firm* was the new owner and jumped to conclusions about what that meant for the Pistons' storied franchise:

> The Detroit Pistons are about to become the first major professional sports franchise in North America to be owned by a private equity fund. Not by flesh-and-blood individuals who made their fortunes in private equity (like the Boston Celtics or Golden State Warriors), but by a \$2.75 billion financial vehicle. What that means is that the Pistons are about to become an investment, not a labor of love. Something bought for the purpose of later being sold, not to keep in the Michigan-loving family for generations.[5]

---

2 "TowerBrook Capital owned the St. Louis Blues of the NHL from 2006 to 2012." Kevin Dowd, *Not Just for Kicks: PE Gaze Turns Toward European Football*, PITCHBOOK (April 18, 2016), https://pitchbook.com/news/articles/not-just-for-kicks-pe-gaze-turns-toward-european-football. Outside of marquee leagues, New York private equity firm Spire Capital Partners purchased a majority stake in Professional Bull Riding in March 2007, which it held until its sale in 2015. Richard Morgan, *WME/IMG acquires Professional Bull Riders for Reported \$100M*, N.Y. Post (April 15, 2015, 11:57 AM), https://nypost.com/2015/04/15/wmeimg-acquires-professional-bull-riders-for-reported-100m/.

3 *Will PE Strategies Score? A Dive into Sport and Entertainment Investing*, BOCCONI STUDENTS INV. CLUB (December 8, 2019), https://bsic.it/will-pe-strategies-score-a-dive-into-sport-and-entertainment-investing/; *see also*, Giles Richards, *CVC Ownership of F1 Should Serve as a Warning to Premiership Rugby*, THE GUARDIAN (September 10, 2018), https://www.theguardian.com/sport/blog/2018/sep/10/cvc-ownership-f1-warning-premiership-rugby-union.

4 *Tom Gores*, L.A. BUS. J. (May 28, 2007), https://labusinessjournal.com/news/2007/may/28/tom-gores/. "A leveraged buyout (LBO) is the acquisition of another company using a significant amount of borrowed money to meet the cost of acquisition. The assets of the company being acquired are often used as collateral for the loans ... many people regard LBOs as an especially ruthless, predatory tactic." Will Kenton, *Leveraged Buyout (LBO)*, INVESTOPEDIA (last updated May 24, 2020), https://www.investopedia.com/terms/l/leveragedbuyout.asp#:~:text=A%20leveraged%20buyout%20(LBO)%20is,assets%20of%20the%20acquiring%20company.

5 Dan Primack, *Why Tom Gores Is Not Really Buying the Detroit Pistons*, FORTUNE (April 13, 2011, 1:21 PM), https://fortune.com/2011/04/13/why-tom-gores-is-not-really-buying-the-detroit-pistons/; Dan Feldman, *Don't Panic about Platinum Equity Buying the Pistons with Tom Gores*, PISTON POWERED (last visited November 28, 2020), https://pistonpowered.com/2011/04/13/dont-panic-about-platinum-equity-buying-the-pistons-with-tom-gores/.

Another sports commentator for Yahoo! noted that the Pistons were "likely to be stripped down" and would be treated "as an asset, rather than a potential champion."[6] In the days after the transaction closed, Gores received frequent questions about whether he had any intentions to spin-off parts of the franchise like the stadium; reporters and fans alike were skeptical of his intentions, in part, because of his firm's history.[7] But Primack was off target: Gores purchased fifty-one percent of the team, and his firm purchased the other forty-nine, leaving the flesh-and-blood individual in control.[8] Fears that Gores would sell off the Pistons' different assets were likewise unfounded, and, in 2015, Gores bought out his fund's entire stake in the team.[9]

---

6 Kelly Dwyer, *The New Pistons Owner Is Not the New Pistons Owner*, YAHOO!SPORTS (April 13, 2011), https://sports.yahoo.com/pistons-owner-not-pistons-owner-20110413-104040-807.html.

7 Bill Shea, *"Shocking" Bargain: Gores Pays $325 Million for Pistons*, CRAIN'S DETROIT BUSINESS (June 5, 2011), https://www.crainsdetroit.com/article/20110605/FREE/306059954/shocking-bargain-gores-pays-325-million-for-pistons; Peter Lattman, *The Detroit Pistons' New Private Equity Driver*, N.Y. TIMES (April 14, 2011, 1:12 PM), https://dealbook.nytimes.com/2011/04/14/the-detroit-pistons-new-private-equity-driver/.

8 Dan Weil, *The NFL's Next Billionaire Owner Won't Be a Person*, INSTITUTIONAL INVESTOR (June 6, 2018), https://www.institutionalinvestor.com/article/b18jhkn8dm9rx8/the-nfl's-next-billionaire-owner-won't-be-a-person.

9 Dan Weil, *The NFL's Next Billionaire Owner Won't Be a Person*, INSTITUTIONAL INVESTOR (June 6, 2018), https://www.institutionalinvestor.com/article/b18jhkn8dm9rx8/the-nfl's-next-billionaire-owner-won't-be-a-person; Scott Soshnick, *Platinum's Gores Buys His Fund's Ownership Stake in Pistons*, BLOOMBERG (September 4, 2015, 8:02 PM), https://www.bloomberg.com/news/articles/2015-09-05/platinum-s-gores-buys-his-fund-s-ownership-stake-in-pistons. At the time of Gores' decision to buy out the firm's stake, there was recognition that doing so was supposed to allay people's fears about his and his firm's original intentions. A partner at Gores' Platinum Equity fund, Mark Barnhill, commented on the decision to this effect:

> Private equity funds have a lifecycle and exit investments over time, and because one of our funds had a minority equity interest in the team, some folks questioned when we bought the team whether Tom was in this for the long haul or not … This transaction should put that question to bed … He's in this for the long haul … and will own this team long after the lifecycle of the fund that originally invested expires. The deal has been in the works for some time. Given the finite lifecycle of the private equity fund, we needed to plan how best to manage the fund's exit.

Report: Gores Buys Remaining Pistons Stake, ESPN.COM (September 7, 2015), https://www.espn.com/blog/nba/post/_/id/8561/report-gores-buys-remaining-pistons-stake.

Similar episodes and commentary have followed other private equity purchases of sports entities.[10] One commentator characterized a private equity firm's ownership tenure at a European sports league as a "raping of the sport."[11] These guttural reactions match up with how private equity, as an industry, has been characterized since its initial boom in the 1980s—namely as "barbarians at the gate."[12] However, these criticisms and suspicions largely overlook what the private equity leaders themselves already appear to know: When it comes to the business of sports, "[w]inning might be the best way to maximize profits."[13] And winning is something that few fans are likely to disapprove of. Other commentators have pushed back on the connection between winning and profits, most notably "Ed Woodward, Manchester United's executive vice-chairman, [who] famously stated that 'playing performance doesn't really have a meaningful impact on what we can do on the commercial side'."[14] However, the introduction of new, industry-specific earnout clauses means that winning has, in many cases, become meaningfully tied to financial performance, especially in the long term.[15]

While firms have been infrequent investors in professional sports teams—primarily because they have been barred from doing so—the executives that run those firms have not. Indeed, a 2016 estimate concluded that twenty-five percent of National Basketball Association teams are

10 Giles Richards, *CVC Ownership of F1 Should Serve as a Warning to Premiership Rugby*, THE GUARDIAN (September 10, 2018), https://www.theguardian.com/sport/blog/2018/sep/10/cvc-ownership-f1-warning-premiership-rugby-union.

11 Giles Richards, *CVC Ownership of F1 Should Serve as a Warning to Premiership Rugby*, THE GUARDIAN (September 10, 2018), https://www.theguardian.com/sport/blog/2018/sep/10/cvc-ownership-f1-warning-premiership-rugby-union. More recently, the announcement of a European soccer "Super League" with backing from JP Morgan Chase was widely condemned, including by a large fan group, Football Supporters Europe, which called it "driven exclusively by greed", "a venture that would only benefit the hedge funds, oligarchs, and … already wealthy clubs"—many owned by private equity groups or executives. Tariq Panja, *Top European Clubs Form Breakaway League*, N.Y. TIMES (April 19, 2021), https://www.nytimes.com/2021/04/18/sports/soccer/super-league-united-liverpool-juventus-madrid.html.

12 Bryan Burrough & John Helyar, BARBARIANS AT THE GATE (Harper Business) (1st ed. 2009).

13 Dan Feldman, *Don't Panic about Platinum Equity Buying the Pistons with Tom Gores*, PISTON POWERED (last visited November 28, 2020), https://pistonpowered.com/2011/04/13/dont-panic-about-platinum-equity-buying-the-pistons-with-tom-gores/.

14 Matthew Taylor, *Private Equity Set to Continue Investment Trend in Sport*, LINKLATERS (March 6, 2020), https://www.linklaters.com/en-us/insights/blogs/sportinglinks/2020/march/private-equity-set-to-continue-investment-trend-in-sport.

15 "[I]nvestments into sports clubs are increasingly tied to longer-term plans dependent on improved team performance and potential entry into the most lucrative competitions." *Id.*

owned by private equity "moguls."[16] At the time, that constituted seven NBA teams that were majority-owned by men with private equity backgrounds.[17] Like Gores with his Pistons, these owners, by and large, have not brought private equity's stereotypical cost cutting and spin-off strategies to the NBA.[18] What they have done is "gone to great lengths to find the right executives to run" their teams.[19] That strategy seems to have paid huge dividends for both this group of owners and the teams' fans: During the 2018-2019 season, the top four finishers in the NBA's Eastern conference were all owned by private equity professionals.[20] Even the owners whose teams have not found runaway success on the court—including Mr. Gores and his woeful Pistons—can take solace that their investments have been enormously successful in financial terms: "In 2012, the English Premier League's Manchester United was the only professional sports franchise valued at $2 billion. Eight years later, more than 57 teams have

16 Kevin Dowd, *Barbarians at the Ticket Gate: The PE Moguls Who Own 1/4 of the NBA*, PITCHBOOK (February 25, 2016), https://pitchbook.com/news/articles/barbarians-at-the-ticket-gate-the-pe-moguls-who-own-14-of-the-nba. Many more are owned by men with backgrounds in venture capital and hedge funds. *See,* e.g., *Hedge Fund and Private Equity Managers That Own Sports Teams*, LITTLESIS (last visited November 28, 2020), https://littlesis.org/lists/963-hedge-fund-and-private-equity-managers-that-own-sports-teams/members.

17 Kevin Dowd, *Barbarians at the Ticket Gate: The PE Moguls Who Own 1/4 of the NBA*, PITCHBOOK (February 25, 2016), https://pitchbook.com/news/articles/barbarians-at-the-ticket-gate-the-pe-moguls-who-own-14-of-the-nba.

18 Kevin Dowd, *Private Equity Is Dominating the NBA in 2020*, PITCHBOOK (February 13, 2020), https://pitchbook.com/news/articles/private-equity-is-dominating-the-nba-in-2020. Arguably, the lone exception is the Philadelphia 76er's, which are owned by David Blitzer, global head of tactical opportunities at Blackstone, and Josh Harris, a cofounder of Apollo Global Management. Under Blitzer and Harris' leadership, the 76er's pioneered "the Process, a controversial strategy of prolonged tanking designed to net" high draft picks. Roger Sherman & John Gonzalez, *The Great Tanking Debate: Which GM Did a Better Job, Sashi Brown or Sam Hinkie?*, THE RINGER (August 21, 2019, 5:50 AM), https://www.theringer.com/nfl/2019/8/21/20813898/sashi-brown-sam-hinkie-browns-76ers-tanking-trust-the-process. However, while hugely unpopular with fans at the time, the tactic seems to have paid off, and the 76er's GM at the time, Sam Hinkie—who was eventually forced to resign because of his tactic—is now widely "hailed as [a] hero[]." *Id.*; Stephen Babb, *Philadelphia 76ers Owner Calls Tank-Tastic Season a "Huge Success,"* BLEACHER REPORT (April 18, 2014), https://bleacherreport.com/articles/2034580-philadelphia-76ers-owner-calls-tank-tastic-season-a-huge-success.

19 Kevin Dowd, *Private Equity Is Dominating the NBA in 2020*, PITCHBOOK (February 13, 2020), https://pitchbook.com/news/articles/private-equity-is-dominating-the-nba-in-2020.

20 *Id.*

reached that valuation worldwide."[21] In the U.S., National Football League team values have increased fivefold in the last ten years, averaging gains of ten percent each year.[22] And in the NBA, team valuations are up fourteen percent in the last year alone.[23] Beneath the burgeoning franchise valuations are "lucrative broadcast rights agreements, which guarantee hundreds of millions of dollars in secured revenue."[24] Case in point, Gores' Pistons, purchased for USD 325 million, are now worth an estimated USD 1.45 billion.[25]

Rule Changes Arrive in the Major Leagues

The trend toward welcoming private equity to American sports kicked off in October 2019 with Major League Baseball (MLB) announcing changes to its ownership rules; the changes would allow investment funds to take minority stakes in multiple clubs.[26] With MLB franchise values at an all-time high, the initial idea behind the change, as stated by Commissioner of Baseball Rob Manfred, was to help minority owners find buyers for their increasingly expensive stakes.[27] Following this initial adoption, similar

---

21 Justin A. Casey & Gregory A. Marino, *A New Game in Town: The Rise of Private Equity and Institutional Investment in Sports*, FOLEY (November 11, 2020), https://www.foley.com/en/insights/publications/2020/11/private-equity-institutional-investment-sports.

22 Russell Hedman, *Professional Sports Opening Up to Private Equity Is a Good Thing, but Questions Remain*, BENZINGA (August 7, 2020, 3:08 PM), https://www.benzinga.com/general/sports/20/08/16993520/professional-sports-opening-up-to-private-equity-is-a-good-thing-but-questions-remain.

23 Russell Hedman, *Professional Sports Opening Up to Private Equity Is a Good Thing, but Questions Remain*, BENZINGA (August 7, 2020, 3:08 PM), https://www.benzinga.com/general/sports/20/08/16993520/professional-sports-opening-up-to-private-equity-is-a-good-thing-but-questions-remain.

24 Justin A. Casey & Gregory A. Marino, *A New Game in Town: The Rise of Private Equity and Institutional Investment in Sports*, FOLEY (November 11, 2020), https://www.foley.com/en/insights/publications/2020/11/private-equity-institutional-investment-sports.

25 *#26 Detroit Pistons*, FORBES (last visited November 30, 2020), https://www.forbes.com/teams/detroit-pistons/?sh=f5e06e03a623.

26 Andrew Woodman, *Hard-Hit Sports World Finds New Fans: Private Equity Firms*, PITCHBOOK (July 20, 2020), https://pitchbook.com/news/articles/sports-private-equity-investments-pandemic.

27 Jabari Young, *MLB Commissioner Talks about Digital Strategy Shift, Falling Ratings and Drawing Millennials in Wide-Ranging Interview*, CNBC (December 17, 2019, 8:01 AM), https://www.cnbc.com/2019/12/17/mlb-shifts-digital-strategy-to-draw-millennial-fans-as-ratings-fall.html; Scott Soshnick, *Investors Get Path to Buy into Major League Baseball Teams*, BLOOMBERG (October 16, 2019, 8:46 AM), https://www.bloomberg.com/news/articles/2019-10-16/investors-get-path-to-buy-stakes-in-major-league-baseball-teams.

changes spread to almost every prominent league in the country. In April 2020, the National Basketball Association confirmed rumors of a similar move and announced that it had asked Dyal Capital Partners to create a fund to buy up minority stakes in NBA teams.[28] A memo sent to owners prior to the announcement gave some of the same justifications that Commissioner Manfred had stated: "This vehicle would provide additional liquidity for the sale of team ownership interests, including by providing access to a new pool of long-term investors that do not currently have access to team ownership opportunities."[29] Finally, in July of 2020, Major League Soccer Commissioner Don Garber told reporters that the league was "pretty close to finalizing something" that would allow private equity investment in its teams.[30]

These moves put pressure on the other major sports leagues to keep up in providing similar liquidity for their team owners. The National Football League currently only allows *individuals* to purchase ownership stakes,[31] and it previously declined to create an investment vehicle like the one announced by the NBA.[32] However, the same week that the MLB announced its rule changes, NFL insiders let leak that the league was considering increasing—dramatically—the amount of money that owners and prospective buyers are allowed to borrow when acquiring a team, from the current limit of USD 350 million to USD 1 billion.[33] The NFL also

---

28 *Dyal Capital Partners Seeks $2B For Minority Stakes in NBA Teams*, SBJ DAILY (May 29, 2020), https://www.sportsbusinessdaily.com/Daily/Issues/2020/05/29/Finance/Dyal-Capital.aspx?ana=register_free_form_2_filled.

29 Scott Soshnick, *NBA Considers Creating Investment Vehicle to Buy Stakes in Teams*, BLOOMBERG (September 2, 2019, 10:00 PM), https://www.bloomberg.com/news/articles/2019-09-03/nba-weighs-creation-of-investment-vehicle-to-buy-shares-of-teams.

30 Jabari Young, *Major League Soccer to Join Other Leagues in Allowing Private Equity Financing*, CNBC (July 11, 2020, 11:15 AM), https://www.cnbc.com/2020/07/11/mls-join-nba-mlb-in-private-equity-financing.html.

31 Thomas Barrabi, *Why Pro Sports Team Investments Are Wall Street's Newest Play*, FOXBUSINESS (November 27, 2019), https://www.foxbusiness.com/sports/pro-sports-private-equity-investments.

32 Eben Novy-Williams, *NFL Owners May Soon Be Able to Borrow a Whole Lot More Money*, BLOOMBERG (October 11, 2019, 4:58 PM), https://www.bloomberg.com/news/articles/2019-10-11/nfl-owners-may-soon-be-able-to-borrow-a-whole-lot-more-money.

33 Thomas Barrabi, *Why Pro Sports Team Investments Are Wall Street's Newest Play*, FOXBUSINESS (November 27, 2019), https://www.foxbusiness.com/sports/pro-sports-private-equity-investments; Eben Novy-Williams, *NFL Owners May Soon Be Able to Borrow a Whole Lot More Money*, BLOOMBERG (October 11, 2019, 4:58 PM), https://www.bloomberg.com/news/articles/2019-10-11/nfl-owners-may-soon-be-able-to-borrow-a-whole-lot-more-money.

announced that it would raise teams' operating debt limits from USD 350 million to USD 500 million.[34] The hoped-for effect would be more or less the same as in the other leagues: an increased pool of potential buyers, even if that pool still did not include private equity firms.[35] It is worth noting, however, that simply raising the debt ceiling for teams has proven insufficient for owners in other leagues:

> In June 2018, the NBA's board of governors approved rules increasing the debt limit for owners from $250 million to $325 million. While the permitted debt increase may be helpful to some ownership groups, when the average NBA franchise is worth $1.65 billion, the leveraged buyout approach is clearly off the table. With financing at slightly less than 20 percent of the purchase price, as well as cash flow needs to drive operations, potential owners cannot rely on third-party indebtedness to acquire teams.[36]

The NFL's proposed much higher number of USD 1 billion might seem to solve this issue, but the average NFL franchise value also currently sits at around USD 3 billion, nearly double the value of the average NBA team.[37] The National Hockey League, meanwhile, does not prohibit private equity ownership, but it has yet to give any clarifying guidance on the types of investments that would make it past the league's extensive review process, i.e., whether it would allow funds to own stakes in multiple teams and what other tweaks to private equity funds' financial operations it might require.[38] Some observers and former National Hockey League (NHL) executives have speculated that, given its most recent financial outlook, the

---

34 Justin A. Casey & Gregory A. Marino, *A New Game in Town: The Rise of Private Equity and Institutional Investment in Sports*, FOLEY (November 11, 2020), https://www.foley.com/en/insights/publications/2020/11/private-equity-institutional-investment-sports.

35 Eben Novy-Williams, *NFL Owners May Soon Be Able to Borrow a Whole Lot More Money*, BLOOMBERG (October 11, 2019, 4:58 PM), https://www.bloomberg.com/news/articles/2019-10-11/nfl-owners-may-soon-be-able-to-borrow-a-whole-lot-more-money.

36 Matt Eisler & Andrew Brandes, *Sport Franchise Transactions: Unlike Anything Else*, SPORTS LITIG. ALERT (December 7, 2018), https://www.hoganlovells.com/~/media/hogan-lovells/pdf/2019/sla-15-24-reprint-eisler-brandes.pdf?la=en.

37 Mike Ozanian, *The NFL's Most Valuable Teams 2019: Cowboys Lead League at $5.5 Billion*, FORBES (September 4, 2019, 7:25 AM), https://www.forbes.com/sites/mikeozanian/2019/09/04/the-nfls-most-valuable-teams-2019-cowboys-lead-league-at-55-billion/?sh=6987cd1f2f1b.

38 Thomas Barrabi, *As NHL Expands, Private Equity Could Boost Hockey's Financial Boom*, FOXBUSINESS (November 30, 2019), https://www.foxbusiness.com/sports/nhl-private-equity-ownership-team-expansion.

NHL is a prime target for private equity investment, although having the league's teams split between the U.S. and Canada adds a wrinkle that some of the other leagues have not had to address.[39]

The Rise of Sports-Focused Funds and SPACs

Developments among the several leagues were immediately followed by a flurry of private equity activity as investors raced to put together sports-focused funds.[40] Galatioto Sports Partners (GSP) was the first to move after the MLB's announcement in October.[41] Sal Galatioto, a decades-long participant in sports finance, created a new vehicle—the GSP Baseball Fund—directly following the MLB's announcement.[42] The fund intends to raise USD 500 million in capital focused on limited partnership investments in professional baseball teams and is restricted to one hundred investors with a minimum contribution of USD 1 million.[43] Then, as noted above, Dyal Capital Partners was tapped by the NBA in April 2020 to create a passive USD 2 billion fund to purchase minority stakes in NBA teams.[44] A couple of months later, in July 2020, RedBird Capital Partners announced the creation of "a $500 million Special Purpose Acquisition Company (SPAC)[45] [to] target sports franchises, media, and data analytics

39 Thomas Barrabi, *As NHL Expands, Private Equity Could Boost Hockey's Financial Boom*, FOXBUSINESS (November 30, 2019), https://www.foxbusiness.com/sports/nhl-private-equity-ownership-team-expansion.

40 Karishma Vanjani, *Chart: Private Equity's Biggest Bet in Sports since 2015*, PE HUB (September 16, 2020), https://www.pehub.com/chart-private-equitys-biggest-bets-in-sports-since-2015/.

41 Thomas Barrabi, *MLB Ownership Rule Change Puts Private Equity in Scoring Position*, FOXBUSINESS (November 29, 2019), https://www.foxbusiness.com/sports/mlb-ownership-rule-change-private-equity.

42 Brendan Coffey, *Move over, Billionaires; The Really Big Money Wants in on Sports*, SPORTICO (July 27, 2020), https://www.sportico.com/business/finance/2020/sports-team-ownership-billionaires-investment-funds-private-equity-1234609947/#!.

43 Scott Soshnick, *Investors Get Path to Buy into Major League Baseball Teams*, BLOOMBERG (October 16, 2019, 8:46 AM), https://www.bloomberg.com/news/articles/2019-10-16/investors-get-path-to-buy-stakes-in-major-league-baseball-teams.

44 Justin Casey & Gregory Marino, *A New Game in Town: The Rise of Private Equity and Institutional Investment in Sports*, SBJ DAILY (November 11, 2020), https://www.sportsbusinessdaily.com/SB-Blogs/COVID19-OpEds/2020/11/11.

45 Special Purpose Acquisition Company. For more information on SPACs, especially their meteoric rise in 2020, *see* Nessa Anwar, *SPAC Listings Hit a Record High in 2020—but What Are These "Shell Companies"?*, CNBC (November 22, 2020, 9:20 PM), cnbc.com/2020/11/23/what-are-spacs-2020-saw-record-number-of-shell-companies-listed.html.

companies."[46] That SPAC—named RedBall Acquisition Corp.—was in talks to merge with Fenway Sports Group LLC, the owner of the Boston Red Sox, the Liverpool Football Club, and other related businesses.[47] For Fenway Sports Group (or another future target), the primary benefit of being acquired by a SPAC would have been, again, to offer liquidity to the Group's existing investors.[48] In October, Arctos Sports Partners announced its debut fund, raising USD 430 million on a target of USD 1.8 billion,[49] with the goal to buy team stakes across multiple leagues.[50] As evidence of the sheer speed with which this area is developing, new groups continue to announce their intentions to seek stakes in teams *almost weekly*, and high-profile individuals from the sports world continue to sign on as their partners or advisors. Since I began drafting this chapter, two more notable groups have joined the ranks of those already mentioned: The newly formed Beautiful Game Group announced that it is building a fund to specifically target sports franchises.[51] More recently, it added two sports power brokers to its list of partners and Oliver Luck, ex-commissioner of the currently defunct Xtreme Football League (XFL), as a member of its board.[52] Another investment advisory firm, The Raine Group, is the latest

46 Karishma Vanjani, *Chart: Private Equity's Biggest Bet in Sports since 2015*, PE HUB (September 16, 2020), https://www.pehub.com/chart-private-equitys-biggest-bets-in-sports-since-2015/.

47 Cara Lombardo & Miriam Gottfried, *Red Sox Owner in Talks to Take Sports Holdings Public*, WALL ST. J. (October 9, 2020, 7:55 PM), https://www.wsj.com/articles/red-sox-owner-in-talks-for-deal-with-redball-acquisition-11602286661. The SPAC acquisition eventually fell apart but not the funding or opportunity for owner liquidity: RedBird, alongside professional basketball star Lebron James, invested USD 750 million into Fenway Sports Group in a private agreement, noting that the deal was a better fit for the private market. Kevin Draper & Marc Stein, *Lebron James Is Becoming a Red Sox Owner*, N.Y. TIMES (March 16, 2021), https://www.nytimes.com/2021/03/16/sports/basketball/lebron-james-red-sox.html.

48 Brandon Kochkodin, *Red Sox Finances Could Stay Secret Even with Stake Sale to SPAC*, BLOOMBERG (November 12, 2020, 5:00 AM), https://www.bloomberg.com/news/articles/2020-11-12/red-sox-finances-could-stay-secret-even-with-stake-sale-to-spac.

49 Karishma Vanjani, *Chart: Private Equity's Biggest Bet in Sports since 2015*, PE HUB (September 16, 2020), https://www.pehub.com/chart-private-equitys-biggest-bets-in-sports-since-2015/.

50 Dan Primack, *Private Equity Firm Formed to Buy into Pro Sports Teams*, AXIOS (April 29, 2020), https://www.axios.com/private-equity-pro-sports-89da1c8f-f7d6-4271-8567-c814a320e937.html.

51 BEAUTIFUL GAME GROUP (last visited November 28, 2020), https://www.beautifulgamegroup.com/.

52 Brendan Coffey, *Beautiful Game Group Adds Oliver Luck, Gary Woolf, Others to Executive Roster*, SPORTICO (October 6, 2020, 2:55 AM), sportico.com/business/finance/2020/beautiful-game-group-executives-1234614298/.

addition, announcing on 28 November 2020 that it would form a SPAC seeking USD 325 million "for a technology-media-telecom acquisition, including the possible acquisition of a sports team."[53] Others will undoubtedly continue to follow.

The Role of the COVID-19 Pandemic

The COVID-19 pandemic accelerated funds' rush to get in on the industry's rapid growth[54] with teams and leagues looking for sources of funding and private equity firms looking for deals. Understandably, the pandemic hit sports leagues harder than many other businesses since it cut off vital revenue streams predicated on in-person attendance, i.e., tickets, concessions, and parking.[55] Even leagues with solid financial foundations, like the NFL, were projected to lose and to lose big.[56] Other sources of funding that normally might have been able to cover these reductions in cash flow—like different types of credit facilities—were available at less attractive terms or are not available at all.[57] But the same environment that made debt hard to come by for teams also made it harder to come by for private equity funds looking to finance large deals; this, in turn, made smaller, easier-to-fund deals—such as minority stakes in sports franchises—a growing focus for firms.[58] And most observing parties are optimistic about

53 Brendan Coffey, *Cubs' Tom Ricketts, Raine Group Form Sports-Focused SPAC*, SPORTICO (November 28, 2020, 8:45 AM), https://www.sportico.com/business/finance/2020/chicago-cubs-raine-group-spac-1234617358/?cx_testId=92&cx_testVariant=cx_1&cx_artPos=0#cxrecs_s.

54 Justin A. Casey & Gregory A. Marino, *A New Game in Town: The Rise of Private Equity and Institutional Investment in Sports*, FOLEY (November 11, 2020), https://www.foley.com/en/insights/publications/2020/11/private-equity-institutional-investment-sports.

55 Justin A. Casey & Gregory A. Marino, *A New Game in Town: The Rise of Private Equity and Institutional Investment in Sports*, FOLEY (November 11, 2020), https://www.foley.com/en/insights/publications/2020/11/private-equity-institutional-investment-sports.

56 Justin A. Casey & Gregory A. Marino, *A New Game in Town: The Rise of Private Equity and Institutional Investment in Sports*, FOLEY (November 11, 2020), https://www.foley.com/en/insights/publications/2020/11/private-equity-institutional-investment-sports. "The NFL, arguably the domestic league with the most solid financial footing, may experience a decrease in revenue approaching $4 billion." *Id.*

57 *Id.*; *see,* e.g., Davide Scigliuzzo & Jeannine Amodeo, *Billionaire Fertitta Offers Record 15% Loan Rate to Save Empire*, BLOOMBERG (April 6, 2020, 2:14 PM), https://www.bloomberg.com/news/articles/2020-04-06/landry-s-brings-first-u-s-leveraged-loan-in-almost-a-month.

58 Selin Bucak & Lina Saigol, *Sports Are Back on the Pitch. So Is Private Equity—and the Competition Is Heating Up*, MARKETWATCH (June 30, 2020, 5:58 AM), https://

sport's long-term outlook: The managing director of the NBA's new investment vehicle at Dyal, Michael Rees, said that he "doesn't think the virus will have any long-term effect on the NBA" and that the pandemic has only revealed "the insatiable appetite for sports and live entertainment."[59] Other fund managers concur, with some viewing the pandemic as a "buy-low-sell-high" opportunity.[60]

COVID-19's challenge to sports in Europe is no different: "[[R]evenues for top-flight European soccer clubs [were] projected to fall by almost $2 billion compared to 2018-19, according to a report from Deloitte."[61] However, unlike sports leagues in the U.S., European leagues and teams had, for some time prior to the onset of the pandemic, welcomed investment from, and even ownership by, private equity firms.

Private Equity's Investment in European Sports

The primary difference between the two regions' disparity in private equity investment lies in comparatively looser regulations among their various leagues, which make it easier, more attractive, or necessary for investors—even foreign ones—to buy in.[62] For one, the sports markets and teams in Europe have much lower valuations than in the U.S.; this means that small family offices in the U.S. that want to own a team but are unable to afford an expensive stake in the NFL, for example, often turn to

www.marketwatch.com/story/sports-are-back-on-the-pitch-so-is-private-equity-and-the-competition-is-heating-up-2020-06-30.

59 *Dyal Capital Partners Seeks $2B For Minority Stakes In NBA Teams*, SBJ DAILY (May 29, 2020), https://www.sportsbusinessdaily.com/Daily/Issues/2020/05/29/Finance/Dyal-Capital.aspx?ana=register_free_form_2_filled.

60 Selin Bucak & Lina Saigol, *Sports Are Back on the Pitch. So Is Private Equity—and the Competition Is Heating Up*, MARKETWATCH (June 30, 2020, 5:58 AM), https://www.marketwatch.com/story/sports-are-back-on-the-pitch-so-is-private-equity-and-the-competition-is-heating-up-2020-06-30. The head of private equity fund CVC's sports, media & entertainment division said that they "expect sport to recover from the crisis, to return to growth, and to make a strong contribution to the recovery … wanted to invest now to support that opportunity." *Id.*

61 Justin A. Casey & Gregory A. Marino, *A New Game in Town: The Rise of Private Equity and Institutional Investment in Sports*, FOLEY (November 11, 2020), https://www.foley.com/en/insights/publications/2020/11/private-equity-institutional-investment-sports.

62 Matthew Eisler, *Opinion: Investors Who Want to Buy Sports Teams Look to Europe, not the U.S.*, MARKETWATCH (August 16, 2019, 12:05 PM), https://www.marketwatch.com/story/investors-who-want-to-buy-sports-teams-look-to-europe-not-the-us-2019-08-16.

Europe.[63] Interest is not restricted to small funds, though, by any means: Large funds, such as the previously mentioned Arctos Sports Partners, are *eager* to invest in European teams.[64] Looser regulations mean that even minority owners can often participate in high-level decisions regarding teams, unlike in the U.S., where leagues typically dictate that the controlling owners must retain jurisdiction over important choices.[65] European teams also tend to be much more leveraged than their American counterparts, creating a need for equity capital either to help clear debt[66] or to maintain balance sheets that have a healthy mix of both sources of capital.[67] Together, these factors and others have made European sports a tantalizing prospect for funds of all shapes and sizes, and from all over the world.

Indeed, 2019 was a record year for private equity investment in the European sports market,[68] and, despite—or perhaps because of—the effects of the COVID-19 pandemic, 2020 built on that record significantly. In advance of a discussion of how the types of private equity deals conducted with teams and leagues in Europe apply to the U.S. market, it is useful to run through some of the notable private equity transactions in European sports from the last couple of years.

---

63 Matthew Eisler, *Opinion: Investors Who Want to Buy Sports Teams Look to Europe, not the U.S.*, MARKETWATCH (August 16, 2019, 12:05 PM), https://www.marketwatch.com/story/investors-who-want-to-buy-sports-teams-look-to-europe-not-the-us-2019-08-16.

64 Dan Primack, *Private Equity Firm Formed to Buy into Pro Sports Teams*, AXIOS (April 29, 2020), https://www.axios.com/private-equity-pro-sports-89da1c8f-f7d6-4271-8567-c814a320e937.html.

65 Matthew Eisler, *Opinion: Investors Who Want to Buy Sports Teams Look to Europe, not the U.S.*, MARKETWATCH (August 16, 2019, 12:05 PM), https://www.marketwatch.com/story/investors-who-want-to-buy-sports-teams-look-to-europe-not-the-us-2019-08-16.

66 Kevin Dowd, *Not Just for Kicks: PE Gaze Turns Toward European Football*, PITCHBOOK (April 18, 2016), https://pitchbook.com/news/articles/not-just-for-kicks-pe-gaze-turns-toward-european-football.

67 "[N]ine of the 20 [soccer] teams in the [English Premier League] carr[ied] over €100 million in debt [in 2016], led by Chelsea at a hefty £958 million. But that's not always the case. Swansea, for instance, had zero debt as of last year." *Id.* In comparison, at the time Chelsea was carrying GBP 958 million in debt, it was valued by *Forbes* at USD 1.7 billion, which would have been approximately GBP 1.27 billion. *#6 Chelsea*, Forbes (last visited December 2, 2020), https://www.forbes.com/teams/chelsea/?sh=6b9868013725.

68 Andrew Woodman, *Hard-Hit Sports World Finds New Fans: Private Equity Firms*, PITCHBOOK (July 20, 2020), https://pitchbook.com/news/articles/sports-private-equity-investments-pandemic. "$911 million injected across 10 deals." *Id.*

Notable European Deals

One of the first private equity deals on the continent was also one of its largest: British private equity firm CVC Capital Partners paid approximately USD 952 million for a majority stake in Formula 1 racing, which CVC eventually sold in 2016 for more than an estimated USD 6.7 billion.[69] Additionally, in perhaps the most active segment of investment, a growing number of European soccer clubs are owned by a broad range of private equity firms, many from the U.S., as well as sovereign wealth funds from around the world:

> Florida-based Tavistock Group … is the owner of Tottenham Hotspur … Paris Saint-Germain … is owned by Qatari Sports Investments, a branch of the Qatari Investment Authority. And Hertha Berlin, an emerging powerhouse in Germany's Bundesliga, is owned in part by KKR, which paid €61.2 million for a 9.7% stake in early 2014.[70]

Other notable acquisitions of soccer clubs include Elliott Management's EUR 400 million "loan-to-own acquisition of A.C. Milan in July 2018"[71] and "Silicon Valley-based Silver Lake's $500 million purchase of a ten percent stake in the vaunted English soccer club Manchester City."[72] Moreover, Italian club A.S. Roma was acquired *again* last year—this time by Texas-based Friedkin Group who purchased a nearly ninety percent stake in the club for a reported EUR 591 million,.[73] and, in France, RedBird

69 Adam Le & Alex Lynn, *The New Playbook: How Private Equity Fell in Love with Sport*, PRIV. EQUITY INT'L (November 3, 2020), https://www.privateequityinternational.com/the-new-playbook-how-private-equity-fell-in-love-with-sport/.

70 Kevin Dowd, *Not Just for Kicks: PE Gaze Turns Toward European Football*, PITCHBOOK (April 18, 2016), https://pitchbook.com/news/articles/not-just-for-kicks-pe-gaze-turns-toward-european-football.

71 Matthew Taylor, *Private Equity Set to Continue Investment Trend in Sport*, LINKLATERS (March 6, 2020), https://www.linklaters.com/en-us/insights/blogs/sportinglinks/2020/march/private-equity-set-to-continue-investment-trend-in-sport. Elliot took over A.C. Milan after the club defaulted on its loan.

72 Andrew Woodman, *Hard-Hit Sports World Finds New Fans: Private Equity Firms*, PITCHBOOK (July 20, 2020), https://pitchbook.com/news/articles/sports-private-equity-investments-pandemic.

73 Tash Barrington, Matthew Taylor & Thomas Geraghty, *M&A in Sports: Has COVID-19 Moved the Goalposts?*, LINKLATERS (May 7, 2020), https://www.linklaters.com/en-us/insights/blogs/sportinglinks/2020/may/m-and-a-in-sports-has-covid-19-moved-the-g oalposts. The price paid actually "represent[ed] a significant decrease from the €750 million agreed between the parties prior to the onset of the pandemic. The new purchase

Capital (previously mentioned in connection with its new sports SPAC)[74] acquired a controlling interest in struggling French club F.C. Toulouse.[75] Rugby is another hot market, especially in light of the effects the sport is feeling during the pandemic.[76] If that sounds like an active deal environment, especially when compared to its counterpart across the pond,[77] it barely scratches the surface of private equity's involvement in European sports.

---

price shows the impact that lost match-day, sponsorship and broadcasting income can have on valuations of sports clubs in the current climate." *Id.*

74 *See* Karishma Vanjani, *Chart: Private Equity's Biggest Bet in Sports since 2015*, PE HUB (September 16, 2020), https://www.pehub.com/chart-private-equitys-biggest-bets-in-sports-since-2015/.

75 Justin A. Casey & Gregory A. Marino, *A New Game in Town: The Rise of Private Equity and Institutional Investment in Sports*, FOLEY (November 11, 2020), https://www.foley.com/en/insights/publications/2020/11/private-equity-institutional-investment-sports. In France, U.S. firms GACP Sport and King Street Capital had also previously acquired F.C. Bordeaux. *Id.*

76 "[CVC] has more recently acquired a minority stake in the Guinness Six Nations Championship international rugby event." Justin A. Casey & Gregory A. Marino, *A New Game in Town: The Rise of Private Equity and Institutional Investment in Sports*, FOLEY (November 11, 2020), https://www.foley.com/en/insights/publications/2020/11/private-equity-institutional-investment-sports. And France's rugby league is currently in discussions with London-based private equity firm Novalpina, which is looking to acquire a twenty percent stake in the commercial entity that owns its broadcast and sponsorship rights. Martin Ross, *LNR Pursues Private Equity Talks, but "Not Just to Pay Off Clubs' Debts,"* SPORTBUSINESS (September 20, 2020), https://www.sportbusiness.com/news/lnr-pursues-private-equity-talks-but-not-just-to-pay-off-clubs-debts/.

77 For instance, a few more transactions show the breadth of deals being done: "In 2019, [private equity firm] Bridgepoint sold its stake in MotoGP owner Dorna to another Bridgepoint fund which now owns it alongside the Canada Pension Plan Investment Board." Matthew Taylor, *Private Equity Set to Continue Investment Trend in Sport*, LINKLATERS (March 6, 2020), https://www.linklaters.com/en-us/insights/blogs/sportinglinks/2020/march/private-equity-set-to-continue-investment-trend-in-sport.

"Norway's trillion-dollar sovereign wealth fund … has a $10 million slice of Juventus, the Turin, Italy, soccer club." Brendan Coffey, *Move over, Billionaires; The Really Big Money Wants in on Sports*, SPORTICO (July 27, 2020), https://www.sportico.com/business/finance/2020/sports-team-ownership-billionaires-investment-funds-private-equity-1234609947/#!.

"Italy's top-flight soccer league, Serie A, has recently entered exclusive discussions with a group led by private equity giant CVC Capital Partners, which is seeking a minority stake in a new special purpose entity created to manage the league's broadcasting rights." Justin A. Casey & Gregory A. Marino, *A New Game in Town: The Rise of Private Equity and Institutional Investment in Sports*, FOLEY (November 11, 2020), https://www.foley.com/en/insights/publications/2020/11/private-equity-institutional-investment-sports.

Lessons from Private Equity's Involvement in Europe

In trying to piece together what the future of private equity could become in American sports, the best crystal ball we have is European sports. This is true when it comes to facing fears that private equity will negatively impact the industry, but it is also true in showing how private equity can improve it.

As a baseline in assuaging fears about the "barbarians at the gate," firms invested in European sports have shown that they are not all tied to their usual timeline of investment, which generally includes an exit in three to five years.[78] In fact, experts predict that eventually, a "transition from the traditional leveraged buyout model tied to a sale or Initial Public Offering (IPO) within 3-5 years to longer-term commercial strategies for growing the profitability of sports investments will be crucial to the success of [private equity] investment in sport."[79] CVC's more than decade-long tenure as owner of Formula 1 is, perhaps, the highest-profile example of private equity's interest in remaining in the game over the long term. Others, however, are quickly following CVC's lead: Bridgepoint, headquartered in London, has moved its ownership of MotoGP's parent company between three different entities that it controls in order to maintain viable long-term ownership, and, in fact, it continues to hold the league after nearly 16 years.[80] For some sports, "investments into sports clubs are increasingly tied to longer-term plans [because they are] dependent on improved team performance and potential entry into the most lucrative competitions."[81] Or, as one fund manager noted: "[T]here are a lot of principles to private equity, so the rules about getting out in a managed timeframe are less relevant."[82]

---

78 Jonathan Dyson, *How Football Clubs Can Cash in on the Game's Changing Investment Landscape*, SPORTBUSINESS (July 8, 2019), https://www.sportbusiness.com/2019/07/how-football-clubs-can-cash-in-on-the-games-changing-investment-landscape/.

79 Justin A. Casey & Gregory A. Marino, *A New Game in Town: The Rise of Private Equity and Institutional Investment in Sports*, FOLEY (November 11, 2020), https://www.foley.com/en/insights/publications/2020/11/private-equity-institutional-investment-sports.

80 Adam Le & Alex Lynn, *The New Playbook: How Private Equity Fell in Love with Sport*, PRIV. EQUITY INT'L (November 3, 2020), https://www.privateequityinternational.com/the-new-playbook-how-private-equity-fell-in-love-with-sport/.

81 Matthew Taylor, *Private Equity Set to Continue Investment Trend in Sport*, LINKLATERS (March 6, 2020), https://www.linklaters.com/en-us/insights/blogs/sportinglinks/2020/march/private-equity-set-to-continue-investment-trend-in-sport.

82 Jonathan Dyson, *How Football Clubs Can Cash in on the Game's Changing Investment Landscape*, SPORTBUSINESS (July 8, 2019), https://www.sportbusiness.com/2019/07/how-football-clubs-can-cash-in-on-the-games-changing-investment-landscape/.

These other principles have risen to the foreground as funds have become more involved in European sports. They include "alignment of interest, governance, and transparency."[83] In fact, many onlookers in Europe now publicly recognize private equity's disciplined approach to investing in sports teams as much healthier and smarter than that of previous owners.[84] Even some critics of private equity recognize funds' effect on leagues' governance and structure: Unlike many other private equity deals in European leagues or teams, CVC's tremendous financial success with Formula 1 has been soundly condemned for hurting the future of the sport.[85] However, opponents of CVC's influence on Formula 1 as a sport also concede, amazingly, that the fund "improved the structure and governance" of the sport.[86] Funds also appear to be improving in how they balance their financial interests with the interests of fans and local communities.[87] In many ways, these realizations were already evident in the way that private equity principals, such as the NBA owners discussed earlier,[88] have chosen to govern their teams in the U.S. However, general acceptance of private equity investment in European sports has also moved the sports industry forward in positive ways that go beyond commonsense financial management and respect for the franchise. Here, I will focus on four primary areas: increased competition for minority stakes, securitization, innovation, and public ownership of franchises.

---

83 Jonathan Dyson, *How Football Clubs Can Cash in on the Game's Changing Investment Landscape*, SPORTBUSINESS (July 8, 2019), https://www.sportbusiness.com/2019/07/how-football-clubs-can-cash-in-on-the-games-changing-investment-landscape/.

84 Jonathan Dyson, *How Football Clubs Can Cash in on the Game's Changing Investment Landscape*, SPORTBUSINESS (July 8, 2019), https://www.sportbusiness.com/2019/07/how-football-clubs-can-cash-in-on-the-games-changing-investment-landscape/.
"I think the financial community coming in is potentially a healthier one. Most private equity investors come with a challenging mindset, a smart mindset." *Id.*

85 *See,* e.g., Giles Richards, *CVC Ownership of F1 Should Serve as a Warning to Premiership Rugby*, THE GUARDIAN (September 10, 2018), https://www.theguardian.com/sport/blog/2018/sep/10/cvc-ownership-f1-warning-premiership-rugby-union.

86 Kiel Porter, *After Pocketing 450% Return, CVC Is Ready to Unload Formula One*, BLOOMBERGQUINT (August 9, 2016, 9:39 PM), https://www.bloombergquint.com/business/after-pocketing-450-return-cvc-is-ready-to-unload-formula-one.

87 Kiel Porter, *After Pocketing 450% Return, CVC Is Ready to Unload Formula One*, BLOOMBERGQUINT (August 9, 2016, 9:39 PM), https://www.bloombergquint.com/business/after-pocketing-450-return-cvc-is-ready-to-unload-formula-one. "A lot of them will have a financial driver but what is clear from the Premier League, for example, is that an individual investor will learn quickly how to balance financial performance with stakeholder interest—and by that I mean the fans and the local community." *Id.*

88 *See supra* notes 14-25 and accompanying text.

First, in their enthusiastic rush to be a part of European sports teams, private equity groups are turning more and more to minority stakes.[89] This is in part due to funds' need for smaller deals.[90] Fortunately for the funds—if not the teams—the stress caused by COVID-19-related shutdowns and lost revenues means that even large clubs have been "more receptive than usual to selling minority stakes to shore up their financial positions and help them see out the crisis."[91] However, while the events causing teams to look for new sources of cash are negative, getting that cash from private equity firms can be entirely positive: Besides providing needed capital, the involvement of private equity in minority stakes brings the added benefit of industry expertise.[92] As one law firm partner noted, "[t]hese funds include some of the most savvy and experienced sports executives around … They can quickly and efficiently do their diligence and execute on deals, even when complicated structures and issues are involved. This can be extremely attractive to leagues, teams, and sellers."[93] Moreover, it is particularly valuable when the industry—like the sports industry right now—"is facing operational difficulties and cannot obtain a bank loan,[94] or … needs an experienced partner with which to work to

---

89 Selin Bucak & Lina Saigol, *Sports Are Back on the Pitch. So Is Private Equity—and the Competition Is Heating Up*, MARKETWATCH (June 30, 2020, 5:58 AM), https://www.marketwatch.com/story/sports-are-back-on-the-pitch-so-is-private-equity-and-the-competition-is-heating-up-2020-06-30.

90 Selin Bucak & Lina Saigol, *Sports Are Back on the Pitch. So Is Private Equity—and the Competition Is Heating Up*, MARKETWATCH (June 30, 2020, 5:58 AM), https://www.marketwatch.com/story/sports-are-back-on-the-pitch-so-is-private-equity-and-the-competition-is-heating-up-2020-06-30 and accompanying text.

91 Ben Cronin, *US Investors "Seeking Preferred Equity Positions" in Premier League Clubs Before Market Rebound*, SPORTBUSINESS (May 27, 2020), https://www.sportbusiness.com/news/us-investors-seeking-preferred-equity-positions-in-premier-league-clubs-be fore-market-rebound/?registered_metered=1.

92 Eva Davis, Sara Cieniewski, & Josh Birenbaum, *The Smart Money: When a Private Equity Minority Investment Can Be Better Than a Bank Loan (and What about a Family Office?)*, 20 THE J. OF PRIV. EQUITY 21 (2016).

93 *As Sports Leagues Resume Play, Hogan Lovells' Sports, Media & Entertainment Group Identifies Seven Key Trends to Watch in the Sports Sector*, HOGAN LOVELLS (September 24, 2020), https://www.hoganlovells.com/en/news/as-sports-leagues-resume-play-hogan-lovells-sports-media-and-entertainment-group-identifies-seven-key-trends-to-watch-in-the-sports-sector.

94 *See Id.*; *see,* e.g., Davide Scigliuzzo & Jeannine Amodeo, *Billionaire Fertitta Offers Record 15% Loan Rate to Save Empire*, BLOOMBERG (April 6, 2020, 2:14 PM), https://www.bloomberg.com/news/articles/2020-04-06/landry-s-brings-first-u-s-leveraged-loan-in-almost-a-month. and accompanying text.

overcome near-term challenges while developing long-term growth strategies."[95] There are other positive effects as well, including that fierce competition for minority shares, as is happening now across Europe, will often increase the value of the franchise as a whole, benefitting the majority owner. Many of the most heated battles for minority stakes in leagues or teams center on their media rights, which I turn to next.

Private equity firms active in Europe are helping advance the development of securitization in sports. Industry observers have imagined for a while that in the future there would be "a system where private investors regularly buy and sell stakes in more complex vehicles tied directly to media rights or licensing agreements."[96] Now, the COVID-19 pandemic appears to have accelerated that reality among European clubs: The teams comprising Italy's top soccer league, Serie A, unanimously agreed at the end of November 2020 to sell a ten percent stake in the league's media business to a private equity consortium that includes Britain's CVC, Boston-based Advent International, and state-backed Italian fund FSI.[97] Moreover, Advent International and London-based BC Partners "are among a handful of private equity firms showing an interest in the … international media rights" of the top two German soccer leagues—Bundesliga 1 and 2.[98] The list of other potential bidders for the minority stake—which includes Bain Capital, CVC Capital Partners, General Atlantic and KKR[99]—reads like a "Who's Who" of private equity,

95 Eva Davis, Sara Cieniewski, & Josh Birenbaum, *The Smart Money: When a Private Equity Minority Investment Can Be Better Than a Bank Loan (and What about a Family Office?)*, 20 THE J. OF PRIV. EQUITY 21 (2016). "In particular, companies that sell minority stakes seek deep knowledge about adjacent industry subsectors and expertise about how to spur growth in new regions. Sellers also place a high value on expertise in mergers and acquisitions and initial public offerings." Antoon Schneider & Cristina Henrik, *Private Equity Minority Investments: Can Less Be More?*, BCG (APRIL 2, 2015), https://www.bcg.com/publications/2015/private-equity-minority-investments-can-less-be-more.

96 Justin A. Casey & Gregory A. Marino, *A New Game in Town: The Rise of Private Equity and Institutional Investment in Sports*, FOLEY (November 11, 2020), https://www.foley.com/en/insights/publications/2020/11/private-equity-institutional-investment-sports.

97 Sam Carp, *Serie A Accepts CVC-led €1.7bn Bid to Move Closer to Private Equity Investment*, SPORTSPRO MEDIA (November 20, 2020), https://www.sportspromedia.com/news/serie-a-cvc-advent-fsi-private-equity-offer-accepted-media-rights-business.

98 Sam Carp, *Report: Bundesliga's Overseas Media Rights Attracting Private Equity Interest*, SPORTSPRO MEDIA (November 25, 2020), https://www.sportspromedia.com/news/bundesliga-international-media-rights-private-equity-advent-bc-partners.

99 Sam Carp, *Report: Bundesliga's Overseas Media Rights Attracting Private Equity Interest*, SPORTSPRO MEDIA (November 25, 2020), https://www.sportspromedia.com/news/bundesliga-international-media-rights-private-equity-advent-bc-partners.

demonstrating the high level of sophisticated interest in being a part of these types of deals. That interest in owning leagues' media rights extends to other countries, as well: TPG Capital, which has offices in Fort Worth and San Francisco, submitted a proposal to the English Football League earlier last year to purchase a twenty percent stake for GBP 375 million.[100] Insiders noted that TPG was primarily hoping to "install a management team to handle the EFL's broadcast and commercial rights," though the proposal was ultimately rejected.[101] And France's rugby league was in discussions with London-based private equity firm Novalpina, which is looking to acquire a twenty percent stake in the commercial entity that owns its broadcast and sponsorship rights.[102] Going forward, increased securitization in European sports may further shift how teams and leagues approach their media rights, including incentivizing teams or leagues to "build 'in-house' media broadcasting companies backed by institutional capital" and/or offer "direct-to-consumer … content to fans on a subscription basis, bypassing traditional broadcast network middlemen."[103]

Third, private equity's investment in European sports teams has led to innovations in deal structures and organizational structures that improve the efficiency of both franchises and the industry as a whole. These innovations include the growing use of industry-specific earnout clauses and partnerships between teams and technology start-ups. Unlike American leagues, European leagues nearly always incorporate the concepts of "relegation" and "promotion," by which the worst teams at the end of the season are shunted off to a lower league, and top teams in those lower leagues are moved up to compete at a higher level. To sum up the challenge this creates for teams, "[t]here is a lot of competition for very few spots."[104]

---

100 *Baldwin to Depart as EFL Chief, £375m Private Equity Proposal "Rejected,"* SPORTBUSINESS (October 13, 2020), https://www.sportbusiness.com/news/baldwin-to-depart-as-efl-chief-375m-private-equity-proposal-rejected/.

101 *Baldwin to Depart as EFL Chief, £375m Private Equity Proposal "Rejected,"* SPORTBUSINESS (October 13, 2020), https://www.sportbusiness.com/news/baldwin-to-depart-as-efl-chief-375m-private-equity-proposal-rejected/.

102 Martin Ross, *LNR Pursues Private Equity Talks, but "Not Just to Pay Off Clubs' Debts,"* SPORTBUSINESS (September 20, 2020), https://www.sportbusiness.com/news/lnr-pursues-private-equity-talks-but-not-just-to-pay-off-clubs-debts/.

103 Justin A. Casey & Gregory A. Marino, *A New Game in Town: The Rise of Private Equity and Institutional Investment in Sports*, FOLEY (November 11, 2020), https://www.foley.com/en/insights/publications/2020/11/private-equity-institutional-investment-sports.

104 Jonathan Dyson, *How Football Clubs Can Cash in on the Game's Changing Investment Landscape*, SPORTBUSINESS (July 8, 2019), https://www.sportbusiness.com/2019/07/how-football-clubs-can-cash-in-on-the-games-changing-investment-landscape/.

Relegation can devastate an investment in a team, with vast amounts of money spent on players or a storied history of being in the highest league being no guarantee of how any future season will end:[105]

> Painful case in point: Fulham owner Shahid Khan, who also owns the NFL's Jacksonville Jaguars, spent $130 million on new players only to see his [2019] season end [last] spring in relegation. Dropped to a lower level of competition, this can cut into potential revenues and expose the team ownership to added business risk, including limited access to capital, simply based on how the team plays.[106]

On a brighter note, the possibility of promotion stands as a potential upside.[107] To deal with both sides of this risk, private equity investors are increasingly building earnout clauses into their purchase contracts by which "a certain portion of the purchase price—typically 20 to 30 per cent—[is] held back and provided only if the club meets certain 'relegation/promotion metrics'."[108] Premier League club Aston Villa is a positive example of such a clause: In 2018, Egyptian group NWSE purchased "a controlling 55-per-cent stake in the club" before it won promotion back to the Premier League in May of 2019; that promotion triggered

105 Matthew Eisler, *Opinion: Investors Who Want to Buy Sports Teams Look to Europe, Not the U.S.*, MARKETWATCH (August 16, 2019, 12:05 PM), https://www.marketwatch.com/story/investors-who-want-to-buy-sports-teams-look-to-europe-not-the-us-2019-08-16.

106 Matthew Eisler, *Opinion: Investors Who Want to Buy Sports Teams Look to Europe, Not the U.S.*, MARKETWATCH (August 16, 2019, 12:05 PM), https://www.marketwatch.com/story/investors-who-want-to-buy-sports-teams-look-to-europe-not-the-us-2019-08-16. Another English team, Swansea City, "were relegated from the Premier League in 2017–18 after seven consecutive seasons in the top flight. A consortium of American businesspeople had acquired a controlling 68-per-cent stake in the club in July 2016." Jonathan Dyson, *How Football Clubs Can Cash in on the Game's Changing Investment Landscape*, SPORTBUSINESS (July 8, 2019), https://www.sportbusiness.com/2019/07/how-football-clubs-can-cash-in-on-the-games-changing-investment-landscape/.

107 Matthew Eisler, *Opinion: Investors Who Want to Buy Sports Teams Look to Europe, Not the U.S.*, MARKETWATCH (August 16, 2019, 12:05 PM), https://www.marketwatch.com/story/investors-who-want-to-buy-sports-teams-look-to-europe-not-the-us-2019-08-16.

108 Jonathan Dyson, *How Football Clubs Can Cash in on the Game's Changing Investment Landscape*, SPORTBUSINESS (July 8, 2019), https://www.sportbusiness.com/2019/07/how-football-clubs-can-cash-in-on-the-games-changing-investment-landscape/.

the remainder of the purchase price to be paid.[109] Other new clauses are also appearing, though not all are in leagues' or teams' best interests: The aforementioned deal for the media rights of Italy's Serie A was nearly derailed, it was revealed, because the private equity groups had moved to insert a "breakaway" clause that would release them from their investment obligations if a rival elite European soccer league was launched.[110]

On the organizational side, leagues and teams are also using their brands and other resources to: (1) launch in-house partnerships with sports/technology start-ups, many of which are backed by private equity money; (2) invest directly in private equity funds that are focused on sports start-ups; or (3) form stand-alone private investment funds concentrated on such start-ups.[111] In 2019, for example, the Union of European Football Associations (UEFA) announced that it had selected three tech start-ups to partner with as a part of its inaugural start-up challenge.[112] Also in 2019, Manchester City owner City Football Group was named the anchor investor in the new, USD 115 million sports venture fund Sapphire Sport,[113] and La Liga mega-club Barcelona launched its own USD 112 million investment fund with the stated goal of "creating a testbed for new technologies" that would benefit from the "knowledge and expertise of [Barcelona's] staff."[114]

Finally—and perhaps most compelling for the truly *invested* sports fan—private equity investment in Europe is moving the sports industry toward more widespread public ownership and trading of teams. Globally, publicly traded teams are still a relative rarity for three primary reasons:

---

109 Jonathan Dyson, *How Football Clubs Can Cash in on the Game's Changing Investment Landscape*, SPORTBUSINESS (July 8, 2019), https://www.sportbusiness.com/2019/07/how-football-clubs-can-cash-in-on-the-games-changing-investment-landscape/.

110 Sam Carp, *Serie A Accepts CVC-led €1.7bn Bid to Move Closer to Private Equity Investment*, SPORTSPRO MEDIA (November 20, 2020), https://www.sportspromedia.com/news/serie-a-cvc-advent-fsi-private-equity-offer-accepted-media-rights-business.

111 Susie Jarrold, *How Sports Clubs Are Investing into Tech Start-ups*, LAWINSPORT (June 19, 2019), https://www.lawinsport.com/topics/contract-law/item/how-sports-clubs-are-investing-into-tech-start-ups?category_id=117.

112 Andrew Cohen, *UEFA Innovation Hub Selects Three Tech Startups as Partners*, SPORTTECHIE (October 21, 2019), https://sporttechie.com/uefa-innovation-hub-tech-startups-wsc-sports-formalytics-livelike.

113 Sam Carp, *Man City Owner CFG Leads US$115m Sapphire Sport Investment*, SPORTSPRO (January 29, 2019), https://www.sportspromedia.com/news/man-city-owner-cfg-sapphire-sport-investment-fund.

114 Sam Carp, *Report: Barcelona Seek €100m for Startup Investment Fund*, SPORTSPRO (March 8, 2019), https://www.sportspromedia.com/news/barcelona-news-technology-startup-investment-fund.

First, public ownership of teams makes it more difficult for leagues to exercise close control over franchises. Second, teams and leagues are generally averse to the increased disclosure requirements and financial transparency that would result from public ownership.[115] And, third, large publicly held corporations have much more difficulty in clearing league ownership approval processes than smaller, closely held corporations, families, or individuals. Still, despite the many different aspects about sports that interest private equity groups, they are, at the end of the day, on the hunt for profits, and profits often require "public exits of private investments."[116] Europe also provides examples in this arena, with portions of internationally renowned teams such as Manchester United and Juventus, among many others, already structured as publicly traded entities: Manchester United Plc, the Cayman Island entity that owns the club, has been listed on the New York Stock Exchange since August 10, 2012,[117] and Juventus FC S.P.A. is listed on Borsa Italiana in Milan where it has been trading since 2001.[118] As the industry continues to mature, European sports will likely provide more examples of just what these long-term relationships between sports entities and private equity will look like, especially when those relationships include long-term public ownership.

---

115 Sam Carp, *Report: Barcelona Seek €100m for Startup Investment Fund*, SPORTSPRO (March 8, 2019), https://www.sportspromedia.com/news/barcelona-news-technology-startup-investment-fund.

116 Justin A. Casey & Gregory A. Marino, *A New Game in Town: The Rise of Private Equity and Institutional Investment in Sports*, FOLEY (November 11, 2020), https://www.foley.com/en/insights/publications/2020/11/private-equity-institutional-investment-sports.

117 *Investor Relations*, MANUTD.COM (last visited December 3, 2020), https://ir.manutd.com/investor-faqs.aspx#:~:text=Manchester%20United%20plc%20is%20listed,plc%20is%20the%20Glazer%20family. Manchester United was technically publicly listed beginning in 1991, but a take-private transaction by the Glazer family in 2005 removed the team from the public markets before it was relisted in 2012. *Glazer ownership of Manchester United*, WIKIPEDIA (last visited December 3, 2020), https://en.wikipedia.org/wiki/Glazer_ownership_of_Manchester_United#Red_Knights_takeover_plans.

118 *Juventus at a Glance*, JUVENTUS (last visited December 3, 2020), https://www.juventus.com/en/club/investor-relations/investing-in-juventus/juventus-glance#:~:text=Juventus%20shares%20are%20listed%20on,63.8%25%20of%20the%20share%20capital.

The Argument for Private Equity Investment in American Sports

Opening American professional sports to private equity investment will prove to be an overwhelmingly positive development for both the leagues and their de facto stakeholders—the fans. In line with the example provided by European leagues and teams, onlookers can expect to see private equity tweak its standard operating procedures in order to be the long-term partner that leagues are both hoping for and, occasionally, demanding. Beyond timelines, however, private equity promises to reshape the American sports industry when it comes to franchises' minority stakes; innovation in deals and structures, particularly with regards to leagues' media; and the ongoing development of opportunities for public ownership. These developments will benefit American sports by increasing the value of and competition for franchise and league equity; producing owners who better fit with their league or team; giving birth to efficiency-enhancing innovations; improving industry governance and structure; and reducing the threat posed by well-funded competitors. As was done in "Private Equity's Investment in European Sports", this chapter treats each potential development in turn.

First, we can expect to see private equity operate in American sports on an extended exit timeline (ten years or more), with related focuses on good governance and aligning fund priorities with those of the team/league. Even with the relatively constricted opportunities available to funds interested in the MLB and NBA, these shifts are already apparent: Arctos and Dyal, mentioned earlier, are both "understood to invest either out of permanent capital vehicles or are able to hold assets for longer periods."[119] Indeed, as seen in Figure 7.1, Arctos' website lists being a long-term partner as a core tenet of their investing strategy. In Dyal's case, investors are subject to a seven-year lock-up period before they have any options to redeem their stake.[120] Such a structure is consistent with the NBA's focus on using private equity to create "a new pool of long-term investors."[121] At

119 Adam Le & Alex Lynn, *The New Playbook: How Private Equity Fell in Love with Sport*, PRIV. EQUITY INT'L (November 3, 2020), https://www.privateequityinternational.com/the-new-playbook-how-private-equity-fell-in-love-with-sport/.

120 Adam Le & Alex Lynn, *The New Playbook: How Private Equity Fell in Love with Sport*, PRIV. EQUITY INT'L (November 3, 2020), https://www.privateequityinternational.com/the-new-playbook-how-private-equity-fell-in-love-with-sport/.

121 Scott Soshnick, *NBA Considers Creating Investment Vehicle to Buy Stakes in Teams*, BLOOMBERG (September 2, 2019, 10:00 PM), https://www.bloomberg.com/news/

its foundation, the league's focus on the long term is about control: One anonymous source noted that "leagues and their partners don't want partners who want or expect significant control or influence … What leagues want is long-term, passive, financial partners."[122]

Other evidence of the shift to more long-term, collaborative investment strategies comes from the PE executives themselves. George Pyne, of New York City-based Bruin Sports Capital, has publicly stated that investing in sports *requires* a long-term approach because value creation in the industry comes from the increase in the value of media rights, "which are typically secured in long-term, complex agreements."[123] He added further that "[i]nvesting in and around that ecosystem necessitates a long-term approach to maximizing returns … If you enter into this space with a sell-by date, you can wind up making decisions that will ultimately stunt your gains."[124] As predicted in connection with the European market, firms in the U.S. have been quick to recognize that long-term strategies will be crucial to both entering the industry and having success once they have arrived.

---

articles/2019-09-03/nba-weighs-creation-of-investment-vehicle-to-buy-shares-of-teams. The head of Dyal also was quoted as saying that sports investments are "very long-dated, sticky assets." Adam Le & Alex Lynn, *The New Playbook: How Private Equity Fell in Love with Sport*, PRIV. EQUITY INT'L (November 3, 2020), https://www.privateequityinternational.com/the-new-playbook-how-private-equity-fell-in-love-with-sport/.

122 Adam Le & Alex Lynn, *The New Playbook: How Private Equity Fell in Love with Sport*, PRIV. EQUITY INT'L (November 3, 2020), https://www.privateequityinternational.com/the-new-playbook-how-private-equity-fell-in-love-with-sport/.

123 Adam Le & Alex Lynn, *The New Playbook: How Private Equity Fell in Love with Sport*, PRIV. EQUITY INT'L (November 3, 2020), https://www.privateequityinternational.com/the-new-playbook-how-private-equity-fell-in-love-with-sport/.

124 Adam Le & Alex Lynn, *The New Playbook: How Private Equity Fell in Love with Sport*, PRIV. EQUITY INT'L (November 3, 2020), https://www.privateequityinternational.com/the-new-playbook-how-private-equity-fell-in-love-with-sport/. Bruin's website, similar to Arctos', describes their value proposition as follows: "We approach things differently than the investor/operator who relies on financial engineering for short term time horizons to manufacture growth. Instead, our mission is to be a value-adding partner that brings a unique combination of resources, skills, and expertise. Our value-proposition of long-term capital, industry expertise, operational experience, global resources, and a genuinely collaborative approach was designed to be the rocket fuel for growth in this era of transformation and innovation." *Built for Now*, BRUIN CAPITAL, https://bruincptl.com/approach (last visited April 12, 2021).

Figure 7.1 Arctos Sports Partners Investment Strategy[125]

Opening American leagues more broadly to private equity investment will also increase competition for minority ownership, which—besides providing owners much-needed liquidity—will drive team/league values, and thus current ownership stakes, higher. Not all of the same impetuses for minority investment exist in the U.S. Most significantly, American leagues' restrictions on leverage leave teams with less need for cash to keep team balance sheets healthy when compared to their European counterparts. However, as leagues continue to raise acceptable debt limits, this need will increase. And the entry of private equity promises to backstop higher debt loads with limited risk to sports organizations' control, as funds are largely barred from acquiring majority ownership interests. Increased competition for equity will also enable teams and leagues to be more selective when choosing new partners, allowing them to find those that fit best with their organization's values and provide a high level of industry expertise. As seen in Europe, industry expertise is one of the primary benefits of having private equity on board in any capacity, particularly when the team or league faces difficult market conditions as with COVID-19. The difference between owners that know what they are doing versus

125 Source: *Our Strategy*, ARCTOS (last visited April 10, 2021), https://arctospartners.com/strategy/?gclid=Cj0KCQjwmcWDBhCOARIsALgJ2QeqGi3_EjDHGkqXBTxnVEP9b2InhWrXCa0lq0wnQrHbXcgpm0Zv5hgaAu72EALw_wcB.

those who are merely rich enough to buy in can be stark, and occasionally dangerous, no matter how storied the franchise.[126]

In terms of innovation, private equity interest in American sports will undoubtedly lead to more complex and pioneering structures within deal documents and, at first, within organizations. In fact, when it comes to the American market, leagues here could quickly leapfrog their European counterparts since American teams and leagues have, for a time, had an active interest in developing businesses beyond those playing on the field or the court. The Atlanta Braves, for example, partnered with the fifth largest tech hub in the U.S.—Atlanta Tech Village—in 2016,[127] while the NBA combined with Intel in 2018 to invest in technology start-ups around the world "that have the potential to impact the future of sports and entertainment from both an athlete and fan perspective."[128] The best example, though, comes from Major League Baseball, whose in-house Baseball Advanced Media is a USD 5-billion-plus technology success story based in New York City.[129] Baseball Advanced Media represents another way in which the American leagues are surpassing their European counterparts by offering direct-to-consumer subscription streaming services either on top of broadcast networks' live airings or by bypassing traditional broadcast networks altogether. Other innovations, such as the new types of industry-specific clauses in deal documents seen in Europe, are only likely to emerge in conjunction with expanded opportunities for private equity ownership of sports entities.

When it comes to public ownership of sports teams, American leagues do not have as clear a path to widespread public ownership and trading as those in Europe—but publicly owned teams are still likely in the cards. While only the NFL outright prohibits public (corporate) ownership of

---

126 *See*, e.g., Molly Knight, *How the Dodgers Went from Mismanaged Failure to One of the Most Valuable Teams in Sports*, VANITY FAIR (July 9, 2015), https://www.vanityfair.com/culture/2015/07/the-best-team-money-can-buy-los-angeles-dodgers.

127 Phil W. Hudson, *Atlanta Braves Partner with Atlanta Tech Village*, ATLANTA BUS. CHRON.(July 19, 2016), https://www.bizjournals.com/atlanta/news/2016/07/19/exclusive-atlanta-braves-partner-with-atlanta-tech.html.

128 Sam Carp, *NBA Partners with Intel Capital to Invest in Technology Startups*, SPORTSPRO (May 9, 2018), https://www.sportspromedia.com/news/nba-investment-partnership-intel-capital-technology-startups.

129 Ben Popper, *The Changeup: How Baseball's Tech Team Built the Future of Television*, THE VERGE (last visited December 11, 2020), https://www.theverge.com/2015/8/4/9090897/mlb-bam-live-streaming-internet-tv-nhl-hbo-now-espn.

teams,[130] leagues in the U.S. have "generally prioritized the privacy and centralized control afforded by private ownership over the fundraising potential of an IPO—which brings with it the disclosure requirements and associated costs of complying with SEC and listing exchange rules."[131] This is in part because the more profitable American leagues also do not need the cash an IPO would raise as badly as European leagues, and if private equity firms are limited to minority ownership for the time being, this trend would seem set to continue. Some onlookers, though, believe that:

> [t]his attitude could rapidly change ... as institutional investors more accustomed to bringing companies public continue to flood into sports. It will be increasingly difficult for leagues to argue that entities valued in the billions of dollars lack the cash or bandwidth to undertake regulatory compliance, and even more difficult to deny the wishes of investors that helped drive such valuations.[132]

Indeed, with the meteoric rise of SPACs—including SPACs, like RedBall, intent on acquiring sports teams or team ownership groups—this could change *very* quickly. As private equity investment in sports increases so will the pressure to exit publicly at some point down the road. This pressure could be tempered by team and league stakeholders' expectations for a long-term partner and their restrictions on majority ownership. However, keeping private equity from being able to control franchises in marquee leagues is unlikely to be in the long-term best interest of those leagues for reasons discussed in the next paragraph. If funds are allowed to control teams (and the public's past reception of private equity ownership is any

---

130 Patrick G. Quick, Kevin R. Schulz, & Jeremy R. Polk, *Sports Industry Practice Guide*, Lexis Practice Advisor, https://www.foley.com/-/media/files/insights/publications/2018/05/foleys-sports-industry-practice-guide-published/files/sports-industry-practice-guide/fileattachment/sports-industry-practice-guide.pdf (last visited April 8, 2021). The NFL's Green Bay Packers have been publicly owned since 1923 and are currently held by 360,760 owners representing 5,011,558 shares; the team remains the only exception, however, as a result of being grandfathered into the current rules regime. *Id.*

131 Justin A. Casey & Gregory A. Marino, *A New Game in Town: The Rise of Private Equity and Institutional Investment in Sports*, Foley (November 11, 2020), https://www.foley.com/en/insights/publications/2020/11/private-equity-institutional-investment-sports.

132 Justin A. Casey & Gregory A. Marino, *A New Game in Town: The Rise of Private Equity and Institutional Investment in Sports*, Foley (November 11, 2020), https://www.foley.com/en/insights/publications/2020/11/private-equity-institutional-investment-sports.

guide to the future), they will likely face increased public suspicion of their motives and calls for financial transparency. The easiest way to soothe stakeholder demands—and exit—might simply be traditional public disclosure requirements.

Conclusion

Regardless, leagues should think deeply and be proactive about opening up further opportunities for private equity investment, including majority ownership. Being proactive about such changes means that they will happen on the league's own terms. Even in the more mature American sports market, further private equity ownership will likely accelerate teams' progress toward increased "financial discipline, operational excellence, proper business planning, data-driven decision-making, customer satisfaction and professional management that will strengthen the industry as a whole."[133] Moreover, in the end, leagues' decisions about whether to open their gates to opportunities for control over franchises may be the determining factor in how the sports landscape looks in the very near future. If the NFL or other leagues continue to eschew accepting private equity money—or restrict investment to a single, limited fund as in the case of the NBA[134]—the funds may find that they are better off supporting, or even forming, a rival league. A prime example is the XFL, which was purchased in August 2020 by a group led by RedBird Capital Partners and Actor Dwayne "The Rock" Johnson.[135] The Raines Group also recently proposed forming a professional golf organization—the Premier Golf

133 N3XT admin, *Private Equity: Why Smart Money Continues Coming into Sports*, N3XT SPORTS (August 10, 2020), https://www.n3xtsports.com/private-equity. This is hardly impartial, coming from a group that has a clear stake in wanting private equity to invest more in sports. However, I think the language accurately summarizes some of the key benefits private equity can bring to leagues, as explored throughout this chapter.

134 Adam Le & Alex Lynn, *The New Playbook: How Private Equity Fell in Love with Sport*, PRIV. EQUITY INT'L (November 3, 2020), https://www.privateequityinternational.com/the-new-playbook-how-private-equity-fell-in-love-with-sport/.

135 RedBird Capital Partners LLC, *Dany Garcia, Dwayne Johnson and RedBird Capital Partners Acquire the XFL*, GLOBENEWSWIRE (August 3, 2020, 9:48 PM), https://www.globenewswire.com/news-release/2020/08/03/2071787/0/en/Dany-Garcia-Dwayne-Johnson-and-RedBird-Capital-Partners-Acquire-the-XFL.html.

League—which would compete directly with the PGA Tour.[136] When the PGA Tour recently approached the European Tour about signing a strategic alliance, negotiations were thrown off because the Raines Group launched a lightning-fast, nearly successful competing bid.[137] This highlights one final danger: Unless American leagues open their gates a little wider to the "barbarians," private equity may decide it is better off investing its vast expertise and resources in teams and leagues in Europe—or other markets around the world.[138]

136 The Daily Upside, *Golf Goes Global*, DEALBREAKER (December 2, 2020), https://dealbreaker.com/2020/11/tdu-pga-european-tour-partnership. "The PGL, for short, would host 'highly-lucrative,' limited-field tournaments with a team element. But the proposed tour was dealt a blow in March when Rory McIlroy, Jon Rahm and Brooks Koepka—at the time the top three ranked players in the world—all publicly rejected the PGL. McIlroy said he objected to its source of financing, which was an investment fund controlled by Saudi Arabia." *Id.*

137 The Daily Upside, *Golf Goes Global*, DEALBREAKER (December 2, 2020), https://dealbreaker.com/2020/11/tdu-pga-european-tour-partnership. "The PGL, for short, would host 'highly-lucrative,' limited-field tournaments with a team element. But the proposed tour was dealt a blow in March when Rory McIlroy, Jon Rahm and Brooks Koepka—at the time the top three ranked players in the world—all publicly rejected the PGL. McIlroy said he objected to its source of financing, which was an investment fund controlled by Saudi Arabia." *Id.*

138 Even Europe, however, is not without its reservations about private equity ownership. There, firms are pushing for greater and greater control of the league itself, as evidenced by firms that were looking to invest in the German Bundesliga backing off due to concerns over how "little influence" they would have over the "league itself."

Murad Ahmed, Kaye Wiggins & Jamie Smyth, *Private Equity's New Bet on Sport: Buy the League*, FINANCIAL TIMES (January 20, 2021), https://www.ft.com/content/24e9fc43-4187-4884-8efe-7a6efb496f24.

Securities Market Regulation Theories and Perspectives on Their Improvement

Otabek Narziev
Doctor of Law, Legal and Regulatory Advisor, Head of Department at Tashkent State Law University, Tashkent, Uzbekistan

Introduction

This chapter attempts to focus on the importance and role of Securities Market Regulation (SMR) theory in the organization and development of active securities markets. According to a relatively extensive study on regulation and growth, which analyzed business regulation across 135 countries, "government regulation of business is an important determinant of growth," "the impact of improving regulations is large," and "countries should put priority on reforming their business regulations when designing growth policies."[1]

The consensus is that regulation is crucial to achieving and maintaining an efficient and fair securities market nationally, regionally, and globally. The securities market needs comprehensive regulation because of its institutional (market), contextual (functional features, unique relations and so on), formal features and the propensity for intermediaries to maximize their income at the cost of investors. The need for regulation in the securities market is more pressing than commodity and real estate markets because of several specific characters of the securities market. These features mostly relate to financial instruments.[2] Every stage of financial instruments starting from their origin (issuance and registration), existence (circulation), and their annulment, requires the direct involvement of legal institutions, rules, and procedures. In the case of other market products, such as commodities, economic factors prevail over legal factors. In general, commodities can be produced and put into circulation without the

1 Simeon Djankov, Caralee McLiesh and Rita Maria Ramalho, "Regulation and Growth," *Economics Letters* 92, no. 3 (2006): 4-5.
2 The phrase of financial instruments here refers to all kind of stocks (including equities, bonds, options, and futures) that might be the object of transactions in the securities market.

direct involvement of legal institutions, rules, and procedures.[3] However, in the case of financial instruments, this is less so due to the unique economic and legal nature of financial instruments and the high systemic risk that can be generated through these instruments. Hence why the design and implementation of effective regulation of such markets with unusual objects, subjects, and relations should be based on a sound theoretical framework, which will provide an ideological basis for regulation and reforms achieving investor protection and lowering the cost of capital of issuers. For proving this statement, it is enough to look back and consider the consequences of the "deregulation stream" just in the last two decades, with a particular focus on the latest financial/economic crisis and the contributions of SMR theory. There are many studies and opinions following the crisis. Nobel Prize scholar Joseph Stiglitz wrote perhaps the most generally accepted view on this matter:

> many of most popular micro- and macro-economic theories aided and abetted regulators, investors, bankers, and policy makers—they provided the 'rationale' for their policies and actions. They made the bankers believe that, in pursuing individual self-interest, they were advancing the well-being of society; they made the regulators think that in pursuing policies of benign neglect, they were allowing the private sector to flourish, from which all would benefit.[4]

A light touch to regulation only ends in losses for issuers, investors, consumers, employees and taxpayers and a belief that inflated unregulated issuance and trading volumes is the norm rather than the exception. Lessons are drawn from the recent financial crisis, and the aim of avoiding such catastrophes in the future places considerable challenges before scholars and professionals on SMR to reconsider the ideological agenda that underpins it, and to provide suitable perspectives based on the realities of current conditions. To such end, a brief overview of theories that directly affect SMR follows where the main problems are highlighted, and a series of proposals are presented for the improvement of SMR.

---

3 Except for certification and standardization, ecological and other necessary procedures, which are common practice for some products and services.

4 Joseph E. Stiglitz, "The Anatomy of a Murder: Who Killed the American Economy?," in *What Caused the Financial Crisis*, ed. Jeffrey Friedman (Pennsylvania: University of Pennsylvania, 2011), 144.

Overview of Basic Approaches

Securities market relations and issues concerning their regulation, by their nature and essence, are interdisciplinary matters that are primarily studied in the fields of economics, the emerging field of behavioral economics and the law but are adopted and often interfered with by Governmental policy makers. The development of the securities market, the enhancement of financial instruments, the emergence of various market intermediaries and participants, and the rising necessity on effectiveness and fairness in securities market relations require laws and regulations to be brought closer with economics and the market. In this sense, Cooter and other scholars mention that the "law needs economics to understand its behavioral consequences, and economics needs law to understand the underpinnings of markets."[5]

The scope of theories that treat law and economics issues is quite broad, but very few theories concern securities market relationships. This brief overview of such theories concerns those directly related to SMRs—namely, the *efficient market hypothesis* (EMH), *behavioral economics*, the *economic dynamics of law*, and the *social business initiative.*

Microeconomic Approach: Efficient Market Hypothesis

The EMH[6] is the basic concept of economic analysis of law,[7] which aims to explain and predict the behavior of market participants to ensure efficiency (positive theory),[8] and to use incentives and political instruments for changing their behavior for ensuring justice (normative theory).[9]

---

5 Robert Cooter and Thomas Ulen, *Law, and Economics* (Berkeley: Berkeley Law Books, 6th Edition, 2016), 24, http://scholarship.law.berkeley.edu/books/2.

6 In some literature this notion is cited as *efficient capital market hypothesis* (ECMH). *See* Burton G. Malkiel and Eugene F. Fama, "Efficient Capital Markets: A Review of Theory and Empirical Work," *The Journal of Finance* 25, no. 2 (1970): 383-417.

7 The history of economic interpretation of law goes back to the eighteenth century CE when Adam Smith wrote about the economic effect of legislation on merchants and commerce. However, the beginning of the modern school of law and economics is often placed in the 1960s. For details, *see*: Robert Cooter and Thomas Ulen, *Law, and Economics* (Berkeley: Berkeley Law Books, 6th Edition, 2016), 24, http://scholarship.law.berkeley.edu/books/2.

8 The positive approach to the economic analysis of law seeks to understand how the behavior of people is affected by incentives created by the law. This approach uses the analogy of the law as a type of pricing machine. The law "prices" various forms of human behavior through the use of fines, penalties, and other measures. For details, *see*: Richard A. Posner, *Economic Analysis of Law* (Wolters Kluwer Law & Business, 2014).

9 The normative approach to the economic analysis of law proposes an efficiency criterion for shaping the legal system based on wealth maximization. In the legal context, this approach asks how much each would be willing to pay to either get rid of

Nobel Prize-winning economist Eugene Fama who argued that stocks always trade at their fair value, making it impossible for investors to purchase undervalued stocks either or sell shares for inflated prices, put the EMH forth in the early 1960s.[10] Some scholars state that the origin of the EMH can also be traced back to the work of Paul A. Samuelson. They point out that Fama and Samuelson independently developed the same basic notion of market efficiency from two slightly different research agendas.[11]

The EMH states that asset prices fully reflect all available information, and therefore there are no undervalued or overvalued stocks because the amount in the stock exchange is the fair value of that particular stock. According to the EMH, it is impossible for investors to either purchase undervalued stocks or sell shares for inflated prices.

Initially asserting the efficiency of U.S. capital markets,[12] the EMH has occupied a significant place in the economics and finance literature since the 1960s,[13] also has a strong presence in the contemporary culture of securities regulation.[14] Belief in the EMH has led Chicago School of Law and Economics scholars, especially those studying financial markets, to conclude that markets are self-correcting and therefore in little need of regulation.[15] However, severe criticisms of the belief in efficient and

---

or keep specific laws or rules. For details, *see*: Richard A. Posner, "Utilitarianism, Economics, and Legal Theory," *The Journal of Legal Studies* 8, no. 1 (1979): 103-140.

10 Later Chicago School of Law and Economics scholars developed this hypothesis. *See* Richard A. Posner, *Economic Analysis of Law* (Boston: Little, Brown, University of Chicago Law School, 1972), 415.

11 *See* Andrew W. Lo, "Efficient Markets Hypothesis," in *The New Palgrave: A Dictionary of Economics*, eds. L. Blume, S. Durlauf (2nd Edition, Palgrave Macmillan Ltd., 2007), https://ssrn.com/abstract=991509.

12 *See* Christopher Paul Saari, "The Efficient Capital Market Hypothesis, Economic Theory and the Regulation of the Securities Industry," *Stanford Law Review* 29, no. 5 (1977): 1031-1076.

13 In the early 1960s economists Ronald Coase and Guido Calabresi working independently from one another published two articles, "The Problem of Social Cost" and "Some Thoughts on Risk Distribution and the Law of Torts," respectively, that revolutionized legal theory and laid the foundation for many of the ideas that were developed in the following years. The movement gained further ground with the publication of Chicago University Professor Richard A. Posner's "Economic Analysis of Law." This work led to an era of economic principles being applied to all aspects of the law, referred to as the "Chicago School of Thought."

14 *See* Donald C. Langevoort, "Theories, Assumptions, and Securities Regulation: Market Efficiency Revisited," *University of Pennsylvania Law Review* 140, no. 3 (1992): 851-920.

15 For further details, *see*: Lynn A. Stout, "Are Stock Markets Costly Casinos? Disagreement, Market Failure, and Securities Regulation," *Virginia Law Review* 81, no. 3 (April 1995): 611-712.

rational markets also exist.[16] According to Lo, even after several decades of research and numerous published studies, economists have yet to reach consensus on whether markets—particularly financial markets—are, in fact, efficient.[17] Opponents of the EMH also question the pure practical rationality of market participants pointing out an existence and sometimes prevailing irrational component in their behavior. As evidence, they cite the securities market crash in late 1987 when stock prices seriously deviated from their fair values.[18]

Another scholar Chang also questions the credibility of this EMH by stating that: "individually rational actions can lead to the collective irrational outcome,"[19] and supports his statement with concrete cases and theoretical arguments. Notably, he mentions a compelling story of two Nobel Prize economists—Robert Merton and Myron Scholes—[20] whose free market concept and practice failed twice, hurting investors and industry.[21] At the end of his critic analysis, Chang poses the following reasonable question:

> When the Nobel Prize winners in financial economics, top bankers, high flying fund managers, prestigious colleges and the smartest celebrities have shown that they don't understand what they are doing, how can we accept economic theories that work only because

---

16 For instance, a detailed analysis could be found in Professor Langevoort's papers. For details, *see*: Donald C. Langevoort, "Theories, Assumptions, and Securities Regulation: Market Efficiency Revisited," *University of Pennsylvania Law Review* 140, no. 3 (1992), 851-920; and Donald C. Langevoort, "Taming the Animal Spirits of the Stock Markets: A Behavioral Approach to Securities Regulation," *Northwestern University Law Review* 97 (2002): 135.

17 *See* Andrew W. Lo, "Efficient Markets Hypothesis," in *The New Palgrave: A Dictionary of Economics*, eds. L. Blume, S. Durlauf (2nd Edition, Palgrave Macmillan Ltd., 2007), https://ssrn.com/abstract=991509.

18 *See* details in Burton G. Malkiel, "Is the Stock Market Efficient?." *Science* 243, no. 4896 (1989): 1313-1318.

19 *See* details in Ha-Joon Chang, *23 Things They Don't Tell You about Capitalism* (USA: Bloomsbury Publishing, 2012), 170.

20 In 1997, these two scholars were awarded the Nobel Prize in economics for their "new method to determine the value of derivatives." In 1998, a considerable hedge fund, the Long-Term Capital Management (LTCM), went bankrupt following the Russian financial crisis. It was founded in 1994 and the two Nobel Prize scholars were on its board of directors. Another failure case is connected to the Platinum Grove Asset Management (PGAM) hedge fund, which was founded in 1999 again by these two scholars. In late 2008 this hedge fund also went bust, temporarily freezing investor withdrawal. For further details, *see*: Ha-Joon Chang, *23 Things They Don't Tell You about Capitalism* (USA: Bloomsbury Publishing, 2012), 170-173.

21 *Ibid.*

> they assume that people are fully rational? The upshot is that we are not smart enough to leave the market alone. We need regulation exactly because we are not smart enough.[22]

The diversity of opposing arguments on EMH makes it burdensome to compile a list of all positive and negative views on EMH. Moreover, this would be outside the scope of this research. The reason for analyzing some key criticisms of EMH is to show that there is room for improvement concerning EMH theory—it should be reconsidered from all angles—microeconomic, macroeconomic, legal and social angles. Next, there will be a brief overview of one of the leading macro approaches that seriously questions the EMH.

Macroeconomic Approach: Economic Dynamics of Law

The economic dynamics of law is a relatively new theory that offers a new vision of law as fundamentally a macro-level enterprise establishing normative commitments and a framework for numerous private transactions, rather than as an analogous to a market transaction. Professor David Driesen proposes the main ideas of this approach in a 2012 book[23] and in a 2014 paper.[24]According to Driesen, the law is not a transaction as claimed by Chicago School scholars. Instead, it is a framework of rules by which deals occur. Because law aims to influence future behavior, rather than the past, its architects must often address surprise, change, and uncertainty. In other words, we must deal with the dynamics of an unknown future. For Driesen, most law is neither efficient nor inefficient. It merely provides the framework under which market actors seek to achieve practical outcomes. Hence, it is often not possible to determine whether a law is efficient. Because the statute provides a framework, it should be thought of as more closely analogous to macroeconomic policy than to the transactions that microeconomics typically focuses on.[25]

As Driesen argues, the microeconomic model of government regulation misconceives the essence of law. Government regulation produces not an immediate transaction, but a set of rules intended to influence future

---

22 *Ibid.*, 170.

23 For further details, *see*: David M. Driesen, *The Economic Dynamics of Law* (Cambridge, UK: Cambridge University Press, 2012), 250.

24 For further details, *see*: David M. Driesen, "Legal Theory Lessons from the Financial Crisis," *Journal of Corporation Law* 40 (2014): 55.

25 *Ibid.*

conduct, often for many years, or during a crisis, the modification of immediate behavior. For instance, in Sri Lanka, the regulator ordered the closure of the Colombo Stock Exchange during the first wave of the corona virus to avoid a stock market crash. Accordingly, regulation provides a framework for private resource allocation, rather than allocating the resources itself, whereas the law can mandate resource allocation. This framework performs a macroeconomic role by reducing systemic risks that might permanently modify important economic, social, and natural systems. As such, government regulation resembles monetary policy, which likewise affects, but does not control, resource allocation.[26]

According to Driesen, the law and economics, which is a microeconomic approach by its content, assume that government regulators should aim to make their decisions efficient by seeking to associate costs and benefits at the margin.[27] The Economic Dynamic approach focuses on the shape of change over time to avoid systemic risk. According to Driesen, "we cannot expect the government to make perfectly efficient decisions or ensure our future happiness, but we should, at a bare minimum, expect the government to ward off catastrophes, leaving much of the fine-tuning to private markets."[28] This approach explains how neoclassical law and economics sparked decades of deregulation culminating in the 2008 financial collapse.[29]

The dynamic economic analysis also proposes a form of institutional, economic analysis as a way to aid regulators in analyzing threats and responding efficiently. This approach requires regulators to study how relevant actors react to financial incentives, taking into account the level of bounded rationality anticipated in each group of regulated actors. Such analysis requires, in particular, consideration of countervailing incentives that may defeat legal spurs.[30]

According to Driesen, efficiency leads to an attempt to quantify, and then convert to dollar values, all of an action's consequences, to formulate "optimal" policies:

---

26 For further details, *see*: David M. Driesen *The Economic Dynamics of Law* (Cambridge, UK: Cambridge University Press, 2012), 250.

27 Speech of Driesen at the Prague Conference on Political Economy (PCPE) in 2012, https://www.youtube.com/watch?v=rQe9xNpnCco.

28 For further details, *see*: *The Economic Dynamics of Law* (Cambridge, UK: Cambridge University Press, 2012), 250.

29 For further details, *see*: David M. Driesen, "Legal Theory Lessons from the Financial Crisis," *Journal of Corporation Law* 40 (2014): 56-57.

30 For further details, *see*: David M. Driesen *The Economic Dynamics of Law* (Cambridge, UK: Cambridge University Press, 2012), 250.

> Unfortunately, cost-benefit analysis (CBA) in a strictly quantitative sense becomes impossible or incomplete and unreliable when we face important future consequences. Instead, law and economics scholars often use neoclassical economic assumptions as a proxy for CBA, because they recognize that reasonably reliable CBA of many legal decisions addressing complex dynamic problems proves impossible.[31]

The economic dynamics approach also provides a systematic method of analyzing the law's effects. It focuses on avoiding significant systemic risks (like financial crises in case of SMR). It assumes implementation of the law through a systematic analysis of its economic incentives and peoples' response to them. Accordingly, this approach could be a broadly applicable framework to adequately address neoclassical law and economics failures, such as the 2008 financial crisis.

Another instance of criticism of EMH relates to the relatively new field of study—namely, behavioral finance—that focuses on the relations between irrationality and human emotions such as fear, panic, hope, envy, confidence, and greed, in financial investment decision-making.

Behavioral Finance: "Not Only and Not Always Rational"

Behavioral finance is the branch of behavioral economics that studies the effects of psychological, cognitive, emotional, cultural, and social factors on the economic decisions of market participants. This is a relatively young and promising field of modern finance theory with remarkable progress in the last decades.[32] Behavioral finance is based on the alternative notion that investors are subject to behavioral biases, and therefore their financial decisions can be less than entirely rational.[33]

There are two main issues that behavioral finance mainly focus on: first, the reason that market participants make such irrational systematic errors that affect prices and returns, creating market inefficiencies contrary to the assumption of EMH; and, second, how do other participants take advantage of such mistakes and market inefficiencies.

---

31 For further details, *see*: David M. Driesen, "Legal Theory Lessons from the Financial Crisis," *J. Corp. L.* 40 (2014): 59.

32 *See* Felicia Ramona Birău, "The Impact of Behavioral Finance on Securities markets," *Annals of the "Constantin Brâncuşi" University of Târgu Jiu, Economy Series* 3 (2012): 45-50.

33 *See* Alistair Byrne and Mike Brooks, "Behavioral Finance: Theories and Evidence," *Research Foundation Literature Reviews* 3, no, 1 (2008): 1-26.

The most continuing critiques of the EMH turn around the preferences and behavior of market participants. Lo brings relatively detailed analysis of behavioral critics of the EMH,[34] and argues that investors are often—if not always—irrational, exhibiting predictable and financially harmful behavior.[35]

It would be better to consider behavioral finance as an alternative solution to the challenges of the EMH in explaining certain financial phenomena, rather than to treat it as a replacement of classical economic theory.[36] In the case of extreme complexity and unpredictability of contemporary securities markets, relying on only EMH and rationalism will not reflect market realities. Just the 2008 financial crisis, when "the supposedly smartest people did not truly understand what they were doing"[37] would be enough to demonstrate the role of behavioral factors in securities market relations. What is clear is that the intermediaries understood the incentives and the regulators and risk managers never understood the risks. In this regard, the best case study on all of this lack of regulation is in gold and benchmark rates like LIBOR (London Interbank Offer Rate). Why did regulators in Europe feel the need to carve out these markets from being surveilled by the first Market Abuse Directive? Both of these markets have had huge scandals because all actors knew that there was no market abuse regulation being imposed. In my opinion, the regulators were negligent.

Critical studies on economics revealed another important theory that not only provides an alternative vision to the issues under review here but also severely criticizes EMH, wealth maximization theory, and other microeconomic approaches, and proposes substantial solutions tested in

---

34 For instance, overconfidence (Fischoff and Slovic (1980); Barber and Odean (2001); Gervais and Odean (2001)), overreaction (DeBondt and Thaler (1985)), loss aversion (Kahneman and Tversky (1979)); Shefrin and Statman (1985); Odean (1998), herding (Huberman and Regev (2001)), psychological accounting (Tversky and Kahneman (1981)), miscalibration of probabilities (Lichtenstein, Fischoff and Phillips (1982)), hyperbolic discounting (Laibson (1997)), and regret (Bell (1982)). For details, *see*: Andrew W. Lo, "Efficient Markets Hypothesis," in *The New Palgrave: A Dictionary of Economics*, eds. L. Blume, S. Durlauf (2nd Edition, Palgrave Macmillan Ltd., 2007), https://ssrn.com/abstract=991509, 9-10.

35 *See* Andrew W. Lo, "Efficient Markets Hypothesis," in *The New Palgrave: A Dictionary of Economics*, eds. L. Blume, S. Durlauf (2nd Edition, Palgrave Macmillan Ltd., 2007), https://ssrn.com/abstract=991509.

36 *See* Felicia Ramona Birău, "Behavioral Finance Paradigm And Its Implications On Investment Decisions," in *Proceedings of the International Scientific Conference, ECO-TREND,* 2011.

37 *See* Ha-Joon Chang, *23 Things They Don't Tell You about Capitalism* (USA: Bloomsbury Publishing, 2012), 170-173.

real life over the last four decades, namely, the *social business approach* briefly outlined in the next subsection.

Social Business: "Not Only and Not Always Wealth Maximization Aim"

Social business is an entirely new, dynamic, and bright notion within the field of economics that was defined and developed by Nobel Prize economics scholar Muhammad Yunus.[38] The concept of social business is based on the following four pillars.[39]

First, it is the business that created and designed to address a social problem, rather than to earn money, maximize profit or wealth, in contrast to the tenets of conventional economic theories. According to Professor Yunus, traditional economic theory is not relevant to the realities of humans; it is misinterpreting human nature focusing only on egoism. However, the human being is not only a "money-making machine" but also multifaceted, and one of its facts may include its selflessness, which is based on the principle of "the best way of being happy is to make others happy."[40]

Second, it is based on the principle of nonloss and nondividend business, which means that investors from the beginning decide not to take any profit of their investment, but only get back their invested amount. Instead, investors look forward to the impact of their investment through a real solution of some social problems. The opportunity of one hundred percent withdrawing investment by investors makes social businesses different to traditional nonprofit organizations or other non-governmental organizations, which usually have a limited profit-making right.

---

38 Professor Muhammad Yunus is the recipient of 55 honorary degrees from universities across 20 countries. He has received 112 awards from 26 countries including state honors from 10 countries. He is one of only seven individuals to have been awarded the Nobel Peace Prize, the United States Presidential Medal of Freedom and the United States Congressional Gold Medal. For further information on Professor Muhammad Yunus, *see*: http://muhammadyunus.org/index.php/professor-yunus/curriculum-vitae-in-brief.

39 For further details, *see*: Muhammad Yunus, *Building Social Business: The New Kind of Capitalism that Serves Humanity's Most Pressing Needs* (Public Affairs, 2010); Muhammad Yunus, *Creating a World Without Poverty: Social Business and the Future of Capitalism* (Public Affairs, 2009).

40 *See* Muhammad Yunus, "Nobel Prize Winner Muhammad Yunus: The Key to Super Happiness" (2013), https://www.forbes.com/sites/erincarlyle/2013/06/07/nobel-prize-winner-muhammad-yunus-the-key-to-super-happiness-video/?sh=63bf98b04463.

Third, unlike a nonprofit, a social business is not dependent on donations or other grants to survive and to operate because, like any other business, it is self-sustainable. Profits realized by the company are reinvested in the industry itself (or used to start other social companies), with the aim of increasing their social impact.[41] This feature makes social businesses a new form of a commercial venture that lies somewhere between for-profit and philanthropy.[42] According to Muhammad Yunus in philanthropy or charity, one dollar has only one life and one chance; in the case of social businesses, one dollar can be used over and over to solve social problems.[43] For Muhammad Yunus, the profit made through social business operations is less important than the beneficial effects it has on society. This is again connected with the purpose of business activity that should be other than merely making a profit as an end in itself. So social businesses could provide an alternative model for utilizing capitalism to address social concerns at the local, national, regional, and global levels.[44]

And, lastly, the social business concept is not a hypothesis any longer. Instead, it is effectively implemented and a developing business model for more than three decades in many countries across the globe. In 2006, the Nobel Prize was awarded to Professor Muhammad Yunus and Grameen Bank which is implementing social business projects since 1976.[45] Today the Grameen Group is a network of nearly 30 sister organizations in around 60 countries, involving 9 million borrowers in Bangladesh and 300 million around the world, with a USD 3 billion loan turnover with 98.4 percent return rate.[46]

---

41 For instance, expanding the company's reach, improving the products or services or in different ways subsidizing its social mission.

42 *See* Alejandro Agafonow and Cam Donaldson, "The Economic Rationale Behind the Social Business Model: A Research Agenda," *Social Business* 5, no. 1 (2015): 5-16.

43 *See* Muhammad Yunus, *Building Social Business: The New Kind of Capitalism that Serves Humanity's Most Pressing Needs* (Public Affairs, 2010); Muhammad Yunus, *Creating a World Without Poverty: Social Business and the Future of Capitalism* (Public Affairs, 2009).

44 *See* Muhammad Yunus, Bertrand Moingeon, and Laurence Lehmann-Ortega, "Building Social Business Models: Lessons from the Grameen experience," *Long Range Planning* 43, no. 2-3 (2010): 308-325.

45 *See* Nancy Wimmer, *Green Energy for a Billion Poor: How Grameen Shakti Created a Winning Model for Social Business*, MCRE-Verlag, 2012, 226; Muhammad Yunus, Bertrand Moingeon and Laurence Lehmann-Ortega, "Building Social Business Models: Lessons from the Grameen experience," *Long Range Planning* 43, no. 2-3 (2010): 308-325.

46 *See* Muhammad Yunus' keynote speech at the Conference "The Future of Finance" at Imperial College Business School in London on April 19, 2018, https://www.youtube.com/watch?v=ccX0pisosB4 (video).

Some of the future challenges deriving from the development of the social business are listed up in the recent research by Agafonow and others,[47] where authors raise a reasonable question: is the development of a capital market that targets social businesses possible? This research attempts to partly contribute to this issue by considering the implementation of the social business model in the securities market relations of CIS (Commonwealth of Independent States) countries.

Contemporary Problems of SMR

One of the tasks of the chapter is to analyze the main theoretical problems currently at play in securities markets, to consider their primary reasons, and to examine their implications for CIS and other countries with transition securities markets.

Here only those problems that are directly or indirectly pertinent to the above basic theories shall be discussed. One of the main problems is connected with the failure of the EMH, and the necessity of adjusting it with the realities of today's securities market.

The Excessive Efficiency of Securities Markets

The first problem is connected to the notion that securities markets are "too efficient."[48] Even though this problem is characteristic of developed financial markets, it can easily have implications for emerging or transition countries in the current information technology and globalization conditions. At the very least, developing countries cannot entirely avoid the harmful consequences of the overly efficient securities markets in developed countries, as has been the case with the financial crisis in 2008.

47 For further details, *see*: Alejandro Agafonow and Cam Donaldson, "The Economic Rationale Behind the Social Business Model: A Research Agenda," *Social Business* 5, no. 1 (2015): 5-16.

48 This problem is widely discussed in various papers, especially after the financial crisis of 2008. *See*, for instance, Ha-Joon Chang, *23 Things They Don't Tell You about Capitalism* (USA: Bloomsbury Publishing, 2012), 231-241. *See also*: Raymond Goldsmith, *Financial Structure and Development* (New Haven: Yale University Press, 1969); Robert G. King and Ross Levine, "Finance and Growth: Schumpeter Might be Right," *The Quarterly Journal of Economics* 108, no. 3 (1993): 717-737; Raghuram G. Rajan and Luigi Zingales, *Financial Dependence and Growth*. No. w5758. National Bureau of Economic Research, 1996.

Chang refers to this problem as having to do with the short-term generation of profits by the financial sector through financial "innovations" in the form of various complicated financial instruments. According to Chang, "these new assets have made the overall economy, as well as the financial system itself, much more unstable."[49] Consequently, there have formed a massive gap between the financial sector with a short-term focus and the real sector of the economy, which has long-term goals. For instance, if in 1980 the total value of all financial assets was approximately five times the value of U.S. gross domestic product (GDP), by 2007 this ratio had doubled. In the U.S., the securities industry increased from 107 percent of GDP in 1980 to 323 percent of GDP in 2007.[50] In the U.K., the financial assets ratio to GDP was around 700 percent of GDP in 2007.[51] In equities, much growth came from an increase in assessment ratios rather than their substantial increase.[52] Before the 2008 crisis, financial derivatives, which Warren Buffet called as "financial weapons of mass destruction," grew about eight times faster than world output. The main cause for this was the creation of more and more financial claims for each underlying asset and economic activity.[53] In 2016, total debt levels globally came in at a record USD 164 trillion, amounting to 225 percent of the world economy's GDP.[54]

So, the root of the problem of excessive efficiency of the modern securities markets goes to the deviation from the basic securities theory, which is the equivalence of issued securities to the amount of existing real assets or economic activity. If under a real asset worth USD 1 a USD 10 derivative is generated, there is 100 percent possibility that the owners of USD 9 derivatives will be in loss. During the high speed of securities

---

49 *See* Ha-Joon Chang, *23 Things They Don't Tell You about Capitalism* (USA: Bloomsbury Publishing, 2012), 231-232.

50 *See* details in Kevin R. Brine and Mary Poovey, *Finance in America: An Unfinished Story* (Chicago: University of Chicago Press, 2017), 361.

51 *See* Ha-Joon Chang, *23 Things They Don't Tell You about Capitalism* (USA: Bloomsbury Publishing, 2012), 237.

52 *See* details in Robin Greenwood and David Scharfstein, "The Growth of Finance," *Journal of Economic Perspectives* 27, no. 2 (2013), 9.

53 The increase was in just ten years from USD 92 to USD 683 trillion or from 2.4 to 11 times the size of global output. *See* details in José Gabriel Palma, "The Revenge of the Market on the Rentiers: Why Neo-liberal Reports of the End of History Turned Out To Be Bremature," *Cambridge Journal of Economics* 33, no. 4 (2009), 837.

54 *See*: Cheang Ming, "Global Debt Is at Historic Highs And Governments Should Start Cutting Levels Now, the IMF Says," *CNBC,* April 19, 2018, https://www.cnbc.com/2018/04/18/global-debt-is-at-historic-high-and-governments-should-cut-levels-imf.html.

market relations, this possibility of failure may seem low, but it is only an illusion.

The best, credible, and initially assumed way of organizing securities market efficiency did not rely on the "artificial increase" of financial assets, as was the case with the "invention" of derivatives, collateralized debt obligations, or credit default swaps, but on ensuring the real sector of economy involved financial flows through the accumulation and redistribution functions of the securities market. Ideal securities market efficiency cannot be achieved based on the lopsided development, i.e., fostering of financial instruments without the growth of the real economy, or in the case with the securities market, which should reflect the real economy will pose it to high risk of destruction.

The financial crisis is not a natural disaster; i.e., all measures and their consequences did not happen accidentally and by chance. Some scholars have further supplied some theoretical background through the notions of "self-interest" and "wealth maximization" theories as well as lack of adequate oversight by regulators. There were "licensed professionals" who "invented" complicated and complex financial instruments and cared mostly about achieving their self-interest and wealth-maximizing aim. There were credit rating agencies whose biased assessment of financial instruments speeded up the circulation again based on higher fees for higher rated products. There were incentive schemes for intermediaries and their employees to promote products and their values without any reference to real-world values. In addition, there were "illiterate" and bargain-seeking consumers, and some regulators could not recognize the actual value of these "financial innovations" and had no or insufficient foresight on their harmful consequences. In addition, there was far too much cheap credit, with no oversight on the credit risk.

The next problem of the modern securities market to be discussed tries to find an answer to the question as to why this had happened, and what were the main factors and driving force. In the opinion of this author, there are two key answers: the imbalance in theoretical supply and the human factor.

Imbalance in Theoretical Supply

The foregoing included a brief discussion as to the importance of theory in SMR, and it was concluded that theory is essential for the design and implementation of effective regulation. In this subsection, an attempt is made to shed light on the deficiency of economic theory that was dominant in the last centuries. There are two main issues in economic theory directly relevant to the securities market and its regulation: first is economic theory focusing on, and by all means aiming to stimulate, self-interest approach of market participants, and the second is the hypothesis that encourages wealth maximization. There is sufficient literature and debate on the advantages and disadvantages of these theories. This research does not aim to review those debates but, rather, to direct the focus on the other side of the issue—the moral side, which was suppressed, and lagged behind the self-interest and wealth maximization streams throughout time. The moral side has had very little academic analysis and has not actually been applied sufficiently by lawmakers, regulators, and risk managers in intermediaries to the detriment of end investors.

Self-Interest Focused Approach Is Imbalance in Interpreting Human Merits

Some ideas and experiences about selfless interest are concisely discussed above within the scope of social business and behavioral finance theory and practices. Briefly, altruistic interest means that human beings, who are the main subjects and take a central position in the market relations, not only are self-interest driven but may also behave in selfless ways, i.e., acting not only for their own ego or their own interest. On the legal and regulatory side, the lawmakers and regulators may have also acted in an irresponsible way allowing immoral activities to take place.

The economic theories of last century mainly focused only one feature of a human being—its self-directness, ignoring and depreciating its moral and social characteristics. As a result, more and more people in society are brought up as self-interested. Existing theories neither provide firm conclusions about the limits of such self-interest behaviors nor could consider its harmful consequences in the personal and public spheres. Moreover, the original natural remedy for the deviation of self-interest conduct—namely, the selfless instincts—was not accounted for by those theories. Therefore selflessness became unsustainable and could not fulfill its original function—to be an antidote for the plague of self-centeredness both in the personal and in public spheres. As a result, there have been overwhelming financial crises, global fraud and manipulation, and loss of trust, which are the core values of both market and social relations.

In conclusion, however, it must be stated that this self-interest imbalance does not necessarily depreciate the essence of self-interest theory and its practice. The present author is merely drawing attention to balancing it through considering the limits of self-interest, and by bringing up possible antidotes, such as selfless directed behavior in practice. In case of securities market, this will contribute to solving such key problems of the modern securities market such as greediness, fraud, demand and price manipulation, insider dealing, Ponzi schemes, and abuse of investor trust—in short: both market and regulatory failures.

Wealth Maximization Approach Is Imbalance in Interpreting Business Aim

The second imbalance in theoretical supply is connected with the misinterpretation of wealth maximization as the purpose of the activity of market participants. As one of the main concepts of market efficiency theory, wealth maximization provided the ideological background for fostering market relations. It seems that there is nothing wrong with it because endeavoring wealth maximization is the consequence of natural self-interest instinct. However, the problem is in the interpretation of wealth maximization as the principal purpose of business. This does not fit with the notion of wealth, which originally tends to be as a means for achieving some greater goals rather than being an end in itself. In this author's opinion, wealth in and of itself does not have significant value. The relation and demand of subjects on the proper item determine its value. For instance, in the case of securities, their value is no more than the value of ordinary paper. However, state guarantees, the company's activity, transparency, and development prospects, along with investor demand, turn such paper into valuable commodities.

The misinterpretation of wealth by existing economic theories is also not in line with the ideal business goal, which is about not only making money but also solving problems, and avoiding loss. According to the 2015 Deloitte Millennial Survey,[55] 75 percent of millennials overwhelmingly believe that businesses are focused on their profit-making agenda rather than helping to improve society.[56] According to millennials in the twenty-first century, business needs to reset its purpose, and it should focus on people and mission, not just products and profits.[57] This kind of necessity is becoming even sharper in the case of the modern securities market.

---

55 *See* more about the 2015 Deloitte Millennial Survey: https://www2.deloitte.com/bm/en/pages/about-deloitte/articles/2015-millennial-survey-press-release.html.

56 *Ibid.*

57 *See* Deloitte Touche Tohmatsu Limited's (Deloitte Global) fourth annual Millennial Survey, https://www2.deloitte.com/bm/en/pages/about-deloitte/articles/2015-millennial-survey-press-release.html.

Today in the securities market, there is massive divergence between two common aims of participating in securities markets as an investor, a speculative aim and an investment aim. The speculative aim is prevailing over the investment aim in the securities market. However, the investment-focused aim was the original purpose of the securities market formation through the accumulation of resources and their redistribution within the sectors of the economy. In this long-term goal, shareholders' primary aim is to gain from the development of the business and industry. In contrast, intermediary participants with speculative purposes care little about the long-term growth of the company or industry. Instead, their goal is to maximize their profit in short-term price fluctuations caused by objective, subjective and market manipulation factors.

The ideal conduct for market participants is to act toward solving some essential economic problems—for instance, in the case of the securities market, to invest their funds (and client funds) to sectors of the economy where there is scarcity in financial resources in order to promote economic development. In this process, investors seek appropriate profit and bear the relevant risk of loss for their investment. Of course, a market participant investing in the securities market can choose a short-term investment, mainly focusing on daily price changes of stocks. It is entirely justifiable in normal conditions when a participant has to sell or buy shares on a short-term basis. However, when speculation becomes a routine business, and this business becomes dominant in the securities market, there is increased risk of a market crash. Consequently, risk and scale of harm will be higher and higher.[58] This is because the circulation of financial instruments is much faster than the financial assets or real sector business. For instance, Professor Chang makes an interesting comparison: "building factory takes at least months, if not years; technological know-how may take decades; but financial assets can be issued and circulated in minutes, if not seconds." According to Chang, "if the financial sector moves too fast, it can derail the real economy."[59]

There is an appropriate link between overgrowths of speculative practice in modern securities markets and wealth maximization, the EMH, and self-interest approaches. The imbalance in securities market business goals is causing several substantial problems that go beyond the financial sphere and a single jurisdiction. It is necessary to reconsider wealth maximization

58 History contains enough evidence on this issue. Cf., for instance, the securities market crashes in 1930, 1980, and 2008.

59 *See* Ha-Joon Chang, *23 Things They Don't Tell You about Capitalism* (USA: Bloomsbury Publishing, 2012), 239-241.

theory in order to adequately interpret the aim of business, to resolve the mentioned divergence between business aims in the securities market, and to return the modern securities market to its initial aim, which is to facilitate investment.

The fostering of moral values already integrated into individuals could be an effective way of achieving these tasks. Primarily, in the case of scarcity of moral values in modern securities markets, this measure will assist in achieving a balance between moral and material merits of market participants, which could consequently lead to fair and transparent market relations in the securities business.

Moral Value Deficit Syndrome

The last problem of the modern securities market discussed in the foregoing has been referred to as the moral value deficit syndrome (MVDS).[60] *Moral value* here means all merits intrinsic to a human being that can be put opposite its material values. This research considers both the moral values and the material interests as being integral parts of human beings. However, due to several factors, these are not always equally developed, and a fair balance between them is not always achieved. For instance, there is a considerable gap between material and moral values in modern securities market relations because of lopsided explanation by abovementioned economic theories and their practice in the last half-century.

It is hotly debated in the relevant literature whether the market and morality are consistent with each other,[61] whether there is a place for morality in the market,[62] or, alternatively, what may be the moral limits of the market,[63] etc. Unfortunately, reviewing these discussions is outside the scope of the present research but suffice to say that morals are allowed to change in the context of greed and incentives and the imbalance between fear of repercussion and greed of returns. The goal of this subsection is to

60 A metaphor coined from the "acquired immune deficiency syndrome" disease.

61 *See*, for instance, Jeffery D. Smith, "Moral Markets and Moral Managers Revisited," *Journal of Business Ethics* 61, no. 2 (2005): 129-141; *See also*: Ian Maitland, "Virtuous Markets: The Market as a School of the Virtues," *Business Ethics Quarterly* 7, no. 1 (1997): 17-31.

62 *See*, for instance, Thomas Clay Arnold, "Rethinking Moral Economy" *American Political Science Review* 95, no. 1 (2001): 85-95.

63 *See*, for instance, Philip Booth, "The Moral Limits to the Market Economy, and the Financial Crash." *IEA Discussion Paper* No. 30, September 2010, https://iea.org.uk/wp-content/uploads/2016/07/upldbook521pdf.pdf.

show the role of moral values in modern securities market relations and to use their potential in potentially solving the problems discussed earlier.

Moral values are connected with the market through the participation of human beings, who, in this author's opinion, should be at the center of market relations.[64] In other words, because moral values are an integral part of human beings, they, by extension, also become an essential part of market relations. Moral values are the main feature that distinguishes human nature from vending machines. By this statement, the present author does not suggest that market participants should be saintlike. Rather, what should be pointed out is the need to use the natural integral "watchdog" of human beings—their moral values in market relations as a remedy—that is to say, their moral values can restrain market participants from such wrongdoings, such as fraud, abuse of trust, insider dealing, manipulation and so on. Unfortunately, neither in current securities market theory nor in practice are moral values duly regarded. Regulators can never keep up with a sufficiently well-defined code of conduct which the market participants abide by, as the latter group are always incentivized to keep many steps ahead of the regulator. In contrast, because of the abovementioned dominant economic theories, moral values have not been taken into account in market relations, which has consequently contributed to the various failures in both market and regulation procedures.[65]

The recent survey shows a clear, negative shift in millennials' views on business motivations and ethics. Today, only a minority of millennials (albeit a substantial one) believe that businesses behave ethically (namely, 48 percent versus 65 percent in 2017), and that business leaders are committed to helping improve society (47 percent versus 62 percent in 2017).[66] In this regard, millennials believe that corporations should set out to achieve a full balance in social objectives, such as making a positive impact on society and the environment; creating innovative ideas, products

64 In the literature, there are various approaches to this issue. For instance, some scholars place institutions in the front line; others corporations and their behavior; and the third group of scholars prioritize regulation, etc. In the present author's opinion, the human is the crucial factor in all of the mentioned aspects; respectively in market relations, its position is central. As there is no institution, corporation, and regulation without human, it is humans who really may develop or debase relations, including market relations.

65 *See* Stan Viorica, "The Actual Collapse and the Importance of Moral Values (Ethics); Some Reflections Regarding the Roots of the Current Crisis," *Procedia—Social and Behavioral Sciences* 58 (2012): 1057-1063.

66 The Deloitte Millennial Survey 2018, "Millennials' Confidences in Business, Loyalty to Employers Deteriorate", https://www2.deloitte.com/bm/en/pages/about-deloitte/articles/millennialsurvey.html.

and services; and seeking to achieve job creation, career development, and to improve people's lives. In their collective view, businesses are out of step with these priorities.[67] In the opinion of the present author concerning the origin of this situation, the dominant theories of the last century have made a substantial contribution to the present situation.

Self-interest and wealth maximization approaches will be the leading cause of the problem in securities markets if they are not equipped with moral values. The recent financial crisis is a clear example of this.[68] The person who owns USD 10 has more intention to earn more than the person who possesses less money. On the one hand, there is nothing wrong with self-interest and wealth maximization—on the contrary, it encourages action in all business relations and creates competition. On the other hand, in the majority of cases, the practice of profit or wealth maximization shows a deviation from moral values.[69] In contrast, the existence of strong moral values helps to use the wealth and money according to their initial purpose—as a means to solve problems, not as an ultimate goal in and of itself. For instance, philosopher Jacob Needleman states that people with strong ethical and religious lives have often stayed quite stable after being rich. According to Needleman, "they have a sense that there's something more important than wealth. That is why, even when they get wealthy, it does not deflect them."[70]

The longest research on happiness, which took about 80 years, also revealed that it is not wealth that is the source of happiness, but things such

---

67 *Ibid.*

68 The core causes of majority financial crisis were fraud, abusing trust, insider dealing, manipulation or other forms of ethical and moral failures. *See*, for instance, Joseph E. Stiglitz, "The Anatomy of a Murder: Who Killed the American Economy?" in *What Caused the Financial Crisis*, ed. Jeffrey Friedman (Pennsylvania: University of Pennsylvania, 2011) 140-141. *See also*: Viral V. Acharya and Matthew Richardson, "How Securitization Concentrated Risk in the Financial Sector," in *What Caused the Financial Crisis*, ed. Jeffrey Friedman (Pennsylvania: University of Pennsylvania, 2011).184-185; Daron Acemoglu, The Crisis of 2008: Lessons for and from Economics, in *What Caused the Financial Crisis*, ed. Jeffrey Friedman (Pennsylvania: University of Pennsylvania, 2011), 255.

69 Professor Jacob Needleman wrote in this regard the following: "[w]hen money can make you feel humble, then I think it's beneficial. However, if it fattens your ego, which it often does, then look out." *See*: Jacob Needleman, "Money and the Meaning of Life" (1991).

70 *See* in details: Needleman, Jacob, *Money and the Meaning of Life* (New York: Doubleday, 1991), 321.

as communication, love and close relationships that provide real happiness.[71] Professor Robert Waldinger, who is the fourth director of this research project, stated that: "what I learned from this 75-year study is that good human relations are a secret of happiness."[72] It is impossible to reach good human relations without strong moral values, whether this is in social or market relations.

Recent research that used data from 73 jurisdictions from 2009 to 2011 examined the existence of social capital thresholds in the securities market development and macroeconomic performance nexus. The empirical results demonstrate that securities market liquidity is significant and positive in influencing GDP and *total factor productivity* (TFP) growth respectively only after the achievement of a certain threshold level of firms' ethical behavior. Until then, the effects of the securities market on both GDP growth and TFP growth are found to be negligible. They mention that even though ethics and trust are as old as humanity, "we are only at the starting point in the journey to better understand the role of ethics and trust, or in a broader sense, social capital, in financial markets."[73] Therefore, modern securities market relations need a proper ideological supply for the activation and development of market participants' moral values, at least up to the level that will provide balance with their dominant material values. This issue would be a promising field of further research and future studies, but the author believes that to embed moral values into securities markets, the moral code needs to be imposed and enforced from the top by lawmakers and regulators, and there need to be real consequences from regulators and for those regulated in the event of noncompliance.

Summary

In this chapter, it was attempted to provide an outline of the basic theories of SMR and some challenges they are facing in contemporary conditions. It was found that theories have a significant impact on SMR and current

71 Robert Waldinger, "What makes a Good Life? Lessons from the Longest Study on Happiness," TEDx Beacon Street, November 2015, https://www.ted.com/talks/robert_waldinger_what_makes_a_good_life_lessons_from_the_longest_study_on_happiness?referrer=playlist-the_most_popular_talks_of_all#t-754153.

72 *Ibid.*

73 *See* details in Adam Ng, Mansor H. Ibrahim and Abbas Mirakhor, "Ethical Behavior and Trustworthiness in the Securities market-Growth Nexus," *Research in International Business and Finance* 33 (2015): 44-58.

theoretical notions focus mostly on self-interest, wealth maximization, and microeconomic issues, and do not adequately reflect the market and human features. Based on the analysis of existing theories and practice of their application, the author proposed a new approach—the MVDS as a remedy for the discussed problem.

There should be substantive research and consideration toward encouraging business (including securities business) to consider alternative aims, market participants to espouse alternative values, and the SMR to shift toward a more balanced approach.

The chapter sends an important message for transition economies, which need to minimize the risk of market crashes. They need to learn from the mistakes of mature markets and embed high moral standards into the industry to create continuous growth of wealth and trust. If they do not take appropriate lessons from the world markets experience, a significant portion of wealth in such countries will continue to circulate outside the formal economy and the financial sector will fail to become an engine of economic and wealth development for the country and individuals.

www.ingramcontent.com/pod-product-compliance
Ingram Content Group UK Ltd.
Pitfield, Milton Keynes, MK11 3LW, UK
UKHW020809290926
15470UKWH00003B/1055

9 789403 531700